Petr Chalupský
Tereza Topolovská

Of Spaces and Ideas
The Novels of Jim Crace and Simon Mawer

CHARLES UNIVERSITY
KAROLINUM PRESS 2024

KAROLINUM PRESS
Karolinum Press is a publishing department of Charles University
Ovocný trh 560/5, 116 36 Prague 1, Czech Republic
www.karolinum.cz

Set and printed in the Czech Republic by Karolinum Press
Layout by Jan Šerých
First edition

A catalogue record for this book is available from the National Library of the Czech Republic.

The publication of this monograph was financially supported by the Czech Science Foundation, project GAČR 20-24867S: "Representations of Space in the Novels of Jim Crace and Simon Mawer".

ISBN 978-80-246-5807-0
ISBN 978-80-246-5816-2 (pdf)

The original manuscript was reviewed by Bożena Kucała (Jagiellonian University in Krakow, Poland) and Sidia Fiorato (University of Verona, Italy).

Contents

Introduction

This monograph seeks to provide a deeper insight into the work of two contemporary British novelists – Jim Crace and Simon Mawer. Their narratives are interpreted primarily from the perspective of their treatment of space and place since they derive a significant part of their meaning from the synergistic relationship between their protagonists and the environment they inhabit. Apart from this noticeable focus on the representation of space, there are also other thematic and aesthetic preoccupations as well as biographical similarities between these authors. Not only are they contemporaries, both having begun their writing careers relatively late – in their forties – but each also has an idiosyncratic approach to the creative process, which adds other levels of complexity to the comparison. This is reflected in their reluctance to unequivocally specify the genre of their works and thus be pinned down by categories, preferring to see their novels as works of ideas which thematise a variety of related topics. Their works tend to be classified as historical fiction, but each views and responds to this labelling differently: while Mawer dramatises his historical narratives with scientific elements and narrative strategies from popular genres, such as the thriller and the spy novel, whose settings are inspired by real-life referents, Crace's stories function on the principle of the parable, whose properties, including the settings, are products of pure imagination. Moreover, neither of the authors has received much scholarly attention, even though their novels deal with some of the focal points of contemporary fiction, namely those of space, place, history and identity.

Out of the many similarities between the two authors and their literary creation, the present monograph is concerned with their embrace of spatial representation as a productive instrument of their narratives.

It therefore seeks to identify, chart and interpret the various forms and roles that space and place assume in their novels. We understand space as a general notion referring to a rather abstract category, while place as a concretised and familiarised portion of space to which personal meanings are attributed by its occupants. In order to ground its spatial analysis within a theoretical framework, a comprehensive overview and taxonomy of approaches to space, place and their treatment in literature is provided. Applied to selected works by Crace and Mawer, they exemplify that the ways in which both authors render the interaction of literary spaces and characters echo contemporary literary theory and philosophy's preoccupation with the mutual interference between humans and their environment. Our monograph stems from an interdisciplinary approach, triggered particularly by what is known as the (postmodern) spatial turn, i.e. the increased tendency to refocus literary study on the treatment of space and place as its point of departure. This tendency to acknowledge the primacy of space and time in determining our existence and identity has further solidified the position of place as a key category enabling humans to comprehend and assess their experience of space.

The focus of the interpretative part of the study was established by means of systematic textual and comparative analysis of the literary representations of place and space in selected works by Crace and Mawer. The resulting chapters address their narratives' thematic concerns, key aesthetic elements, structure, and the conception of the protagonists, which are shown to adhere to and complement the novels' treatment of spatial properties and vice versa. They illustrate the authors' preferences in terms of genre, themes, structure, characters, and treatment of place and space. There are two major determining and inherently intertwined features of Crace's novels: the creation of imaginary environments which, despite their historical and geographical differences, evince a number of idiosyncratic properties that make them seem real to the reader; and the theme of communities in a transitional moment of their existence in which their members are forced to readjust their values and the very essence of their identity to these newly emerging circumstances.

Identity plays a prominent role in both Crace's and Mawer's novels. This preference corresponds with one of the pivotal elements marking Mawer's narratives – liminality. This quality is shown to permeate all aspects of his writing and can be seen as determining its position between serious and popular fiction, being a mixture of the historical novel, the spy novel and the thriller. The characters' borderline position is often expressed by means of their bilingualism and hybrid cultural and personal identity, but the most explicit form of liminality in his novels is his choice of historical and geographical settings. Mawer mostly opts for culturally complex areas in the midst of profound historical transformations. This, together with the (auto)biographical elements he projects into his writings, results in a predominance of the two regions where he tends to situate his novels – central Europe and the Mediterranean.

The first analytical chapter outlines the character of Crace's imaginary landscapes as it is introduced in his first two novels, *Continent* (1986) and *The Gift of Stones* (1988). *Continent* comprises seven thematically linked stories that are variations of a fictitious realm, an imaginary seventh continent whose inhabitants are going through an identity crisis that, symptomatically for Crace, is reflected in their spatial experience. The chapter provides a geocritical analysis of the novel and explores how it dramatises the intricate interaction between the geographic and topographic properties of the landscapes and the protagonists' psyches. *The Gift of Stones* not only depicts a community in transition, but also elaborates on the significance of making up stories in human life. This chapter demonstrates how the novel's physical environments intertwine not only with the main protagonist's mental world, but also, and above all, with his talent for imaginative storytelling.

The parallels between Crace's construction of characters and the fictional landscapes they inhabit in *Signals of Distress* (1994) and *Quarantine* (1997) are discussed in chapter two. It shows that the power of his writing rests in the combination of distinctive main characters and the conception of unique fictional topographies. Through the form of a satirical parable, *Signals of Distress* explores the position of an individual in the process of a community's transition due to larger historical, social and economic circumstances, and the formative role that landscape plays in such a character's development. The chapter also demonstrates the various roles that space, place and landscape assume in the lives of *Quarantine*'s protagonists, and argues that Crace's approach transcends that of phenomenological spatial representation by making the environment a deciding agent within the narrative's ethical framework.

The third chapter focuses on Crace's urban novels, particularly on *Arcadia* (1992), and discusses the diverse particularities of the author's fictional cityscape. The novel brings to bear a wide range of thematic perspectives, such as the ambivalent symbiosis of the rural and the urban, the archetypes of modern city dwellers and the importance of the agora for a functioning urban social life. Moreover, it integrates a celebratory narrative voice with a satirical one. Its story takes place in an unnamed

English city, which allows the author to employ a mixture of genres, namely the psychological novel, sociological and urban studies and the quasi or mock-pastoral. The first part of the chapter shows how *Arcadia* contributed to the transformation of the British urban novel and, consequently, to the overall process of the hybridisation of the genre of the novel in general. The second part argues that, along with *The Melody* (2018), *Arcadia* can be subsumed within so-called transmodern fiction, and that it carries out its critique of globalised capitalism through so-called *entre-deux*, or in-between, places. Accordingly, it observes that the novel's liminal and heterogeneous places display non-linear and complexly interrelated temporalities that are indicative of their role in the city's progress.

Crace's employment of literary cartography, or mapping narratives, in *The Pesthouse* (2007) and *Harvest* (2013) is elaborated on in the fourth chapter. *The Pesthouse* is set in a devastated America of an imagined future, a country that has reversed and deteriorated into a pre-modern and pre-industrial wasteland so hostile to sustainable existence that most of its inhabitants have become refugees travelling eastward to set sail for a new life on another continent. These refugees are leaving their homes behind to flee not only misery and destitution but also the trauma and pain from the fateful loss of their relatives. This chapter presents and analyses the ways in which Crace's novel maps and explores its spaces, landscapes and places, as well as how it links them with the transformation of the protagonists' psyches and mental worlds. *Harvest* is even more complex in this regard as it includes the map-making of its imaginary landscapes as one of its main themes. The chapter thus shows that the novel is a remarkable example of literary cartography in that it combines subjectivist and objectivist approaches to the textual representation of space.

Mawer's debut novel, *Chimera* (1989), which outlines all the dominant aspects of his poetics, his thematic focus and his chief structural and formal preferences, is the subject of chapter six. *Chimera* marks Mawer's first immersion in the subject matter of war, resistance movements, and espionage, as well as his first work set in the Mediterranean. The novel also aptly incorporates a field of science, namely archaeology, in both its thematic orientation and its narrative structure. Pioneering Mawer's distinctive fusion of protagonists and their setting, *Chimera* derives a considerable part of its meaning from its profound sense of time and place.

The seventh chapter revolves predominantly around Mawer's arguably most famous novel, *The Glass Room* (2009), which helped to establish his position as both a well-known and critically acclaimed novelist. *The Glass Room* revisits a number of signature aspects of Mawer's works, such as a tempestuous historical period, a culturally and geopolitically complex region, and protagonists whose identities are intertwined with radical historical, social and cultural transformation. Finally, and perhaps most importantly, the novel introduces a spectacular central conceit which simultaneously encapsulates the central dilemma of the novel and embodies the essence of its poetics. It is the eponymous Glass Room, a spacious room with walls made entirely of glass, whose austere geometrical frame braves the course of the tumultuous twentieth century in central Europe and shelters the histories of individuals against the backdrop of the traumatic period. Along with *Mendel's Dwarf* (1997) and *Prague Spring* (2018), *The Glass Room* represents Mawer's venture into central Europe and its turbulent modern history. Both *Prague Spring* and *Mendel's Dwarf* are mentioned to illustrate the aspects of the spatial poetics Mawer employs in connection with the depicted region. The former is presented as a paean to the liminality of the Prague Spring as a historical period, echoing the liberating efforts of the First Czechoslovak Republic evoked in *The Glass Room*. The latter introduces one of the most memorable of Mawer's creations in the character of an undersized geneticist while skilfully combining two parallel but historically distant plotlines and situating a part of its action in the area of the present-day Czech Republic.

The final chapter focuses on the duo of critically acclaimed spy novels, *The Girl Who Fell from the Sky* (2012) and *Tightrope* (2015), set in France and England during and in the aftermath of WW2, charting the ways in which Mawer's ability to merge the protagonists and their psychological states with the rendering of space and place contributes to the overall sense of excitement, suspense and unease that is typical of the genre. These two novels, as well as the rest of the works analysed in this volume, exemplify Mawer's ability to thematise subjects as diverse as archaeology, architecture or espionage while shedding light on forgotten or lesser-known historical developments.

The analytical chapters thus not only attempt to theoretically conceptualise Crace's and Mawer's renderings of space but also, and more importantly, to demonstrate the various ways in which the authors make use of these spatial representations in order to express, exemplify or accentuate the principal ideas lying behind their novels' framework of meaning.

1. After the Spatial Turn

Throughout the second half of the twentieth century, literary theory and criticism began to focus on the representation of space and place, which gradually acquired the significance that time and temporality had enjoyed for centuries. This focal shift, which insisted that the spatial properties of the narrative should not be confined to mere background setting, emerged from the recognition that the relationship between human beings and their environment is reciprocal and highly interactive. The fact that human beings live in space-time, and that these two dimensions significantly determine our existence and are equally crucial for the formation of our identity, opened up a fruitful field of interest for theorists, culminating in what has been called the postmodern "spatial turn". Its immediate consequence, as Emmanuelle Peraldo notes, is that space "is now considered as a central metaphor and *topos* in literature, and literary criticism has seized space as a new tool and stake" (2016, 1). This relationship is reciprocal: not only do the spatial properties of our existence shape who we are and how we perceive ourselves and the world around us, but our perception and interpretation of space, whether in the form of mental projections, scientific delineations or artistic representations, also determine the character and significance of our living environments. Their temporal and spatial coordinates are thus supplemented by a social one as we try to make them intelligible by (self-)projecting meanings onto them. These endow spaces with new layers of meaningfulness, both private and public, which combine and interact, appropriating them discursively and thus allowing them to get narrativised. The study of textual representations of space is therefore one of the ways in which we can better understand not only the spaces in question, but also our own spatial, and possibly even social, experience.

In order to clearly define the object of a textual spatial inquiry, it is crucial to make a distinction between space and place. The first is a general notion, a broad concept that refers to any environment in which a person finds him/herself. As such, it is rather loose and indeterminate in terms of the individual's personal relation to it. Place is a segment of space which is particularised and localised on the basis of an individual's more intense attachment, formed through the ascription of meanings, the projection of ideas and the making of interpretations. Space is concretised into place by "being named" by the flows of power and negotiations of the social relations of its occupants (Carter et al. 1993, xii). Therefore, place is "a setting to which individuals are emotionally and culturally attached" (Altman and Low 1992, 5), a section of space "enriched with human experience and understanding; an organized world of meaning" (Tuan 2018, 179). Prieto (2012, 13) suggests that it is "any geographical site [...] that is meaningful to someone, for whatever reason," and immediately mitigates this definition's vagueness by stressing its two principal features: first, it involves a human relation; we can speak of a place only when "a person comes along and enters into a meaning-generating relationship with it"; and second, it is an unstable relationship, which may vary depending on the context of who thinks of a given site in terms of place and why and when they do so.

It follows that place has a much more immediate impact on our existence and identity than space and that it also represents a much more "formable" entity in that it can be unrestrictedly infused with new discursive meanings, which, in effect, prove more determining of the place's significance than its actual physical and historical attributes. If we understand place as being defined by human relations, then we have to accept their inherent variability and recognise the resulting contestatory and dialogical dimension of place. Rather than focusing on individual distinct places, we are then concerned with "place" as a mode of human existence or of being in the world. Any meaning of any place can be contested by other individuals and/or other contexts, so "any given site is going to be subject to a dialogical struggle over the meaning of that site" (Prieto 2012, 14). Approached and appropriated by a multiplicity of subjects, places evince a multiplicity of meanings projected upon them, often of a disparate or even contradictory character, which is precisely the case of interstitial territories, and fiction can serve as an apposite and illustrative medium for this dialogic contestation. Humanistic geographers, neo-humanists and phenomenological philosophers can be seen as the practitioners of this stance (Creswell 2015, 56).

Finally, the notion of "landscape" should be clarified in relation to the above-established space-place dyad. It can be defined as a middle term between the indeterminate space and the more fixed place since it "typically consists of several places, and yet it is linked to an area, a region, in a way space is not" (de Lange et al. 2008, xvi). Landscape is thus a greater geographical, but also meaningful, unit than place, formed when several places interconnect as a result of a person's longer-term habitation in, recurrent visits to or journeying through them. Endowed with meanings, places and landscapes are embedded with narratives, just as narratives allow us to comprehend and organise places. Reading and studying literary representations of places and landscapes, both real and imaginary, therefore enables us to think about them more thoroughly and systematically and be more attentive to how the ways in which we perceive and mentally appropriate places leave traces in our inner universe.

As a result of the above-mentioned spatial turn, a number of critical approaches investigating literary representations of both real and imaginary space and place have been developed since the late 1970s. All of them are intrinsically interdisciplinary, complementing and enhancing literary studies and poetics with an insight from other disciplines, such as psychology, philosophy, sociology, cultural anthropology, ecology and geography. Such a broad scope necessarily produces a diversity of theory-practices, as can be demonstrated on the examples of geopoetics, ecocriticism, psychogeography, humanistic geography and geocriticism.

Geopoetics challenges what it sees as a "separation of human beings from the rest of the natural world" and proposes "that the various domains into which knowledge has been separated can be unified by a poetics which places the planet Earth at the centre of experience" (Scottish Centre for Geopoetics). Kenneth White, the creator of the concept of geopoetics, advocates an alternative treatment of the space we inhabit to the prevailing quantitative approach, one that would attempt to restore the principles of natural philosophy towards what may be called "cosmoaesthetics". In this sense, geopoetics represents a particular fusion of poetry and geography, a higher unity of the two in which the poet discovers the nature of the explorer in themselves (White 1992, 165–176). Geopoetic thinking forces and equips us to revise not only our relationship with the world, but the very relationship between language and our being in this world. Geopoetics is thus far more than a literary or critical school, it is an interdisciplinary field that invites all like-minded thinkers, poets, and writers to share ideas and experience, an umbrella platform "where poetry, thought and science come together, in a climate of reciprocal inspiration" (The International Institute of Geopoetics). One of the more specifically oriented approaches that this platform has generated is ecocriticism, which is concerned with how written texts respond to modern environmentalism and the most acute ecological issues. Compared to geopoetics, ecocriticism is more avowedly ideological, tying its "cultural analyses explicitly to a 'green' moral and political agenda" (Garrard 2011, 3).

Like geopoetics, psychogeography strives to critique the dominant, mainstream Western thinking of rational and pragmatic materialism. Yet, being an ultimately urban practice, psychogeography rests in spontaneous, solitary acts of unrestricted strolling or wandering along the "off-centre" paths and terrains of the city. It is walking with the aim of subverting the politics and ideology of the authorities by deliberately avoiding officially promoted routes and places in favour of exploring and mentally mapping territories and spaces unlikely to be utilised for commercial purposes and thus destined for oblivion, the "landscapes of the id" as Iain Sinclair calls them (Sinclair 2003, 306). Psychogeography searches for experience, not knowledge, of the present through the prism of the past. This practice is fundamentally nostalgic and in practical terms ineffective as it does not strive to save or protect these vanishing aspects of the cityscape but merely records their existence and their impact upon the explorer's psyche through mental projections, textual discourse, and visual mediation. It is also reactionary in that it deliberately undermines the commonly held ideas of modern urban progress and planning, cherishing what in most cases stands in their way. A literary psychogeographer aims to reconstruct, though in an inevitably fragmentary and eclectic manner, the city's physical and mental topographies through "a superimposition of local and literary history, autobiographical elements and poetic preoccupations" (Coverley 2018, 12). This strolling practitioner attempts to expose the hidden layers and lines of force of impalpable urban experience and transform them into a representation, fusing the political, the visionary and the artistic: "Walks for their own sake, furiously enacted but lacking agenda [...] Walks as portraits. Walks as prophecy. Walks as rage. [...] Walks that release delirious chemicals in the brain as they link random sites (discrete images in an improvised poem). Savagely mute walks that provoke language" (Atkins and Sinclair 1999, 15). The result of such a practice cannot be other than subjective, biased, eclectic and fragmentary, based on layering, superimposition and juxtaposition rather than on logical causality and correlation.

However, although geopoetics and psychogeography have been inspiring for literary studies and criticism, their actual applicability as a general method of textual analysis and interpretation is rather limited. The former is too broadly conceived and too embedded in various extra-textual realities, while the latter is narrowly focused on a specific segment of human experience. Critical theories that are much more universally applicable to literary studies are humanistic geography and geocriticism, which are methods of analysis that combine literary theory with the study of geographic space. Unlike geopoetics, they are primarily concerned with the interaction between physical space and its literary rendering. Unlike psychogeography, they involve all kinds of spaces that are meaningful from the perspective of their inhabitants or observers.

Humanistic geography originally evolved as a branch of critical geography, a blend of geography and left-leaning social sciences and humanities responding to acute issues such as human rights, female emancipation, environmental problems, and anti-imperialism in the early 1970s. In the late 1970s and 1980s, humanistic geography gradually separated from the more radical Marxist and feminist currents of critical geography, focusing generally on the multi-layered relationships between geographic properties of space and place and human beings, its aim being to examine "how geographical activities and phenomena reveal the quality of human awareness", and, by doing so, show "human experience in its ambiguity, ambivalence, and complexity" (Tuan 2018, 84). In order to achieve the necessary empathy to do so, geography needs to seek assistance from various branches of the humanities, especially history, philosophy, the arts, theology, and literature. Drawing also on Bachelard's spatial poetics, Yi-Fu Tuan, the main proponent of this practice, is particularly interested in the ambivalent human experience that is generated by the interaction of opposing forces of place and space, that is, between the intimate, secure, and rooted on the one hand, and the remote, intangible, and expansive on the other. Literary representations of place and space assume a crucial role in his investigations as he believes that language and communication, especially in the form of written texts, play a crucial role in people's creation of a sense of geographical environment, and, as such, can serve them as a useful guide in their dealings with the potentially progressive dialectical tensions between the existential poles of place and space.

Lately, psychogeography, whose field of research has been restricted almost exclusively to urban landscape, has proved to be an inspiration behind the development of new approaches, such as *deep topography*, developed by Nick Papadimitriou (Self), or *deep locational criticism*, demarcated by Jason Finch in his *Deep Locational Criticism: Imaginative Place in Literary Research and Teaching* (2016). Both of these approaches involve archaeological research as one of the key aspects of their respective fields of inquiry and both study real places and their artistic reflections. What both of these disciplines share is their aspiration to provide a deeper and wider-reaching analysis of the functioning of a place, focusing mainly on the effects of environment, both natural and man-made, on the human psyche (Finch 2016, 199). Deep locational criticism is an interdisciplinary practice merging a number of techniques based on several academic disciplines grounded in empirical study, such as "architectural history and the study of the built environment; local history; cultural geography; industrial-age archaeology" (Finch 2016, 21). Deep topography focuses on natural rather than man-made landscapes and is mostly concerned with their ethical and ecocritical implications. It acknowledges "the magnitude of response to landscape" (Coverley 2018, 179), which Nick Papadimitriou, its key proponent, considers to be insufficiently featured "in most accounts that I read of landscape" (Coverley 2018, 179). Both deep locational criticism and deep topography regard the literary text as an irreplaceable aspect of imaginative places as it "participates in [their] construction" (Coverley 2018, 22). The privileged position of place as the centre of the study echoes the position of scholars such as Betrand Westphal, who formulated the essence of so-called geocriticism.

Geocriticism, which aims to create a more universal use for literary studies, is a method of analysis that incorporates literary theory into the study of geographic space. It explores how different recipients engage with the spaces and places that are formative for them in terms of their identity and sense of being in the world and, along with this, how their lived spatial experience is translated into textual discourse and its interpretation. Like Lefebvre's Spaces of Representation and Soja's Thirdspace, it is based on the premise that all lived spaces are, at the same time, "real-and-imagined" (Soja 1996, 11) in that they exist both as geographic entities and their imaginary projections, and that the relationship between them, and their very nature can, in consequence, best be discovered through the study of their textual representation. Geocriticism believes that it allows us "to understand 'real' places by understanding their fundamental fictionality. And vice-versa, of course. We understand fictional spaces by grasping their own levels of reality as they become part of our world" (Tally 2011b, x). As such, it can cast some light on the ways in which we attempt to make sense of our world and our place in it, through an in-depth examination of the diverse ways in which we approach and process our spatial experience.

Developed at the beginning of the millennium by the French scholar Bertrand Westphal, and formulated in his 2007 comprehensive study *Geocriticism: Real and Fictional Spaces* (*La Géocritique: Réel, Fiction, Espace*), geocriticism soon proved to be an effective tool for looking into the convoluted relationship between human beings and the environment they occupy. In its original form, it is a set of critical practices that explore the ways in which literary representations of space interact with the geographic reality of the world. Owing to these practices, various people – readers, critics, scholars, geographers – can "engage with the spaces that make life, through lived experience and through imaginary projections, meaningful" (Tally 2011b, xii). Westphal is primarily interested in spaces of heterogeneity, in what Deleuze and Guattari call smooth spaces, which are characterised by nomadic free action as opposed to the systematic workings of the State apparatus in striated spaces, organised around points rather than lines and directioned in open rather than closed intervals. As a result, they evince a strong tendency towards deterritorialisation (2000, 480). Similarly, Westphal's geocriticism is based on three underlying principles: the first – spatiotemporality – denotes an increasing tendency of modern theory to entwine space and time, that is, not only to temporalise space as before but also to spatialise time. This tendency ran simultaneously with another paradigmatic shift when the historical perception of time was challenged by the relative laws of space-time, breaking down the continuous and steady timeline into a dynamic profusion of (time)lines or even points. Therefore, the most apt metaphor to express this new perception of space-time is that of entropy, i.e. the property of a system that is characterised by a state of disorder, randomness, and uncertainty in which, as this state intensifies, the system eventually evolves into a new state. The result of this increasing disorder, or turbulence, is nonequilibrium. Unlike orderly equilibrium, which is immune to metamorphoses and, persisting only in one condition, is a nonstory, nonequilibrium is far more interesting since it offers a complexity of stories corresponding to its disarrayed lines and separate points of instability (Westphal 2011, 18–19). Two more metaphorical concepts related to entropy that Westphal makes use of are bifurcation and isotropy: while bifurcation refers to the fact that a profusion of timelines tends to organise in forking paths, an isotopic system of (time)lines is one whose progression defies hierarchy as the directions and configurations of all the timelines possess equal properties. The paramount consequence of this spatialisation of time is that "space appears as heterogeneous as time" (Westphal 2011, 25), defined by movement, mobility, and temporariness.

The second principle, called transgressivity, refers precisely to this characteristic feature of contemporary space, namely its capacity for movement and mobility. As said above, such space is inherently heterogeneous, in fact limitless, since it unfolds between points that connect an infinite number of lines. However, this space is always subject to homogenising (or striating to use Deleuze and Guattari's term) forces through which the various institutions of the state apparatus impose boundaries and limits on it. However, all boundaries and limits call for crossing and trespassing, just as rules and norms call for violation and deviation. This transgression, that is, the intentional leaving of one's own space and stepping into a foreign one, is in essence inseparable from movement and change, but can be random and spontaneous rather than the result of some organised activity or impulse. However, when it becomes recurrent and continual, it develops into a state – transgressivity, the perpetual operation of peripheral and destabilising processes that operate upon heterogeneous spaces. This permanent transgressivity of movement, transition, transformation, and transgression in defiance of established norms renders the given space incessantly volatile and it is "eventually governed by an almost impalpable deterritorialising and evolutionary dialectic" (Westphal 2011, 52),[1] particularly in the tension between the centre and the periphery. Spatial representation of such a territory is therefore inevitably palimpsestic in order to capture all the ongoing successive changeovers as "erasures and overwritings" (Westphal 2011, 60).

Accordingly, referentiality, the third of these principles, which speaks of the relations between real spaces and their textual renderings, claims these links between the referent and its representation are also constantly moving and oscillating. Drawing on Lefebvre's notions of conceived space and lived space, Westphal notes that a textual representation of space can be quite consistent without directly corresponding to the actual reality, sometimes forming a wholly fictional space of representation. In any case, such a representation never reproduces the referent,

1 Such a system evinces all the defining properties of Deleuze and Guattari's rhizome, namely the principles of connection, heterogeneity, multiplicity, signifying rupture, cartography, and decalcomania. Although every rhizome contains lines of segmentarity according to which it is stratified and organised, there is a rupture in it whenever these explode into lines of flight and deterritorialisation. It may be broken but it will always start up again, either on its old lines or on its new ones (2000, 6-12).

but constitutes a discourse that establishes it. The representation thus reproduces an experience of the real, and human spaces exist only in the modes of this experience (Westphal 2011, 80–85). However, the distinction between the real and the represented becomes blurred as the represented becomes part of the real or even participates in its formation. The relationship between the fictional and real place (if there is one at all) is volatile due to the transgressive nature of the referent, based on the highly variable degree of correlation arising from the oscillating interaction between the world and the virtual, discursively produced reality of textual representation.

These major principles of spatial-discursive heterogeneity are supplemented with other consequent phenomena, namely multifocalisation, that is, inviting a multiplicity of views on a geographical referent without privileging any of them; polysensorality, that is, promoting the experience of an environment using all the senses; stratigraphy, that is, highlighting the temporal variability of spaces that never unfold in pure simultaneity but through a permanently reactivating layering caused by the concatenation of diverse temporalities; and intertextuality, which refers to the architecture/architexture of space, that is, the inherent interplay between spaces in texts and texts in spaces (Westphal 2011, 114–164, Tally 2011b, xiv–xv). The pivotal aspect of Westphal's geocriticism is its strictly geo-centred focus, which means that it takes the actual spaces/places at the centre of debate and draws on their textual representations in order to grasp them more thoroughly. In other words, it is a comparative mode of analysis aimed at "understanding a given place (through the problematics of representation) rather than studying a given set of representations (through the thematics of place)" (Prieto 2011, 21). What follows from this restricted scope is not only the absence of an ego-centred dimension that would be concerned with how the sense of a place affects those who encounter it, but also that it can only be used for textual representations of real-life territories. However, he does not present his concept in a doctrinaire manner that would delegitimise the other approach, but rather aims to build on it so as to conceive "a kind of metacritical endeavor" that "extends literary studies into the realm of the geographical referent in a way that transcends the aesthetic function of literature and seeks to show how it can actually participate in and inflect the history of the places in question" (Prieto 2011, 21–22). Given all this, Westphal's geocriticism operates somewhere between the geography of the real and that of the imaginary. Moreover, its defining principles are formulated in such a way as to legitimise alternatively focused geocritical approaches.

A more markedly ego-centred form of geocriticism, though admittedly derived from Westphal's, has been developed by the American literary scholar Robert T. Tally Jr. in so-called "literary cartography". This is a form of narrative that takes into account both the social and psychological experience of space/place and the possibility of reflecting such spatial experience through a wholly imaginary literary environment. In his view, geocriticism can become a tool with which we can examine how our spatial experience and awareness determine the very nature of our being in the world. It should therefore include as a subject of its interest not only the spaces, both real and imaginary, that we experience through texts, but "also the experience of space and place within ourselves" (Tally 2011a, 3). He believes that just as textual representations can establish and mobilise spaces, spaces are infused with meaning and thus possess a unique potential for narrative. As he puts it, literary cartography is a "practice by which writers figuratively represent, or attempt to represent, the social space of the narrative or text, as well as the relationship of the individual or collective subject to a larger spatial, social, and cultural ensemble" (Tally 2016, 25). A crucial part of these meanings and narratives is linked to the spatiotemporal and transgressive character of spaces, which is why spatial criticism should pay attention not only to representations of the actual places, but also to "the experience of place and displacement, while exploring the interrelations between lived experience and a more abstract or unrepresentable spatial network that subtly or directly shapes it" (Tally 2014, x). In other words, his geocriticism concerns not only spaces that readers get to know through textual representation, but also their mental reflections, through which it "can examine how the ways in which we are situated in space determine the nature and quality of our existence in the world" (Tally 2011a, 8). In doing so, it goes far beyond the reproduction of real-life referents towards imagined and mental spaces, thus accentuating the experiential and aesthetic dimensions of spatial representation and appropriation.

Tally's aim is to pay attention not only to places that writers and readers experience through texts, but also to the very nature of that experience and its impact on how we see ourselves. He speaks of so-called "mapping narratives", which attempt to map the real-and-imagined spaces of human existence, and which are expressions of a "productive ambiguity" – something that maps while also being something to be mapped (Tally 2014, 3). Such a narrative provides a textual cartography of actual and/or fictitious spaces, but is also "mapped" by readers' interpretations and the interpretative frameworks and socio-spatial contexts in which they are situated and which make them meaningful to those readers. Literary cartography has a wide field of interest as "its activity requires the meticulous coordination of different registers, from the individual subject's subjective experience of spaces and places to the vaster, abstract or even scientific apprehension of a spatial and historical constellation of forces" (Tally 2016, 21). It is based on the premise that the narrative both represents and shapes the spaces depicted in it, thus creating the fictitious environment of the story while also projecting a certain reality into it, and that this real and imaginary can then be comprehended at once. Mapping narratives thus "make possible novel spaces" (2014, 12), and the geocritical explorations of these literary cartographies can help us better understand our own spatial experience.

From this understanding of geocriticism, it is only a step to the phenomenological conception, which places emphasis on the interaction between the physical environment and the human psyche. As Jonathan White puts it, as humans, we cannot discount the psyche, i.e. "the mental perspectives with which we endow spaces and places" and the fact that "place, and the way that it is imagined, is imbued with attitude" (2019, 5, 6). This premise informs the phenomenological conception of geocriticism, which emphasises the interaction between the physical environment and the human psyche and, drawing in part on Tuan's humanistic geography, examines the relationship between the psyche of individuals and the physical environment they occupy by "emphasizing the embodied, environmentally constrained nature of human consciousness" (Prieto 2011, 16). It is subjectivist in that it looks at places from within, giving "precedence to the density, complexity, and qualitative aspects of place experience", while the opposite, objectivist or scientific, approach "relies on the analytic abstraction and decentred perspective associated with maps" (Prieto 2012, 187). However, by focusing on the geocritical inquiry into "place as a manifestation of the dynamic interpretation of consciousness and world" (Prieto 2011, 25), Eric Prieto argues for a comprehensive theory of space that would reconcile these two visions by bringing them together and looking for ways in which to adopt both perspectives simultaneously.

Prieto tries to combine the two approaches in his geocritical analysis of fictional representations of space, seeking to find out how they shape our attitudes towards the environment and how they imprint themselves on the mental space of our consciousness. In line with the current understanding of spaces as inherently heterogeneous and transitional, he emphasises the concept of the *entre-deux* or in-between place, that is, the borderlands situated between the officially recognised landscapes/cityscapes and what lies beyond their limits, where the entropic, transitional, and transgressive momentum is most palpable. It designates "the many different kinds of sites that fall between the established categories that shape our expectations of what a place should be and that often tend, therefore, to be misunderstood, maligned, or simply ignored" (Prieto 2012, 1). These emergent, liminal and interstitial territories, although generally perceived as "defective variants of more-established, better understood places", possess a substantial productive potential which tends to be largely overlooked and underappreciated, but which makes them "unexpectedly resourceful loci of innovation and development" (Prieto 2012, 1). Prieto thus argues for this latent dynamic potential of these interstitial "non-places", such as borderlands, edges, peripheral areas, brownfields, backstreets, and the need to "examine the ways in which literary representations help us to understand the often misunderstood properties of emergent forms of place" (2012, 1–2).

Prieto notes that although these sites have always existed, they have taken on a particular significance within the unprecedented rapidity of recent socio-cultural transformations, as these transformations have allowed for new forms of spatial organisation and modes of habitation that have generated areas "destined to become an enduring part of the physical and cultural landscape even if they are not yet fully understood or accepted" (2012, 9), particularly on the margins of established habitats. As such, they naturally attract imaginative appropriation, including literary representation. Thus, according to Prieto, the *entre-deux* can be said to be "a kind of master trope for our era" (2012, 9), as they appositely reflect the transitional moment of history in which we live and thus prove a particularly useful object of geocritical study. Imaginative literature, which tends to be preoccupied with the productive potential of the peripheral, the liminal, the transitory, and their underappreciated properties, can thus become a crucial mediator in our understanding of lived spaces. Drawing also on the premise that the loss of one kind of place leads to the emergence of new spatial alternatives, Prieto calls for a systematic inquiry into literary representations of *entre-deux* places, not only in order to better comprehend the overlooked properties of borderline and emergent forms of place, but also to provide further insight into our experience of place/space in the current, globalised era.

The tendency to examine the ways in which (literary) texts render the intersection of human consciousness and the environment links geocritical conceptions, and especially the perspective of Eric Prieto, to another equally influential and inclusive contemporary approach, ecocriticism. Ecocriticism is generally understood as an attempt to connect literary theory and criticism with environmental concerns (Garrard 2011, x). However, its field of study is not limited to natural landscapes or wilderness areas, but "also includes cultivated and built landscapes, the natural elements and aspects of those landscapes, and cultural interactions with those natural elements" (Wallace and Armbruster 2001, 4). According to Kathleen R. Wallace and Karla Armbruster, the editors of *Beyond Nature Writing* (2001), a collection of scholarly essays dedicated to expanding the boundaries of ecocriticism, environment need not only refer to "natural" or "wilderness" areas. Therefore, ecocriticism should assess even those texts which feature "less obviously 'natural' landscapes and human attempts to record, order, and ultimately understand their own relationships to those environments" (Wallace and Armbruster 2001, 4). Cheryll Glotfelty, the author and editor of a pioneering work of ecocriticism, *The Ecocriticism Reader: Landmarks in Literary Ecology* (1996), proposed a path of more "interdisciplinary, multicultural, and international" (1996, xxv) ecocritical scholarship, believing that "the environmental crisis has been exacerbated by our fragmented, compartmentalized, and overly specialized way of knowing the world" (1996, xxii). Glotfelty's message concerns mainly humanities scholars, whom she urges to gain knowledge of scientific disciplines so that they are able to meet the demands of the interdisciplinary nature of the ecocritical approach. Ecocriticism thus echoes the universal call for the merging of individual scientific and artistic fields in order to overcome the traditional dualistic division.

At this point, one more crucial spatial concept should be mentioned – that of Michel Foucault's heterotopia (1986, 24–27). Heterotopias are places of heterogeneity with the curious property of reflecting and being linked to all other places, while simultaneously contradicting them and challenging the set of relations that they happen to mirror. They are counter-sites, absolutely different from all the other real sites to be found within the culture, in which all these other sites are both represented and designated as well as contested and inverted. Heterotopias can be specified by five defining principles: They exist in all cultures and take varied forms. Although each heterotopia has its precisely given function, it can assume one or more other functions as society evolves. The heterotopia can juxtapose several other places within itself, even if these are incompatible in themselves. The temporal arrangement of heterotopias is that of heterochrony, since they are usually linked to slices of time and function best when liberated from traditional temporality. They also presuppose a system of openings and closings that somehow isolate them and make them freely inaccessible. In order to enter, one either has to perform a ritual or rite, make a gesture or obtain permission, or the entry is compulsory only for selected individuals. Finally, they have a function in relation to all the other places, that is, they mirror them.

Foucault also distinguishes several types of heterotopia, namely crisis heterotopias (special places reserved for individuals who are in a state of crisis according to the standards of their culture, for instance pregnant women or elderly people), heterotopias of deviation (for individuals whose behaviour is not compatible with the required norms), heterotopias of indefinitely accumulating time (immobile places in which different time periods are perpetually accumulated), heterotopias of fleeting, transitory temporality (temporary, provisional sites that, through cyclical recurrence, are oriented towards the eternal), heterotopias of illusion (illusory places that expose the real places outside as even more illusory), and heterotopias of compensation (sites that are supposed to be orderly and well-arranged in order to compensate for the others that seem chaotic, messy, and ill-conceived). The list of examples of such places includes the boarding school, the barracks, the prison, the asylum, the rest home, the psychiatric hospital, the cemetery, the garden, the museum, the library, the fairground, the holiday village, the hammam, the Scandinavian sauna, the brothel, the Puritan colony, and the ship. Heterotopias, Foucault concludes, are essential for every culture, especially because they represent "the greatest reserve of the imagination" (1986, 27), a reserve that propels the freedom of dreams, and, as such, helps to defy the potentially authoritarian and repressive tendencies of the state apparatus.

As Michel Foucault predicted in his 1967 lecture entitled "Of Other Spaces", "[t]he present epoch will perhaps be above all the epoch of space" (1986, 22). Throughout the second half of the twentieth century, the humanities, especially philosophy and literary theory, have acknowledged the significance, if not the primacy, of the category of space. Acutely perceptive of other branches of knowledge, literary theory generated a number of interdisciplinary approaches and proved to be a formative influence on other disciplines, architectural theory and practice being one of the most prominent. Just as literary theory underwent a spatial turn, with a wide range of works dealing with the spatial practices behind the poetics of a literary text, contemporary architectural theory and practice underwent a textual turn. Of the theories that most affected architectural theory and steered the direction of its thinking towards the inclusion of a linguistic approach, Roland Barthes' "The Death of the Author" (1967) and his emphasis on semiotics, and Julia Kristeva's concept of intertextuality (1969) are the most widely acknowledged (Hauptmann 2020, iv).[2] What followed was a swift embrace by architectural theory and practice of various aspects and approaches developed mainly in the context of literary theory.[3] This development testifies to the precedence of interdisciplinarity as a universal approach to different aspects of human creation, both practical and theoretical. It also highlights the reciprocal nature of the relationship between human beings and their environment, which is acknowledged by the plethora of theoretical disciplines presented throughout this chapter. The key postulate they all develop is also the one behind this monograph – the textual representation of space proves to be an irreplaceable part of spatial experience, and the mutual influence of these two components of human perception enables a more complex interpretation of our living environment.

1.1 Approaching Crace's and Mawer's Spatial Representations

From what has been said so far, it can be assumed that the fictional rendering of varied spaces, places, and landscapes is one of the idiosyncratic features of both Simon Mawer's and Jim Crace's novels. Their narratives therefore naturally invite critical examination based on spatial theories of textual representation. Given their protagonists' outspoken experience of being in such milieux, Yi-Fu Tuan's approach suggests itself in the

2 Diana Agrest and Mario Gandelsona's "Semiotics and Architecture: Ideological Consumption or Theoretical Work" may be regarded as one of the first Anglo-American theoretical works viewing architecture through the lenses of the contemporary French intellectual postulates as well as the Italian focus on semiotics. The article was first published in the first issue of *Oppositions*, an architectural journal produced between 1973 and 1984 by the Institute for Architecture and Urban Studies in New York (Hauptmann 2020, iv).

3 Currently, the textual turn in architecture has taken a number of different forms. This is reflected in contemporary architectural discourse, which is beset by the simultaneous and contradictory processes of the abstraction of space on the one hand, and its materialisation and commodification on the other. Some authors see the textual turn as a means to an end, helping to communicate other functions of architecture, such as its ethical function. The more radical perspectives focus on the current proliferation of technologies and developments in mapping, and examine their influence on the process of reading buildings and architecture. This merging tendency has mostly been embraced by architects, who see it as the premise of their practice: architecture that does not exist in a vacuum but within a larger stream of images and ideas (Steffens 2009, 14).

first place, for both novelists depict places as a way of human existence in the world. Moreover, both authors tend to situate their plots in times and places of profound historical transformation. Their preferred subject matter is transition, that is, the way their characters deal with the sudden need to face up to an impending change and to adapt rather quickly to new circumstances. These processes are always closely linked to the physical environments in which they take place. Both Mawer's and, even more so, Crace's novels depict the turbulent and frustrating process during which the traditional and habitual are challenged and undermined by the modern and unfamiliar. In some of their novels, this transition is individual and personal, in others, it concerns whole communities, though mostly metonymically portrayed through the fates of a few protagonists. The power of their narratives lies precisely in how they interweave the actual environments with these transitional events and their impact on the physical and mental lives of their characters.

Each author, however, develops a major narrative element through which he expresses the theme of transition. For Crace, a theme related to that of transition – the human impulse to tell stories and the centrality of storytelling in human life – is always explored not only within the framework of the transitional historical moment he depicts, but also in relation to the psychic and experiential properties of the physical environment inhabited by the main protagonist. Rather than storytelling, Mawer projects the theme of transition onto the pronounced liminality of his characters and their milieux. The former move between linguistic, cultural, and national identities, often exploiting this capability for the sake of both the thematic enrichment of the novels as well as the pace of the action. The latter category of places and spaces is closely connected with the liminal, if not hybrid, nature of their inhabitants. Both Mawer's and Crace's writings thus provide rich material for an in-depth analysis from the perspective of humanistic geography.

Although some of Crace's novels feature urban settings, and three of them are set entirely in a city, psychogeography would be difficult to employ as an appropriate lens through which to approach his literary treatment of the cityscape. His protagonists, though often "townies" through and through, can hardly be described as solitary subversive walkers in search of the vanishing undersides of the city's topography and its psychogeographic lines of force. Rather, they are walkers with a practical purpose who, when the environment and their state of mind allow it, enjoy being part of the streets, or, on the contrary, when things go wrong, they project their unease and suffering onto the cityscape, which thus becomes an indirect accomplice to their misfortune. Therefore, even in these cases, the experiential and introspective character of humanistic geography, and to some extent of deep topography and ecocriticism, complemented by the perspective of other concepts of patterns of modern urban existence, such as Michel de Certeau's survey of practices of everyday life, is a far more applicable methodology for exploring the relationship of such characters to their urban milieu.

Mawer's treatment of urban milieux mirrors Crace's to some extent – his protagonists rarely perceive urban spaces and places as realms of subversive potential, mapping the half-forgotten terrain in search of ideologically unrestricted paths. On the other hand, as his novels often develop parallels between the present and the past, there is also a tendency to emphasise connections through spatial representation. Ancient paths, ruins, and landscape alterations of past civilisations are referred to on occasion as the characters strive for a better understanding of the present by means of acknowledging the past. The importance of the built environment and the use of the house as a powerful spatial trope, motif, and setting testifies to the results of Gaston Bachelard's topoanalysis. His study of intimate places discusses the role of houses and their employment in literature, stressing the decisive, defining role they play in the way people experience other places. Moreover, as Mawer often exemplifies in his novels, houses as archetypal representations of place, have the potential to bind together individual temporal layers and thus become perfect vehicles for exploring the connection between the past and the present. In addition, this focus on the house further contributes to the study of place as a category, elaborating on humanistic geography.

Mawer's habit of situating his works in existing environments and historical events, and his meticulous use of period detail, invite a type of reading that encompasses both real places and their artistic renderings. In order to be able to compare and contrast actual places and their artistic reflections, an interdisciplinary approach is necessary. Mawer's texts, which focus mainly on the built environment rather than the landscape, benefit from an analysis that highlights aspects of architectural history, but also local history and cultural geography. All these aspects of analysis are developed by deep locational criticism and deep topography, whose elements provide a suitable framework for a deeper understanding of the functioning of places and spaces in his fiction.

Another critical approach that has proved effective in analysing spatial representations in both Crace's and Mawer's fiction is geocriticism, especially its more ego-centred variants. One of these is Robert T. Tally's literary cartography as an experiential form of the geocritical method, which requires "the meticulous coordination of different registers, from the individual subject's subjective experience of space and places to the vaster, abstract or even scientific apprehension of a spatial and historical constellation of forces" (Tally 2016, 21). It is a type of mapping of fictional landscapes that far transcends the mere reproduction of a geospatial referent, as the author not only figuratively (re)presents the social space in his/her narrative, but also seeks to situate the story's protagonists in a larger matrix of relations in which spatial factors play a crucial role. Exploring such a literary cartographic narrative then offers its readers the opportunity and the tools to encounter and empathise with the experience of others, as well as to better understand their own. This is most evident in stories that trace the protagonists' progress in space and time, and their physical as well as mental movement on the narrative "map" of the fictional world, as is the case in several of Crace's and Mawer's novels. Tally's concept can thus help us to explore the ways in which both authors link their protagonists' mental, emotional, and spiritual worlds to the geography and topography of the territories they journey through, and consequently how their novels' fictional space-time follows a thematic trajectory from pain, despair, and confusion to hope, consolation, and promise.

Along with Tally's mapping narratives, Eric Prieto's phenomenological geocritical approach can shed more light on Crace's and Mawer's spatial representations, especially on spaces of and in transition. The pivotal turns of events in the destinies of Crace's and Mawer's communities in transition also impact and transform the defining properties of the environments in which they occur, to the extent that they become reflections of the shifts in their inhabitants' consciousness, or even one of the inner movers and mediators of the transformation process itself. One of the immediate results of these social, economic, and cultural changeovers is the disappearance and emergence of places/spaces as part of the transformation of the original landscapes and cityscapes, as well as the production of a number of liminal, borderland, and transitory places.

For this reason, Prieto's concept of the *entre-deux* territories and their latent creative powers offers a fruitful analytical tool for examining their role within the narrative and thematic frameworks of the novels. Moreover, with their capacity to simultaneously reflect, appropriate, and contest the other places within the given culture, several of these inherently heterogeneous, emergent, and in-between sites fall into some of the categories of Michel Foucault's heterotopia, including their potential as means of resistance to the totalising measures of the dominant establishment, through which they allow Crace to subtly incorporate his political outlook into the stories. Mawer expresses his political and ethical stance rather indirectly, mostly by means of his narratives. Mawer's choice of key historical events, the hybrid nature of his protagonists, and the radically moral preoccupations which govern their actions all testify to the author's deeply rooted democratic and liberal thinking, while also echoing the concerns expressed in the similarly minded works of Jim Crace. Although both authors tend to set their plots in tumultuous and often historical situations, the majority of their works illustrate their hopeful attitude to the human condition.

One of the aspects that contributes to the relatively positive outlook is the spatial rendering of Mawer's novels, which is most emblematically imprinted in the prominence of spatial conceits, which make the novels decisively topocentric. Mawer focuses on in-between stages, spaces, and places, which is reflected in the linguistic, cultural, and personal identities of his protagonists. His predilection for unstable environments, heavily influenced by a range of heterogenising forces, mostly echoes Westphal's conception of geocriticism and his concept of "non-equilibrium" (Westphal 2011, 19). In accordance with Westphal's emphasis on the creative capacity of this state, Mawer's approach to literary space exemplifies its inclination towards bifurcation and entropy. In other respects, however, it deviates from this theoretical perspective, since the spaces of Mawer's novels seem to be defined by their adherence to real-life topography, and yet their representational nature is usually challenged by their close connection to the characters and their mental states, expressed through the multisensory nature of Mawer's spatial descriptions. The vividness of Mawer's imagery, and most importantly its spatiality, enables the identification of readers with his texts, bringing the direction of the study closer to Prieto's and Tally's conception of geocriticism. Mawer's and Crace's novels thus become illustrations of the mutual influence and interaction between the spaces of the novels, their protagonists, and their influence on the psyche of the reader.

2. Jim Crace

Jim Crace (b. 1946) is an award-winning writer and author of thirteen novels. He is known for his gripping and humane narratives written in idiosyncratically rhythmic and melodious prose in which minute, exact, and often crude details alternate with inventively poetic turns of phrase. Although he is very self-deprecating about his fame, describing his writing as enjoyment rather than hard work or even real work (Jim Crace Website), two of his novels – *Quarantine* (1997) and *Harvest* (2013) – have been shortlisted for the (Man) Booker Prize. He has also been awarded a number of prestigious prizes in Britain and the United States, where his books have enjoyed considerable popularity, as they also have in continental Europe.[4] The critical acclaim[5] for his novels and their popularity with readers has placed Crace in the same league as other members of the strong generation of British writers born in the immediate post-war period; namely Julian Barnes, Ian McEwan, Martin Amis, Salman Rushdie, Peter Ackroyd, Graham Swift, Simon Mawer, and Kazuo Ishiguro, although he is not as widely and internationally known. This may be one of the reasons why he does not see himself as part of the official literary scene or literary circles, claiming to have no close friends among the celebrated British novelists, preferring rather, as he notes with a dose of ironic overstatement, "to hang out with jazzmen" (The Free Library

4 These awards include the Whitbread Award, the James Tait Black Memorial Award, the International Dublin Literary Award, the American Academy of Arts and Letters Award, the National Book Critics Circle Award and the Windham-Campbell Literature Prize.

5 Although the majority of Crace's novels have not only been positively reviewed but also well--received by academia, only two scholarly monographs dealing with his writings have been published so far; namely *Jim Crace* (2006) by Philip Tew and *Jim Crace: Into the Wilderness* (2018), edited by Katy Shaw and Kate Aughterson.

2012). His status as a writer who stands apart from mainstream literary production is partly due to the fact that he has lived outside London, spending a large part of his life in Birmingham before moving to rural Warwickshire. Most importantly, it is his writing style and approach to narrative that have primarily distinguished him from his fellow writers, whose work also began to gain recognition in the 1980s.[6]

Unlike most of his peers, Crace has never shown much interest in the employment of distinctively subversive, self-consciously ironic and self-reflexive postmodernist themes, techniques, and narrative strategies; namely metafiction, intertextuality, parody, pastiche, and experimental playfulness, or the various ways in which narrative authority is contested, such as the use of unreliable narrators, a multiple-narrative perspective, and the deliberate mixing of the factual and the fictitious. Instead, he professes what he calls the traditional approach to writing, derived from the ancient storytelling tradition of legends, myths, and folk tales, which are impersonal in the sense that "the character of the storyteller is completely absent – but the invention is entire" (Begley 2002). He prefers to erase himself from his stories and immerse himself in the realm of pure imagination, relying on the power of the narrative to steer him where necessary. That is why he always begins his novels with the idea, the general theme of the novel, with little or no idea of the plot, characters, narrative voice or other technical details: "I wait for the book to express itself and then let the story unfold in front of me. Narrative is giving; it does the work for you" (Guidarini 2013). Writing is therefore a largely intuitive process for him.

Corespondingly, Crace subscribes to a neo-Darwinian theory of the narrative impulse, insisting that humankind has a "storytelling gene" and that spreading made-up stories is an "adaptive strategy" (Begley 2002). It is something that has been perpetuated for evolutionary reasons since the principal purpose of stories that either reimagine the past or project the future is "to prepare communities for problems and rehearse them for hard times" (Bookgroup.info 2007), "to play out decisions before we make them, to plan routes before we take them" (Begley 2003), and "to encounter experiences without having the experiences" (*antae* Editorial Board 2015), thus giving people the "evolutionary advantage" (Proctor 2000) of being equipped with systems of ideas, experience, and wisdom that can be activated in case of impending crisis. One of its crucial func-

6 While Crace does not associate himself much with modern British literature, he claims to feel European and admits that he prefers to read European novelists such as Gunther Grass, Italo Calvino, and Primo Levi (Lawless).

tions is to provide narratives of comfort that people might turn to when faced with things beyond their understanding or acceptance, especially when dealing with death.

Crace is an atheist but he acknowledges the transcendental human desire for a consolatory narrative, only he does not call it God; he calls it nature or landscape, but sees no great difference between them.[7] This is why he believes that providing comfort in the face of death is one of the crucial tests of what his books are about (Mahmood 2015), and why he sees them as hopeful despite their often dark stories and settings. As he explains, what he wants to do "is to go to dark places and see humankind in its worst moments, yet still find the narrative of comfort and optimism there" (Naidu 2015). He considers himself a sentimental yet strong optimist who believes in fundamental human goodness, only his optimism is always well-hidden "in the murkiest of corners where it will have had to have been strong in order to survive" (Biblio Blog 2007). This perspective must always be fought for and redeemed by painful personal sacrifices, dramatising the author's conviction that "[e]verything new worth having is paid for by the loss of something old worth keeping" (Begley 2002). It is this ethical paradigm that allows readers to assign shared archetypal patterns of thought and wisdom to each of Crace's imaginary landscapes, no matter how exotic or uncanny, to produce meaning that is understood across cultures. This is why the feeling of familiarity readers may experience in his stories stems from their parabolic meaning rather than from their mirroring of the real world, even though they were originally triggered by real-life events. In this, Crace refers to the tradition of oral storytelling in which useful and engaging content goes hand in hand with a pleasing form that is finely measured and melodious[8], full of evocative and often unusual figurative expressions that are complemented by a sense of close-up specificity, which are also qualities that Crace's narrative style aspires to.

He is a storyteller who acknowledges the primacy of imagination, strictly avoids using autobiographical and realistic elements in his novels, and refuses to carry out research to achieve a greater degree of plausibility. He believes that imaginative invention can "deliver a grander, more metaphorical portrait of our lives and landscapes than would result from a photographic approach" (Tayade 2011), asserting that if "[his] writing holds a lens up to the real world, then it is a cracked lens" (Tayade 2011).

7 This need for stories of consolation is where he sees himself related to religious belief since, as he notes, "we both embrace the power of narrative" (Proctor 2000).

8 Andrew Lawless, for instance, describes Crace's literary language as "beautifully rhythmic".

In his opinion, the need for storytelling is innate, and it has proved invaluable for the development of humankind – "if it were not we wouldn't still be storytellers" (The Free Library 2012), he insists, and attributes his own narrative capacity to this deeply embedded trait of human nature. He is convinced that stories not only help us to make better sense of the world but also, by revisiting the past and imagining the future, enable us to practice and plan our potential decisions and strategies without requiring excessive verisimilitude.

He is well aware that engaging and thrilling storytelling inevitably involves a certain degree of concocting lies and presenting them in a realistic way so that they seem more credible and convincing than some nebulous truths about the world. It is the kind of narrative playfulness he gladly espouses: "Literature and storytelling have got to have wisdoms and insights, they've got to be useful; but if they're mischievous, than that is really valuable" (*antae* Editorial Board 2015). Of course, a good storyteller should be able to present the often contingent and disparate fabric of the narrative in a coherent and logical manner and revolve it around a distinct and sensible plotline, but this may not be sufficient for their story to have the desired impact on the audience. Any story that does not contain the fantastic and the embroidered runs the risk of being found dull and narrow. However, when it comes to fabulation, Crace distinguishes between being mischievous and being malicious, considering the latter to be incompatible with his notion of storytelling, as he asserts: "The kind of lying I do and always did was never to deceive you. It was to be amusing and entertaining and generous" (The Free Library 2012). In other words, the fabricated must be subordinate to the story and its audience, not the other way around.

Crace stresses the distinction between traditional and conventional writing, the latter being temporally and geographically anchored in reality and thus, in his view, referring to mainstream realism. He claims that he "lacks realist skills" but possesses "an uncanny talent for making invented places and events feel here-and-now real" (Begley 2002). What may be mistaken for a realistic or naturalistic aspect in his stories is rather an exceptional "preciseness of observed detail" (Tew 2006, xiii), especially from the natural world. He thinks his fiction is too inventive and metaphorical for a realist approach, which is why he prefers to be described as a "fabulist" (Mahmood 2015, Cross 2013) rather than a realist, or even a magical realist. His novels are full of invented words for objects, animals, and natural phenomena disguised as scientific facts, which is his deliberate strategy for making readers "mistake the make-believe for realist detail" (Begley 2003). He wants his fiction, by means of its imaginativeness, to "dislocate the issues of the real world and place them elsewhere" (Begley 2002). However, despite being wholly made up, his settings are not those of fantasy worlds but are grounded in realistic detail and are therefore plausible rather than disorienting to readers, while at the same time being sufficiently different from the worlds that those readers inhabit. As he notes, he likes "trying to dislocate the readers by taking them to invented places, where the realism is magic and disconcerting rather than familiar" (Tayade 2011). For him, the mere fact that people tell stories based on their experience does not make them storytellers if their accounts are instinctively realist, that is, concerned with verisimilitude, fidelity, and coherence (The Free Library 2012), and their manipulation of facts is reduced to exaggeration and emphasis of one point of view over another. The essence of truly evolutionarily adaptive storytelling rests in confabulation and embroidery, which are in fact forms of spreading falsehood. However, he adds that this kind of lying, though driven by mischievous urges, is not intended to harm, mislead or deceive the audience, but to make the narration attractive and absorbing.

For similar reasons, Crace refuses to have his books labelled as historical fiction. Although many of his novels are set in diverse, more or less explicitly characterised, historical periods such as the late Neolithic age, the Renaissance period, the outset of the Victorian era and the early twentieth century, their stories do not seek to provide an image of a particular historical reality but are meant to be read as metaphors through which contemporary preoccupations can be recognised.[9] In order to support his claim, he demonstrates that his stories violate Hilary Mantel's two absolute golden rules for historical novelists (Wroe 2013): first, he is not interested in historical precision, he does not research or verify facts, he invents, and this invention is propelled by the subject matter he wishes to render and relies on the power of his vocabulary; second, he does not avoid projecting modern concerns onto historical environments; on the contrary, he claims that he is not "interested in writing any novel that isn't drenched in the twenty-first century sensibilities, whenever or wherever it's set" (Guidarini 2013). His settings thus "create provocative and complicated parallels with our own world and inspire dynamic and problematizing questions that often remain unanswered

9 As examples, Crace mentions *The Gift of Stones* (1988), a novel set in the stone age that refers to the socio-economic situation in Thatcherite Britain, or *Harvest*, set in an unspecified Renaissance world but inspired by the present day South American soya barons as well as asylum seekers in Birmingham (i.e. Wroe 2013, Hewitt 2013).

at the conclusion of his narratives" (Shaw and Aughterson 2018, 4). But while his stories may be read as allegories of the contemporary world, their focus is on "the aesthetic act as a redemptive force", which records "the semiotic via the symbolic" (Lane 2003, 37–38). Crace is convinced that the purpose of the novel as a genre is primarily to explore weighty human and social concerns rather than the fates of individuals. This is why his books tend to be moralistic and serious in the way they treat "big lofty moral issues"[10], such as the inevitability of death, the importance of religious belief, the decline of the Western world, love, and our loyalty to the land (Mahmood 2015), but they manage to do so playfully and poetically without being schematic, patronising or dogmatic.

Crace's writing also possesses an undeniable political dimension, particularly in the sense of being engaged with social and ethical issues. As an egalitarian socialist and a person of strong left-wing views, he "has long expressed regret that his novels aren't more directly political" (Wroe 2013)[11], but the very nature of his fiction, based as it is on ambiguity and metaphorical parallelism, requires a degree of authorial self-effacement, which precludes direct projection of his political views. Nevertheless, his political convictions do remain in his novels, albeit sometimes rather indirectly and latently expressed. While some of the novels, such as *Continent* (1986), *Arcadia* (1992), and *The Melody* (2018), reflect his "deep antipathy to trade and capitalism" (Proctor 2000) quite explicitly, the political message of others is rather "all smoke and mirrors" (Hewitt 2013) and may remain undetected by many readers, as the actual sources of inspiration are missing from the final version of his texts. For example, *The Gift of Stones* (1988), set in the late Stone Age, was intended as a political allegory of Thatcherite Britain and the decline of the Midlands car industry (Wroe 2013, Hewitt 2013), *Harvest*, set during the onset of modernity, owes its theme to an "article in *The Guardian* about soya barons and to current-day asylum seekers in Birmingham" (Wroe 2013), and the immediate impulse for *Quarantine*, a retelling of the story of Jesus Christ's demise, did not come from reading the Scripture but from Crace's "visit to a care-in-the-community hostel near Moseley" (Wroe 2013). Acute concerns about the present-day globalised world are thus at the core of Crace's narratives, albeit disguised behind various historically and geographically distant settings.

10 Crace even claims himself to be the most "pompously moralistic" novelist since William Golding (Ehrenreich 2004).

11 Accordingly, he names George Orwell as "one of his major literary influences" (Battersby 2018).

All the above mentioned properties of Crace's writing allow him to explore his major aesthetic and thematic preoccupations; namely the mythic and parabolic understandings and symbols that persist despite modernity, humankind's place within the greater evolutionary scheme of nature, belief and the self, the problematic dialectic of the individual within communities, the crisis of faith and meaning, the elusive quality of love, interrogating the essentials of identity within a broader social context, the crises of modernity considered in terms of its mercantile/capitalist instincts, and the human narrative impulse (Tew 2006, 24). It is the combination of Crace's imaginative diversity, allegorical and mythopoetic sensibility, distinctive narrative style, and recurrent thematic preoccupations that results in the creation of unique fictional worlds which, though highly varied, share a set of common features and properties.

Thanks to his talent for mixing the invented with the factual without differentiating between them in terms of their convincingness and authenticity, in each of his novels, Crace has been able to create a distinct milieu which, though wholly invented, has properties that allow the reader to perceive it as if it was real. These places and spaces, vaguely anchored in actual temporal and topographic reality[12], thus feel generic yet highly specific, strange yet recognisable, elsewhere yet nearby, and timeless yet historically precise, which is why critics and reviewers have coined the term "Craceland" (Begley 2002, 2003) to refer to this idiosyncratic universe that reconciles the tensions between the uncanny and the commonplace, the distant and the near – "a somewhere familiar, but not quite here" (Sansom 2001). Even if it appears strange and exotic at first sight, it grows familiar from within as the narration progresses, "a world proportioned to reality, and yet largely a system within itself" (Tew 2006, 4), one that is, by means of metaphor and parable, identifiable and palpable to the reader in spite of its otherness. Such fictional worlds then possess within themselves a potential to fuse the poetic with the spatial, social, and political.

Though reluctant to use the term Craceland, Crace describes himself as a "landscape writer" (Guidarini 2013) since he possesses what he calls a "landscape sensibility" (Naidu 2015). He ascribes this capacity to his life-long love of walking and his amateur enthusiasm for natural histo-

12 Crace insists that while realistic writing locates the reader in the real world, he strives for dislocation, that is, for conjuring a world that looks real but which is taken away from reality. And so, because he does not want to "slur" any real places, he has no other choice but to invent his own (antae Editorial Board 2015).

ry, which is why he revels in rendering his settings in elaborate detail, showing his mastery of geography, geology, botany, and anthropology (Kermode 1998), and why his stories always feature many "neat and organic landscapes" (*antae* Editorial Board 2015). However, he believes that a keen walker such as himself, who spends so much time out in the countryside, should delve beyond the names of vegetation and animals and the good feeling from the fresh air and physical exercise. It makes him meditate on the various ways in which humankind is attached to the landscape and, consequently, how and why people "take a lot of solace and a lot of meaning from the land" (Naidu 2015). In terms of walking, his personal life and his fiction match each other as each of his novels features some kind of walking, the protagonists' deliberate moving through and across places and spaces, which is where the natural world and the landscape itself inevitably come in. As a result, the role of the landscape in his books exceeds that of a setting as it simultaneously assumes those of a narrative device, metaphor, theme, and even stand-alone character, though the diversity of his settings and subject matter does not allow him to conceive a recurrent spatial leitmotif or symbol that could be traced throughout his oeuvre.[13] The act of walking also has a crucial epistemological dimension as it takes the reader back and forth through the landscape, which makes them curious about it and familiar with it along with the protagonists. Moreover, Crace as the narrator does not stand aside but joins them in their progress, "discovering" these surroundings as they unfold before them, making up their topography for them as they see it. His method is "to explore [the landscape] at the same time as the reader is encountering it" (Barry 2015), thus avoiding the conventional omniscience that maps it out for the reader from a bird's eye perspective.

Interestingly, although he is very familiar with the British countryside thanks to his walks, Crace rejects it as a particularly stimulating source of inspiration for his writing, calling it too small, too trodden on, and too spoken for (Wroe 2013, Grimble 2016), unlike, for instance, the vast American landscape. Indeed, only two of his novels – *Signals of Distress* (1994) and *Harvest* – are set in what could be described as a distinctly English landscape.[14] But the fact that most of his novels are set in places outside Britain, some of which are very remote, does not imply that his

13 Frank Kermode (1998) observes that due to this intense focus on a particular environment, rather that some distinct thematic continuity, Crace's novels share "imaginative power" and "variously obsessed landscapes and cultures".

14 Unless we take into consideration the speculations of some critics and reviewers that the cityscape in *Arcadia* owes much to that of the centre of Birmingham or Moseley (Williams 1992).

intention is to spice up his stories through the exoticism of their environment. Crace believes in the concealed potential of such an environment to bear the various mental projections of its inhabitants or travellers, which tend to be relatively similar across cultures and regions. As he observes, the "archetypal things belong in landscape, which are rivers, mountaintops, the seashores, deserts [...], you and I and everyone else can assign to each of those kinds of landscape a shared meaning – a universality of meaning that will be the same in Chennai as it is in Birmingham" (Naidu 2015). The otherness of the settings thus enhances the universality and consequent weightiness of the subject matter of his stories.

Many of Crace's novels deal with what the author terms "communities in transition" (Begley 2002), that is, communities, societies, and groups of people, such as settlements, tribes, religious groups, villages, and towns, who find themselves on the verge of some momentous historical transition – political, economic, social or cultural – to which they have to respond if they wish to survive. He depicts the turbulent and frustrating process when the traditional and habitual is being challenged and undermined by the modern and unfamiliar, in particular, how the impending and ensuing socio-economic changes affect their members' individual and collective identities. Forced by circumstances beyond their control, they struggle to come to terms with and cope with the demands of the impending situation, which frequently necessitates a thorough revision or even abandonment of their former values and beliefs. As a result, the very foundations of their identity are shattered as they are exposed to the pressures of the uncertainty, insecurity and volatility of their future existence.[15] Through the fate of an individual, Crace exposes the damaging effects of this transformation process while simultaneously offering a "narrative of recovery" (Lane 2003, 37) as his protagonists always somehow find a way to adapt to the new reality. This allows the narrative to assume a perspective which is both inside and outside the flow of events, one that is subjective in relation to the protagonist yet somehow detached and observant in relation to the social group as a whole.

One of the crucial aspects this transition affects is the community members' relationship to the land and/or landscape: for instance, they are forced to leave it and search for a new place to settle in, their land ceases to serve its former function and they need to adjust to such

15 In some of his novels, such as *Being Dead* (1999), *Six* (2003), and *All That Follows* (2010), this transition is individual and personal, in others it concerns whole communities, though metonymically portrayed in a few protagonists.

a change, they are only passing through it or they settle in it only temporarily. The places and spaces in which these stories are set not only help to develop the plotline, evoke an atmosphere and enrich the narrative's sensual aesthetics, they also reflect and at times even determine the characters' mental and spiritual states. Therefore, in all these cases, the landscape, as an inherent component of such a transition, functions as a meaningful and meaning-generating catalyst of the narrative. This inherent interconnectedness between the human and the spatial generates the common plot pattern of all Crace's narrations: an individual physically and mentally bound to their environment faces up to an unavoidable evolutionary transformation and has to adapt to and come to terms with its immediate consequences, while the landscape/cityscape becomes a determining medium of such a change as its textual representation reflects both the protagonist's resistance to and compliance with the emergent state of affairs.

3. Imaginary Landscapes and Landscapes of the Imagination in Jim Crace's *Continent* and *The Gift of Stones*[16]

3.1 *Continent*

What makes Crace's protagonists accessible to the reader, regardless of concrete geo-historical parameters, is the fact that they are undergoing a painful personal and community crisis that forces them to question and/or revise their values and relationships within a changing social system. However, the places and spaces in which these stories are set not only help to develop the plotline, evoke an atmosphere, and enrich the narrative's sensual aesthetics, they also reflect, and even at times determine, the mental and spiritual states of the characters. Crace's fictional milieu is always a unique amalgam of the imaginative, the uncanny, the familiar, and the commonplace, an alternate landscape whose spatial coordinates are deeply embedded in the text's narrative and thematic framework. Crace's debut novel, *Continent* (1986), assumes a specific position in this regard: it is structurally made up of seven stories, linked thematically by the fact that their protagonists are individuals facing up to great changes that often involve their own displacement, both territorial and identitarian. Through the mosaic of these stories, Crace composes an imaginary seventh continent[17] whose inhabitants experience various forms of crisis. This section explores the ways in which Crace links

16 Parts of this chapter were published in Petr Chalupský's articles "The Imaginary Landscapes of Jim Crace's *Continent*" in *Athens Journal of Philology* 5, no. 3 (2018) and "The Gift of Stories – Imagination and Landscape in Jim Crace's *The Gift of Stones*" in *American and British Studies Annual* 12 (2019).

17 Many reviewers have tried to situate *Continent*'s made-up places, their suggestions ranging from Latin American via postcolonial to developing countries. Crace himself admits that the novel's location was strongly inspired by Sudan and Botswana, though it also owes much to places outside Africa (Tew 2006, 35-36).

and interconnects the psychic, emotional, and spiritual worlds of the protagonists with the geography and topography of the territories they inhabit or find themselves in, and, consequently, how the seven physical and mental landscapes make up the novel's unique fictional space-time. The term "imaginary landscapes" then stands for the spaces produced by the author's, and his characters', imagination, while "landscapes of the imagination" refer to both the "topographic" structure of the characters' imagination, as well as to how their spatial experience affects their imaginative creativity.

3.1.1 *Continent's* Imaginary Landscapes

Lowdo, the main protagonist of the first story, entitled "Talking Skull", is a university student of biology. Almost all his fellow students are children of prominent townsmen, which is why he, as a country person, attracts a lot of their curious attention. When asked by his schoolmates' fathers about his ancestry and his family's apparent riches, he often resorts to vagueness and reticence as he is ashamed of the fact that the money that allows him to live a comfortable city life and train as a forward-looking natural scientist comes from his father's capitalisation on superstition: selling the "milk" of freemartin cows for its supposed miraculous healing properties, especially its curing of infertility and impotence. The more Lowdo gets accustomed to the modern industrial world and acquainted with biological knowledge, the more he is irritated by what he sees as his father's ignorant narrow-mindedness and stubborn irrationality. This is further intensified by the father's bullying tendency to mock his son by pointing out that while his "unenlightened" business has generated wealth and social status, Lowdo's studies have produced nothing but unproductive chatter.

Born and bred in the countryside, Lowdo is particularly associated by his fellow students' fathers with the place and landscape in which he grew up. To satisfy their inquisitiveness, or at least to fend it off, he invents for them a neo-Arcadian image of rich land whose peacefulness and plenty are achieved thanks to methods of modern agriculture and labour management:

> We sit and contrive between us answers which invent a wide flat valley, a leisurely shoulder-deep river, a contented village of a thousand compounds. Six thousand acres of fertile ground provide nourishment for plantations of

> black-bark tarbony, fields of maize and sunflower, herds of milk cattle. At the benevolent centre of this paradise, my conjured father, his accountant and estate manager discuss agricultural strategies. (Crace 2008, 4)

The reality, however, is quite different. The village where his father lives is situated at the very edge of a flat valley in its almost barren backwater, full of "odourless thickets of thorn and acacia" (Crace 2008, 6), where there are no plantations, no road, no dairy cattle, but "belted aurochs of the scrub-people" (Crace 2008, 7), slow to mature and give beef. It is the part of the valley in which the prosperous landowners show no interest, where the farmers are poor because their herds provide only modest amounts of food, rough hides, and dung for fuel and manure. The limited fertility of the soil and cattle makes the populace value sexual potency highly, and their limited outlook and education make them turn to superstition and myth. And the point of intersection of these two coordinates of their daily existence is the source of Lowdo's father's income.

"Talking Skull" is a story of a person caught between the old and the new and his subsequent need to make an irreversible decision to keep up with the changing world. The freemartin farm itself is an in-between place – one that seeks to pander to primitive beliefs and irrational fears while profiting from the strictly mercantile instincts of supply and demand – a peripheral, border territory whose latent, unacknowledged properties enable it to reflect such evolutionary transformations. This transgressive potential of the seemingly homogeneous and anachronistic homestead with its hermaphrodite cows is clearly detectable in the way Lowdo projects its future in his dreams. Following the townsmen's advice that a profit-making superstition, no matter how ludicrous and outmoded, should be harnessed and turned to advantage rather than eradicated, he no longer envisions a corn and milk farm in the wide valley, which he would run effectively thanks to his scientific knowledge. Instead, his dream contains the same freemartin "homelands far off in the scrub" (Crace 2008, 25), but run with a progressive system of management and logistics, extending the range of local customers to include tourists and city dwellers. This imagined place is thus ultimately one of movement and transgression, defying established spatial, temporal, and social categories by combining within itself contradictory forces and tendencies: deep-rooted, unvarying beliefs and the dynamism of modern trading methods, the circular seasonal temporal pattern and the forking timelines of investment planning, enclosed communality, and trans-local financial flows.

"The World with One Eye Shut" is the most minimalistic of the stories in terms of spatial construction, being reduced to one confined place – a prison cell. The story takes place in a country governed by an authoritarian military regime that severely punishes even the slightest hints of opposition. This is why the main protagonist, a young man with no ambition to undermine the establishment, becomes a political prisoner after getting drunk in a pub and shouting a few offensive remarks at soldiers who were making fun of him and his simple-minded sister. Accused of being part of an organised dissident group, his hopes of being released are negligible as his interrogators do not believe in his innocence. Far from being a dynamic in-between or heterogeneous place teeming with entropic energies and susceptible to transgression, the prison cell is, on the contrary, a no-place intentionally preserved in its state. In fact, it evinces features of Foucault's heterotopias, which contain a moment of exclusion as they "presuppose[s] a system of opening and closing that both isolates them and makes them penetrable" (Foucault 1986, 26), and thus require a special act, gesture, ritual or procedure to get into them, and, in the case of prisons, also out of them.

Isolated from the town, the cell not only stands outside the other places, but it also breaks with traditional temporality since it represents a kind of timelessness made up of accumulated temporal mass, layered cyclically through the fates and experiences of the individual inmates. The prison cell of the story reflects the protagonist's previous life in that he was never free but always in a mental cell of paranoid fear of the regime's repressive measures, but it also contests and inverts it in that he can say whatever he likes in there. His only chance of release seems to be the women who protest on a daily basis at the prison gate with photographs of their missing male relatives, particularly his mentally handicapped sister. The sad irony is that, unlike the other women, his sister comes to stand at the gate because she has fallen for a soldier who works there as a guard. The only "landscape" his cell offers is the little he can see from the small window with his face pressed close to the wall and one eye closed. This view is not only very limited but also utterly monotonous since it only includes the barracks with the squads marching and exercising in the yard and the bustle of women looking for and waiting for their men at the prison gate. In its narrowness and ironic distortedness, it is an ominous landscape of despair, a constant reminder of his impasse: the power of the system and the powerlessness and lack of interest of the outside world.

"Cross-country" is set in a remote mountain village that has recently been reached by the achievements of civilisation in the form of a newly established school where each year a volunteer teacher from the developed world arrives to educate the local children. The latest newcomer, however, a Canadian named Eddy Rivette, differs from his predecessors by being a keen track runner who will not abandon his daily practice even in the hilly countryside where there are no suitable routes for long-distance running. He finds an adequately long, though arduous, circuit from the school across the hills to the village store and back home, which soon becomes his familiar physical as well as mental landscape, a landscape of effort and strain, but also of joy and freedom, an experience "more noble and more worldly" (Crace 2008, 59) than competitive running:

> Alone on the tracks worn by animals and borrowed by men, he encountered everything which he had expected: sunset, warm earth, a sense of liberation amongst a landscape and a people equally dispossessed. He picked his way, running all the time but choosing, heading for landmarks and favouring distance to the hard work of gradients. (Crace 2008, 52)

His regular evening run is thus the most gratifying part of the day, as he experiences first the beauty of the landscape and then a sense of connection with the villagers as the elders who gather at the local store watch him pass by and greet him with cheers. They have gradually got used to the teacher's peculiar activity, which they at first perceived as foolish and disturbing. Although it has not stopped Eddy from being seen as a quirky and embarrassing stranger, it has made him an enjoyable, harmless attraction, someone to be tolerated and joked about rather than feared or detested.

However, the growing popularity of the teacher's running annoys 'Isra-kone, the most skilled member of the last pre-modern generation of boys who never attended school and whose life training consisted of traditional horsemanship and farming, as well as a series of ancestral initiation rituals. The elders like him because he embodies all the age-old values and strengths that they have respected all their lives, unlike the new ways of education and manners they look upon with mistrust and scorn. As a genuine highlander, 'Isra sees Eddy as a rival not only because the foreigner's eccentric daily workout attracts more attention than his horse-riding skills, but also because he is making a claim to a unity with the landscape that 'Isra considers to be exclusively his habitat. As the teacher gets acquainted with the terrain and his movement across the ridge becomes faster and more natural, the sight of him, paradoxically enough, evokes in the elders a somehow comforting prehistoric image of their species as he "seem[s] to tell them something about man and their mountain which they have never guessed – that men were like hares who could bounce across the black-studded basalt earth around which they had stumbled for centuries until the horse had come" (Crace 2008, 57). The race that 'Isra challenges Eddy to is thus for him a vital duel for status and prestige, as well as for the preservation of his territorial ascendancy.

Eddy soon realises that running along the usual hilly path "amongst the slipping soils and half-chewed thorns" (Crace 2008, 59) would mean losing the race as 'Isra on his horse moves faster on these tracks. Eddy therefore pragmatically opts for the longer but more comfortable and obstacle-free route along the flat floor of the valley, which allows him to speed up and be almost level with 'Isra when entering the home stretch leading to the store. The fact that the horse collapses just a few metres before the finishing line, too weary from labouring its way "amongst the treacherous descents" (Crace 2008, 65), and that the teacher comes in first, can therefore easily be interpreted as a confirmation of nimble and resourceful modernity displacing cumbersome and inadaptable tradition. However, the story also implies that a significant role in this process will be played by a radical revision of the community's current socio-spatial arrangements and, consequently, a redefinition of the inhabitants' territorial identity. What they see as an organic bond with their homeland would inevitably undergo a transformation, no matter who the racers were: the loser would become a local antique folk curiosity, the winner would be back home "in Montreal with his colour slides and a life-long commitment to this seventh and shabby continent" (Crace 2008, 58), cherishing nostalgic memories of a lost world.

"On Heat" opens with the narrator's childhood recollection of how she and her two younger sisters assisted their father, a professor of biology, to photograph and measure mating tiger crabs on a shingle beach at the summer solstice. The memory itself is based on a family photograph, published on the back cover of the father's monograph, with the background of a beautiful seascape and a tranquil, empty beach swarming with the coupling crustaceans. But the narration is soon to reveal that this idyllic image of an esteemed professor's life and work is a kind of redemption for the more obscure moments in the family's history. Long before taking an interest in tiger crabs, the young natural scientist's object of interest was anthropological – a rare primitive community living in a tropical forest. Accompanied by his newly-wed wife, he sets out to research the tribe's peculiar, animal-like reproductive habits and rituals, which consist of synchronous conception and communal parturition. However, ending up at odds with the tribe, who showed no willingness to be subjected to the professor's measurements and experiments, the expedition returns home empty-handed, save for Puppy, a thirteen-year-old native girl who expressed her wish to be taken away to their world.

Prompted by a few photographs, the narrator, now aged seventy, is trying to compose a comprehensive image of her parents' life prior to her birth, but her only sources of information are her semi-deranged and forgetful mother and her late father's diary notes. She learns from her mother that her father had been secretly observing, sampling, and computing Puppy's menstrual and ovarian cycles, and that he had included his wife in the experimental sample to see whether or not the two women's reproductive systems would synchronise. However, the mother, tired of being the object of her husband's unrelenting scientific scrutiny and of his consequent ravenous libido, sabotages his research and spoils the results of the measurements, leaving Puppy as the sole object of the father's examination. It is only when the narrator consults her father's measurement notes in detail and pays better heed to the differences between her and her mother's and sisters' physiognomies, that she realises, to her dismay, that her real mother was Puppy. The narrator's central memory of the seaside and the shingle beach where she spent so many happy moments recurs as she gathers and composes bits and pieces of the unknown and evasive past as a firm landmark, a certainty. Yet this is only until she understands that the true point of reference in her life story occurred long before this, and that her father's scientific interest in the reproductive behaviour of animals was expressed out of necessity, very likely as a means of escaping his personal and professional failure when carrying out research on a human being. The soothing imaginary landscape of her childhood memory thus turns out to be illusory and collapses when it is disturbed by intrusive images, particularly that of the closing of the door of her father's study in which he was about to begin the fateful examination of the "kidnapped maid" (Crace 2008, 90).

The narrator of "Sins and Virtues" is "the last and certainly the most distinguished of calligraphers in the old Siddilic script" (Crace 2008, 103). An old man with arthritic hands that are no longer capable of firmly drawing letters and characters, his only ambition is to live peacefully on his savings, spending his days having simple meals and working three shifts at his desk out of habit but producing nothing but worthless doodles. He is in fact getting ready for the very last script of his life – his Sins and Virtues list that will be buried with him when his time comes. Since no one else can produce such calligraphy anymore, his works since his retirement have become scarce and valuable art; rich people from America and Europe buy them up for galleries and private collections. Consequently, many forgeries of his works are produced to satisfy the increasing demand. Only at this moment does the government realise that they are losing money by letting foreigners take the artefacts from the country and they decide to prohibit the trade. It is too late, however, as most of the narrator's works have already been sold, which is why the Minister himself pays a visit to his house and urges him, on the promise of money, to produce ornamental canvases decorated in the ancient script for a travelling exhibition with an auction. Trapped in a commission he cannot fulfil, the narrator continues his unproductive daily routines, listlessly waiting for what his fate will bring him.

He was born and grew up in the country but made his career and name in the city, and both places still play a determining role in his life. The first is a small village, which he visits once a year on his birthday. As the custom used to be to plant an acacia tree when a son was born, he always goes to see "his" tree and also shows reverence to those of his ancestors. So, for him, his birthplace is reduced to the acacia grove at the edge of the village where he goes to meditate, perform a few private rituals, and pray for a tolerable death. It is a peripheral place even in the context of the distant village, a relic the villagers respect more out of superstition than tradition, waiting patiently until the last surviving contemporary dies and the trees will be withered enough to be cut down for firewood, but for the narrator it is also a present reminder of his imminent end. The latter is represented especially by the marketplace, where he used to have his calligrapher's booth and where he spent the best parts of his professional career, when almost all public places were decorated by his hand. But this market is also a cityscape of his mind that no longer exists – the dilapidated booths are no longer in use, replaced by modern air-conditioned stores with fake shop fronts, the owners having sold the original ones to the Americans, and the narrator no longer goes there, sending his apprentice instead.

It is only when the situation becomes truly desperate that the narrator starts taking evening walks to the former marketplace, enjoying the status of a local celebrity and the reminder of his former fame and reputation, and ending his strolls in the Syrian's bar with a cup of tea and a chat with the owner. After one such conversation, the narrator has the brainwave to pass off the Syrian's collection of forged canvasses to the Minister as his own work, despite their many errors. Not only does he pretend to have authored the second-rate fakes, but he even adds his own Sins and Virtues parchment to them. By doing so, he secures peace and comfort in his remaining days, yet at the cost of losing his professional honour and moral credit, violating the customary maxim that "the sin-lister must be free from sins" (Crace 2008, 101). However, this abandonment of his principles does not bring him contentment; it pollutes his mind, and he loses all interest in life, which is reflected in the consoling landscape that dominates his imagination. It is no longer the bustling marketplace or a fashionable Western gallery, but the tranquil acacia resting place where his ashes will be taken: "a forest of trees, almost bare and leafless, with the moon hovering over the horizon. Is it dawn or dusk? Soon we all shall know" (Crace 2008, 123).

"Electricity" tells the story of how a small backwater town gets electrified. Awni, the pathetic warden of the local restaurant called the Rest House, naively believes that this achievement is the result of his countless petitions to the Minister, when the real reason is that the Minister's personal secretary intends to purchase a piece of land there cheaply and build a small gourd farm with a comfortable lodge on it. Awni dismisses the schoolteacher's warnings that electricity can become addictive and easily enslave rather than serve those who do not use it wisely and orders every electrical appliance imaginable, including a monumental ceiling fan with huge propellers, to be switched on as a gesture of thanks and tribute to the Minister, who is going to pay a personal visit to the opening ceremony. The deluded Awni cherishes the idea that with electricity, the town will quickly turn into a modern city, with his Rest House as its progressive centre, an emergent place symbolising the town's transitional, evolutionary changes. However, following Awni's fawning speech to the pompous Minister, the oversized fan's fiercely spinning propellers damage the building and injure many of the assembled people, including the Minister, on whom the fan eventually falls.

The motif of the townscape plays a key role in the story: it is somnolently still, with bad and dusty roads connecting the small gourd farms with their hand pumps and the administrative buildings. It is lit by oil lamps at night and people enjoy communal life on the veranda of the Rest House. The majority of the townspeople like their place as it is, being rather suspicious and superstitiously fearful of change, and they watch the electricians erecting pylons and laying cables with an aloof curiosity rather than eagerness and expectation. An exception is Awni, who already pictures a radically transformed town with new roads, an airstrip, a cinema, a factory, and an abattoir. The Minister's Secretary, however, has no interest in what he sees as a one-horse town, and as he drives towards his planned estate, he is already mentally transforming the serene and semi-wild landscape into one that generates profit:

> He has seen maned deer, quibbling flocks of ground-thrush, a mesmerized bandicoot caught mid carriageway by the engine roar. [...] All good pot animals, and sitting targets, too. The thought of land here becomes more attractive. The comfortable family lodge with a small gourd farm transforms into a hotel for hunters, weekend marksmen keen on game but untempted by treks and danger and patience. (Crace 2008, 141)

The businesslike Secretary continues to scheme to select "a good site, close to the road and the police station, but wind and neighbour free" (Crace 2008, 142), a strip of land ready to be exploited and commercialised to the full, regardless of the rest of the place. Sadly for Awni, the resulting reality is in the Secretary's image: the only modernised part of the town is that adjacent to the Secretary's property, the damaged Rest House is closed and avoided by the locals as a place of bad omen, and the luxurious Huntsman Hotel with its garden bar, pool, patio restaurant, cane settees, and glass-topped tables (Crace 2008, 150), stands out in the townscape as a bitter reminder of the warden's foolish ambition.

In the last story, "The Prospect from the Silver Hill", a mining company agent is sent to the mountains in the vanguard of a government project to exploit the country's potential mineral resources. Posted in a cabin on a hill called Ibela-hoy, his task is to inspect the soil and rocks for signs of precious metals and send samples and reports to the company. Wishing for a family but having none, leading a solitary and joyless life and suffering from chronic insomnia, the deprived agent gradually develops severe depression combined with exhaustion from lack of sleep. The main symptoms of his disturbed psyche are vivid daydreams and frenetic soliloquies, and he eventually reaches a state of psychotic delirium. The more futile his attempts to get some sleep and the greater his desperation, the more attached he grows to the landscape around him – he takes long walks along the cliffs and rocks, collecting pebbles and stones more for his sheer pleasure in their shape and colour than for any geological inspection. Dreaming himself a wife and two children, he at first entreats the boulders to materialise this imaginary projection for him, and later embraces and kisses them as if they were his family. Having nothing and no-one else to lean on, the stones and pebbles become for him the whole of his world, the miniaturised and condensed space of his imagination, evoked by his hopes and memories:

> He was struck how – held and turned in the daylight – each stone was a landscape. Here was a planet, a globe, with the continents grey and peninsular, the seas cold and smooth to the touch. And here a coastline, one face the beach, four faces cliff, and a rivulet of green where the children and donkeys could make their descent. And here [...] were the muddied banks of rivers and the barks of trees modelled and reduced in deep, toffee earth. [...] He remembered how, when he was a child, they had buried his father. The grave was open when the body came. They were clays and flints piled on the yellow grass. (Crace 2008, 157–158)

Realising that the barren, rocky area offers him a hideout from the failures and pressures of his previous life, he makes up his mind to protect it from any kind of intrusion. After burying the stones back in the earth and hiding the minerals and gemstones in places in the valley where they would be impossible for others to find, he deliberately sends the company samples of worthless clay and sandstone.

However, his strategy is jeopardised when the survey team find pebbles with fragments of silver on the valley bluffs and ask him for an expert confirmation of the rare metal's presence. Knowing that the metallic veins in the pebbles are indeed silver, he immediately envisions the imminent uncompromising transformation of the secluded landscape, and of his own place in it:

> Once the word Silver was spoken in the company offices, Ibela-hoy could count on chaos; there would be mining engineers, labour camps, a village, roads, bars, drinks, soldiers. Bulldozers would push back the soil and roots of silver would be grubbed like truffles from the earth. Dynamite, spoil heaps, scars. And he, the company agent, the man who spilled the beans, would have no time to reconcile the stones, the dreams, the family, the fatigue, the sleeplessness which now had reached its final stage. (Crace 2008, 163)

Intimidated by such a prospect and by the noise of the company jeeps sent to drive the deranged agent away from the station, he decides to take the silver pebbles that were found and climb up to the ultimate "location of his dream" (Crace 2008, 164) – the sunlit summit of the highest rock, where he and his wife and children would lead a primitive life like prehistoric people, "where the rocks were hot and moving, where quakes and volcanoes turned shales to schists, granite to gneiss, limestone to marble, sandstone to quartz, where continents sank and rose like kelp on the tide" (Crace 2008, 165). Having reached the sought-for landscape, he first hides the silver in the snow and then gives himself over to the safety of his familial daydreaming until a helicopter or death takes him away.

3.1.2 Experiencing Spaces in Transition

Although the individual stories feature different characters in different life situations, they are linked thematically in that they deal with communities in the process of a socio-historical transition through the fates of individuals. They all dramatise various forms of conflict between the rural and the urban, the outdated and the modern, the customary and the pragmatic, the intuitive and the rational. The strength of the novel lies in the fact that it does not present the two evolutionary stages as binary opposites – one good and beneficial, the other devalued and detrimental – but as two concurrent drives whose seemingly countervailing lines of force actually show a strong tendency to appropriate and complement each other rather than to cancel out or annihilate each other. In order to achieve this thematic narrative coherence, Crace makes use of several devices in order to render and contemplate the manifest discord between the persisting, or surviving, and the coming, or superseding. Prominent among these are recurring motifs and symbols and, crucially, the multi-layered portrayal of diverse geographic locations.

With its complex treatment of diverse fictitious environments, Crace's debut novel anticipates his later works that revolve around portrayals of specific spaces and places. Due to the diversity of the presented landscapes, *Continent* allows a geocritical analysis, especially with regard to the principles of spatiotemporality and transgressivity. Most of its stories rest on the same principle: a homogeneous – orderly, steady, and self-sustained – place/space gets heterogenised by the forces of modernity into a place/space of transition, transgression, and disorder, from a stable and clearly demarcated spatial organisation into entropic deterritorialisation. These traditional socio-spatial units, such as the remote villages in "Talking Skull" and "Cross-country", the market town in "Sins and Virtues", and the provincial townlet in "Electricity", are governed by regular temporality consisting of the successive events and routines of the natural cycle of the year. This is violated by the stern dynamic of the lines of transformation, which strive to invert these cycles or level them off. The progressive impacts distort and uproot the former rules and values and, at the same time, subject the destabilised environment to other homogenising tendencies by imposing on it its own regulations and limits. However, these are by no means accepted unconditionally, but are rather defied and transgressed by resistant impulses, social as well as spatial. The outcome of the activities of these colliding forces are in-between, liminal places in a state of dialogical struggle to maintain their meaning and identity in the face of great turbulent changes. Crace shows how the overlooked and underestimated productive potential of such places empowers them to fight back and have a substantial say in the resulting form of emergent modes of socio-spatial arrangement, be it the reconciliation of pragmatic business with superstition in the modernised freemartin farm, the mountain village tentatively opening its landscape to modern leisure activities, or the bizarre cohabitation of a backward town and a posh, high-end hotel. Although these places cannot completely resist modernity, they still manage to retain their interstitial, border character.

The novel also explores various ways of experiencing place/space and how the physical environment interacts with the protagonists' psyches. The running teacher's mountain trail of joy and liberation, the biology professor's daughter's nostalgic childhood snapshot of the tiger crab beach, the elderly calligrapher's memory of the bustling marketplace, or the company agent's daydreamed family among the rocks and boulders are all examples of mental and imaginary landscapes that the characters create in order to come to terms with the places and with themselves. However, Crace never lets readers immerse themselves in these made-up landscapes for long as he always confronts them with rather exact descriptions of the actual environment, combining minute detail and aesthetic evocation. His prose thus precisely achieves the effect of reconciling the objectivist and the abstract with the emotional and the experiential, which Tuan and Prieto call for in their humanistic geography and phenomenological geocritical inquiry, respectively.

The diverse environments of the individual stories – the villages, the town, the city with its marketplace and prison, the beach, the valley, and the mountains – compose a representation of an imaginary realm, a big country, or a continent, at the dawn of a technological and mercantile modernity whose rapidity and instantaneousness often clashes with the deep-rooted customs and prejudices of the slow-moving old world. Rather than forming a consistent, comprehensive narrative, they constitute a jigsaw puzzle, a topographic patchwork of disparate but related pieces. *Continent* is thus also a specific example of a mapping narrative that, by assembling fragmentary spatial images, achieves a complex landscape with an exceptional unity of geographic, aesthetic, symbolic, experiential, and mental dimensions. This intrinsic richness of the rendered territories makes them integral to the novel's narrative framework, proving crucial at the level of character construction and thematic composition.

3.2 *The Gift of Stones*

The Gift of Stones (1988), Crace's second novel, also touches on his major thematic and aesthetic concerns, namely the invariable human values that persist despite modern, capitalist progress, the often paradoxical position of human beings within the natural world and its evolutionary schemes, the formation and maintenance of one's self and identity under adverse socio-historical circumstances, love and its elusive and unpredictable quality, and the importance of the human need to create made-up narratives. It is especially articulate in terms of the last-mentioned preoccupation – the centrality of the human impulse to tell stories. This section attempts to demonstrate how the novel explores the theme of storytelling not only within the framework of the transitional historical moment it depicts, but also in connection with the psychic and experiential properties of the physical environment the main protagonist inhabits.

3.2.1 A Narrative Animal[18]

The capacity and the need to spin and tell tales are undoubtedly defining aspects of the human condition. In fact, the mind of an individual rushes off to create, recall, or rehearse various kinds of narratives related to his or her life whenever it is not engaged in a mental task which requires intense concentration, which is why most of the stories our mind conceives remain uncommunicated. Although a coherent and comprehensible narrative should adhere to a logical and plausible causality and temporal arrangement, the process of narrativising our experience of the world is not wholly governed by rationality. We build stories on facts we know

18 Crace mentioned this term in an interview with Andrew Lawless.

and pieces of information we receive; yet these may be disparate, incomplete, and jumbled, and so we tend to rearrange them or even invent the missing pieces to establish connections in order to produce a meaningful pattern that could be imposed on the sometimes chaotic and coincidental circumstances of our lives. Our very existence is thus permeated by the stories we tell others and, perhaps even more crucially, ourselves.

Because we crave meaning and order in life, we are addicted to stories, which supply us with these qualities when we cannot have them in reality. On a very basic level, stories entertain us, stir our emotions, and nourish our imaginations. However, by "turn[ing] the experiences of one into the knowledge of all" (Currie 2010, v), commonly shared narratives, ranging from folk tales to novels and movies, also perform far more important roles. Within the demands and difficulties of social life and the ever-changing world, stories offer us opportunities "to practice reacting to the kind of challenges that are, and always were, most crucial to our success as a species" (Gottschall 2012). This is why there is a discrepancy between what we wish for in life and what we expect to have in fiction, where we crave stories of misfortune – hardship, despair, frustration, injustice, violence, and death – and we take pleasure in learning about how such difficulty can be overcome. Stories thus fill us with hope that problems can be faced up to, that goodness is worth fighting for, but they also reassure us that we cannot be blamed for everything bad that happens to us because some events and their consequences are simply random and unpredictable. A successful story thus requires characters "endowed with salient and robust principles of action" who can satisfy our prevailing "desire for order, coherence, and the mental mastery of circumstance" (Currie 2010, 220) in situations when these circumstances get beyond our physical control.

These narratives also possess a significant moral dimension in that they support and proclaim the underlying principles on which the functioning of our society rests, the most important being the belief in a system of justice that punishes vice and rewards virtue. They "make societies work better by encouraging us to behave ethically" by means of which they reduce "social friction while uniting people around common values" (Gottschall 2012). Traditional stories generally inculcate values like kindness, generosity, compassion, tolerance, and diligence, regardless of the particularities of a specific situation (Spaulding 2011, 134). In short, stories are highly beneficial for humankind as they prepare us for a range of predicaments and, by reinforcing moral values, they bind societies together and make us better equipped to resolve crucial life dilemmas. Although every human being is unique and inimitable and people's life stories are manifold and multifarious "anecdotes of destiny" (Cavarero 2000, 2), we do not expect something completely other and new from commonly shared narratives, but rather seek "the old comforts of the universal story grammar" (Gottschall 2012), in other words, those examples and paradigms that help us survive the various trials of life in an effective and yet ethical manner.

Crace is an avid storyteller who acknowledges the primacy of imagination. In his opinion, the storytelling impulse is an innate human property that has proven to be an invaluable device for the development of humankind. He attributes his own narrative ability to this deeply embedded trait of human nature: "I'm often mystified by the way I write [...], but the truth of the matter is that I don't have any explanation. It's just something that is there [...], it's intuitive" (Lawless). Subscribing to a neo-Darwinian conception of storytelling, he sees it as an evolutionary adaptive strategy which makes it easier and less frightening for us to confront misfortune. Given their purpose of preparing people for hard times, most folk stories deal with problematic or dysfunctional communities. Likewise, Crace's novels tend to be rather grim and bleak, which is not to say that they lack hope and consolation. This prospect must, however, always be fought for and redeemed by painful personal sacrifice. It is the presence of this ethical paradigm that allows readers to assign shared archetypal patterns of thought and wisdom to each of Crace's imaginary landscapes, no matter how exotic or uncanny, in order to produce meaning that is comprehensible across cultures. This is why the feeling of familiarity readers may experience in his stories stems from their parabolic meaning rather than from their mirroring of the real world.

Crace admits that gripping storytelling must rely on a certain form of fabrication, that is, making things up and then presenting them as real, but only for the sake of the narrative's effective impact on the audience, both in terms of the attractiveness, coherence, and plausibility of the storyline and the moral message the story aims to deliver. It is the kind of narrative playfulness, of reader-friendly mischievousness, that he considers essential for a successful narrator. Crace renders this persuasion in *The Gift of Stones*, which is set at a precise moment in history in a seaside village whose landscape is influenced by that of western Cornwall and the Isles of Scilly (Begley 2002), but the made-up elements of the novel take over the supposedly realistic ones in order to provide its story with a universally meaningful interpretive framework.

3.2.2 From Wild Plant to Raconteur

The story of *The Gift of Stones* is set in a coastal village whose stonecutter community has made a living making stone tools and weapons. Proud of their craft, the hard-working stoneworkers are confident and complacent, convinced that their prosperity is not imperilled as long as there are enough traders to buy their products and sell them elsewhere. These people like who and where they are, they are earthbound and, having no nomadic or belligerent inclinations, most of them have never been beyond the perimeter of the village, their only connection with the outside world being the traders and the occasional visits of horsemen who come to trade "exotic" goods, such as fabrics and perfumes, for spears, axes, and arrow tips. On such occasions, the serene and purposeful village temporarily succumbs to commotion and turmoil, as if it were a kicked anthill whose decent and disciplined inhabitants have been "sent wild and spirited by the unheralded disorder of the day and by this thin excuse to shout and smile and swagger" (Crace 1997, 21). The next morning, however, everything returns to normal and their life is again one of order, routine, and custom. As a result, the community is enclosed and withdrawn, rigid in their values and beliefs, suspicious and fearful of any form of otherness. While the outside world is believed to be one of chaos, peril, and viciousness, full of "blows and careless brawls and sudden gusts of hardship to blow good fortune down", the village life makes people "tame, secure and virtuous by labour", seeming to be "as snug as poppy seeds. Such was the gift of stones" (Crace 1997, 119). However, fostering this illusion proves more harmful than protective for them.

The problem with these self-contained and inflexible people, whose horizon ends at the limits of their settlement, is that they are unable to see that the world around them is changing to their disadvantage. Year by year, the trade in flint and weaponry is getting worse and fewer and fewer traders and horsemen are passing through the village to barter goods for stone, but the villagers can only seek an explanation within the realm of their own experience, that is in war, diseases and natural disasters. None of them leaves the village to find out what is actually preventing their trade from thriving as hitherto, they just lament, wait, and hope for a reversal, though they would not have to go too far, just to the nearby seashore, to see the merchant ships from which the sailors were bringing ashore tools and components made of bronze. It is not until one of the fruits of these transformations literally arrives on their doorstep, in the form of a bronze arrowhead so thin, hard, and sharp that it easily outdid even the best flint, that they fully realise they have been hoping in vain and are finally willing to admit the naked truth: "The outside world was closing in like lichen on a stone. [...] And all our world was shrinking, breath by breath. [...] We lived like rabbits, sociable and bored and easy prey" (Crace 1997, 169, 195). The question is whether such a destiny could have been averted and, if so, how.

Typically for Crace, the main protagonist of the novel is a misfit in his community. Even as a small boy he showed little interest in helping the adults to mine flint; instead, he liked to slip away from the village and spend the day roaming the countryside and playing with other boys in a horsemen's encampment. He is an orphan adopted by his uncaring uncle, and when he returns to the village, he soon realises that no one misses him the whole day, and so he runs away more and more frequently. On one occasion when he does so, he is unlucky as his arm is badly injured by a young bowman's arrow and later has to be amputated to save his life. From this moment on, he is taken as a true outsider as he is now "officially" useless for stonecutting, and as not even his foster family takes the trouble to find him some useful occupation, he grows up ignored and unloved, irritating the stoneworkers by hanging about and idly gawping at what they do. His wandering expeditions beyond the limits of the village thus become for him a practical necessity rather than a boyish adventure, the only way in which he can flee the insults and scorn of his foster family. It is no wonder that he grows bitter and frustrated, as he himself admits: "Malice and my elbow stump are twins" (Crace 1997, 36). "An arrow ruled my world; it made me what I am [...] the vengeful sort" (Crace 1997, 157). Things change for the better, however, when he discovers in himself a talent for telling stories.

The pivotal moment of his transformation "in that village, overnight, from the wild plant, not much use, into their raconteur" (Crace 1997, 66) happens when he decides to respond to his uncle's annoyed, conventional rhetorical question, "Where have you been?", after he returns from a journey on which he met a husbandless woman living with her child in a hut near the coast. The very mention of the strange woman rivets the cousins, and their avid curiosity proves to be "an invitation far too good to miss" (Crace 1997, 62) for his storytelling mind. During his earlier wanderings, he had already rehearsed in his mind stories he could tell the villagers if they were interested, but this unusual encounter emboldens him to speak up. However, he knows that a mere retelling of what actually happened to him would not do, so instead of telling his tale straight, he showers his listeners with a large number of seemingly unrelated details – colourful and figurative descriptions of the seaside, the birds, and the ships upon the sea – in order to stir their imaginations and increase the suspense. As the storytelling phrases spring from his mouth, he realises that to make the story sound really attractive, these "crafted and well turned" (Crace 1997, 63) descriptions must spice up the bare facts and give them a dramatic aspect. His real experience is thus reduced to a template for his story, to a backbone plotline encased in rich and exciting fabrication. "This is my moment of betrayal, both of the woman and the truth" (Crace 1997, 63), he notes, knowing that being truthful to the story at times rules out being truthful to reality.

The new-born storyteller gradually converts the bitter reality he has been suffering into a bottomless source of well-plotted stories, ranging from those explaining his injury to those describing marvellous ships offloading ever new and more remarkable merchandise. First and foremost, his storytelling represents for him a protective, auto-therapeutic mechanism that makes him forget the injustices of the real world and allows him to show his fellow villagers his worth. He thus becomes two persons: the disdained roamer with a personal life of misfortune and failure, and the mesmeriser who can "hold a household silent with the magic of his words" (Crace 1997, 66), the "minstrel-king of lies" who can "concoct from, say, geese, ships and smells, a world more real than real" (Crace 1997, 97). In fact, he has turned himself into fiction for his audience, having told and retold the stories of his life so many times in so many different versions. Although people know his tales are full of lies and manipulated truths, they are so transfixed and delighted by them that they desire to hear more each day: "The paradox is this – we do love lies. The truth is dull and half-asleep. But lies are nimble, spirited, alive. And lying is a craft" (Crace 1997, 73). They no longer mind his wanderings, knowing that the material for his narratives can only be sought elsewhere, and they cannot wait for him to come back and, with all his storyteller's tricks, transport their pragmatic, mundane minds to "simple, freer, less ordained" (Crace 1997, 68) imaginary worlds. Having learnt to adapt his fictions to match the expectations of different kinds of audience – men, women, and children – his stories gradually become the only diversion for the villagers, a much-prized escape from the drudgery of their daily lives.

Although his narrative gift provides his audience with much pleasure and amusement, he cannot really be regarded as a true bardic figure as his stories tend to lack an ethical dimension. Although he often leaves crucial parts of the story unsaid to make the listener ask questions and seek answers, these always remain on the level of the action. His implied questioning does not lead to an abstract moral framework by forcing the audience to contemplate and reflect on their own acts and decisions and confronting them with those of the fictitious characters. However, it would be unfair to say that he did not try at all – when he brings Doe and her daughter to the village to find refuge for them and the reception from his fellow villagers is rather cold and hostile, he invents a number of versions of how she might have lost her husband and son to provoke sympathy in them. The stoneworkers listen eagerly as long as these stories do not concern them personally. But when, in the final version, he suggests that they might have been guilty of not helping a woman in need, the atmosphere changes instantly from interest to amazement and consternation as his audience quickly creeps away "unamused and angered by the venom in his voice" (Crace 1997, 133). Some of them in their smug conceitedness consider themselves too righteous and principled to be criticised or reprimanded, others fear that their hidden insecurities, worries and anxieties might be brought to life. In either case, they still look down on the loquacious amputee, and even though they condescendingly allow him to be their entertainer, they cannot really stand the thought that he should be the voice of their conscience. As a result, his stories entertain but fail to perform the other two crucial functions: they neither prepare and rehearse the audience for hard times, nor do they foster and strengthen their moral qualities.

After experiencing the community's reaction to a displeasing story, he decides not to give them even a hint of unsettling truth any more. As a result, they remain fully isolated from and unaware of the radical transformations that are reaching their village. He often wonders how calm and cheerful they are while the world around "was tumbling, spinning, wild" (Crace 1997, 158), but in reality, it is also his fault; as village storyteller he rejected the potentially unpopular ethical dimension of his craft while enjoying his position as a well-liked entertainer. And so, even though his mind is full of unease as he watches new ships and people coming from the sea, he keeps the information to himself: "The ritual of our trade was this – I did not tell the truth. They looked to me for comfort, not for gloom" (Crace 1997, 162). The problem is that to see storytelling as a trade in which you merely barter pretty tales for laughter and applause is to fatally misunderstand its public function, for one of the crucial, though admittedly most demanding and thankless, roles of a raconteur is to cleverly confront his community with inconvenient truths in order to make them conscious of their flaws and encourage them to rectify them. He is, however, forced to change his strategy when the villagers eventually understand that leaving their settlement is unavoidable, and they turn to their temporarily out of favour storyteller to guide them as the only "worldly-wise" member of the community. Although he is at first happy to have his former authority restored, he soon realises that the power of his fanciful tales will be exhausted after a two-day journey when the travellers enter territories that he himself has never been to. "At last his lies had caught him out. [...] The stories that he'd told were now our past. His new task was to invent a future for us all" (Crace 1997, 201–202). The stories he is then asked to concoct to retain his status as communal storyteller must do far more than just amuse – they must give his community hope, courage and moral strength to withstand the trials of the days to come.

3.2.3 A World That's Upside Down – the Landscapes of the Imagination

As is typical of Crace's novels, the narration of *The Gift of Stones* pays substantial attention to the landscape in which its story is set and how it is interconnected with the characters' minds. The central landscape pattern of the story is based on the contrast between the village, surrounded by stony hills, and the nearby seashore. While the first is appreciated by the villagers as safe, orderly, and stable, the latter is perceived as unruly, unpredictable, and unusable, something that defies any attempt to impose order, control, and meaning: "Our village looked inland. [...] The sea brought no one luck so we stayed away. Lives were passed in this one place, working stone and seeking respite from the wind" (Crace 1997, 16). Uneventfully comfortable as the village is for the stoneworkers, it is too monotonous and uninspiring for the main protagonist's restless and wayward nature. The village is an example of a homogeneous, or striated, space, which is why the disabled young man's storytelling mind is so attracted by the places beyond the surrounding hills, especially those of the seashore. And so, the barely trodden clifftop path becomes for him a gateway into the limitless realm of the imagination.

The climate and the landscape of the seashore, with its winds and storms, its cliffs and coves with narrow paths and thickets, prove exceptionally stimulating for his imagination because each time he finds himself in this territory, they seem to be somewhat distinct, which is why they invite a variety of narrative renderings that depend not only on reality, but also on the character of the story and the listeners' expectations. One day, for example, when he spots a ship on the sea passing briefly on the horizon, he knows immediately what kind of story he will tell that night – one in which the ship comes to the shore, for which he needs the weather and the waves to be calm: "I could invent for you a sea and wind and sky that flung saltweed in my face and emptied water from the pools and cast a light so dark and feeble that even lugworms took the day for night, mistook the wind for tide [...] But I will keep it calm and windless" (Crace 1997, 41). The seashore not only provides him with a narrative stimulus and material for his stories, it also enables him to assume a new viewpoint, both literally and metaphorically, one that is detached from and unfettered by the mundane reality of his village, one that allows him to see even familiar objects from a fresh perspective: "The sea viewed from the clifftop is a world that's upside down. Its gulls have backs. You are looking down on wind. The shallows, from above, are flat and patterned, green with arcs of white where the water runs to phlegm" (Crace 1997, 43). It is the excitement derived from the different landscape and seascape that drives him to walk further along the beaches into the low heathland where he comes across a hut inhabited by a young woman with her baby girl, another source of his tale-telling inspiration.

However, he soon realises that the otherness of this environment is of a different kind to that of the unpeopled seashore. The presence of various kinds of human beings, whether long-term, temporary or only fleeting, imbues it with contrary connotations that are absent in the natural world, such as negative emotions, hostility, rage, and violence: Doe callously rejects her one-armed benefactor's offers of help, preferring to resort to occasional prostitution in order to obtain food and other necessities; people from a distant village arrive on the coast to slaughter wild geese that have destroyed their crops; gangs of raiding horsemen ride through the countryside looking for settlements to plunder, women to rape, and men to kill. Accordingly, the landscape and his perception of it modifies to correspond with these meanings. When going to see Doe for a second time, the description of the environment foreshadows the hardships and misfortunes he is going to encounter: "The sea, that night, curled and lisped and whispered in a voice which said, Dismay, Dismay, Dismay. [...] The landscape and the tide conspired to chase him off the beach" (Crace 1997, 78, 79). And before the slaughtering of the geese begins, Crace offers the image of the stinking moorland that seems to anticipate the brutal act to come: "The saltland heath – saddened and yellowed by the winter – was sweating in the sun. It smelled like rotten fruit, like beer, like cow's breath. The earth was passing wind; it belched at every footfall; its boil had burst; it was brackish and spongy with sap and pus and marsh" (Crace 1997, 88).

This heterogeneous world does not lack story-generating potential, but it is different from that of the almost fairytale-like seashore where each imaginary ship that came ashore "could offload a new and untried plot; a different set of characters with untold loves and enmities could disembark" (Crace 1997, 67). While the landscape of the shore worked as a stepping stone for concocting sensational tales, the eventful valley makes the protagonist construct stories in order to fend off the vicissitudes of distressing reality. His stories deceive the villagers by concealing from them the truth about the changing socio-economic conditions of the outside world, but he also deludes himself into believing that Doe is a woman who could love him as a husband. When he realises that not even her relocation to the village will turn her into the caring wife he desires, he is not able to accept the truth and instead runs away to the imaginary safety of the shore in search of herbs for "his" Doe, consoling himself in his mind with images of their fulfilled relationship when he returns home: "You know the route. I'll not detail the landmarks that are old friends to us. [...] I picked her fill. My filling her was all I had in mind. I marvelled at my speed and skill, and at the luck which brought me through the bracken, over rocks, without a sprain or scratch" (Crace 1997, 166). He has associated the landscape of the seashore, which inspired so many of his successful tales, with escapist nostalgia and illusion, making it the only place where he can feel contented. Similarly, his stories make the stonecutters believe that their village is a secure oasis of happiness, a delusion to which they are so susceptible that when they see the bronze arrowhead, they think it is one of his tricks and demand a comforting story that would explain the appearance of this mysterious object.

With the collapse of the trade in stone and flint, the village gradually transforms into an in-between place. Its homogeneity breaks down as the former routines, hierarchies, and value systems lose their legitimacy and people no longer feel bound by them. Although some still persist in stoneworking, foolishly believing that the good times will return again, the majority are forced to leave the shells of their selfish complacency and seek the company of others to face the sad reality together. "The village seemed a shabby and a friendly place at last. People did not shut themselves inside. They strolled. [...] They took an interest in each other's grieving, empty inside worlds and in the outside world as well"

(Crace 1997, 194). The heterogenising forces thus generate positive, creative energies that make the community stronger and more evolutionarily adaptive, thanks to which they finally make the decision to leave their homeland. At this point, the vital significance of stories emerges again as they prevent their will and courage from faltering and their minds from dwelling on memories. But the storyteller knows that his old stories will not suffice this time as his new task is "to invent a future" (Crace 1997, 202) for his fellow refugees. Out of habit, he seeks inspiration in the landscape:

> He closed his eyes and what he saw was the shingled margin of the sea with horses wild and riderless close by. He tried to place a sail upon the sea, but could not. He tried to fill the air with human sounds. But all he saw were horses in the wind, the tide in loops upon the beach, the spray-wet rocks and stones reflecting all the changes in the sky, and no one there to notice or applaud. (Crace 1997, 202)

Once again, the landscape becomes a metaphor for the character of his storytelling – it is different from what he is used to, rich and promising but stern and unyielding, just as his new stories will have to be. He is facing the greatest challenge of his craft: to create stories that would entertain and instruct at the same time, and that would be told for the sake of the community as a whole rather than for the benefit of their maker.

3.2.4 Consolatory Spatial Narratives of Transition

Like most of Crace's novels, *The Gift of Stones* renders, through the perspective of an outsider as its main protagonist, the fate of a community in transition, set in a landscape made vivid through the use of precise and minute descriptive detail combined with a distinctive poetic diction. However, it differs from his other similarly constructed narratives by strongly accentuating and foregrounding the theme of storytelling and its significance for humankind. In many respects, the novel exemplifies its author's conviction about the defining properties of good and effective storytelling, namely the primacy of imagination and the necessity of inventive fabulation. However, although the novel features a gifted and well-liked storyteller, he cannot be regarded as a fully-fledged one because, for the sake of his own popularity and comfort, he fails to provide his listeners with a moral which would, by depicting troublesome situations and the virtues and vices of imaginary characters, prepare them to cope with potential hardships. By being self-complacent in the role of entertainer, a conceiver of sensational worlds, his tales fail to perform the function of an evolutionary adaptive mechanism that would enable the community to make better sense of the changing world in which they find themselves and force them to reflect on their own stances because instead of seeking consolation in the most demanding tests of human will and strength, they make do with mere escapist fabrication. However, the humanist optimist Crace gives his protagonist a second chance at the end of the story in the form of a challenge to come up with stories that would make the stoneworkers' passage into a new future more bearable and hopeful.

In *The Gift of Stones,* the theme of storytelling is closely linked to the motif of landscape. Since the village, dominated by routine and hard work, offers the storyteller's imagination no stimulus, he seeks it along the seashore, which becomes for him the landscape of his imagination. The sea and its coastline prove to be a rich source of stories, but these are bound to the realm of the fantastic, and not only the audience but even the storyteller himself turns to them to flee the pressures of the real world. Although he is a sensitive observer of space and place and always projects his feelings and emotions into the environments in which he finds himself, not all of them turn out to be suitable material for the kind of tales he wishes to tell. The landscape of his imagination, like his stories, thus remains illusory, with little or no overlap with the listeners' actual or potential experience. Also typically for Crace, the novel depicts a homogeneous place which, affected by heterogenising forces, evolves into an in-between place, a liminal territory temporarily stuck between two socio-historical developmental phases. As such, this transitory dynamic generates new energies that transform the place into that of a turbulent non-equilibrium with a latent capacity for a multiplicity of stories. And so, although he no longer needs to travel far for his narrative inspiration, the storyteller faces a true ordeal by fire: he must make up stories that are imaginative enough to allow the listeners to wonder but that are also implicitly linked to the socio-spatial reality of the listeners so as to retain their reflective and instructive capacity.

4. Character and Landscape Construction in Jim Crace's *Signals of Distress* and *Quarantine*[19]

4.1 *Signals of Distress*

Signals of Distress (1994) illustrates that Crace's characters, often exposed to changes beyond their control and forced to cope with conflicting demands in order to survive, tend to be loners and outsiders who live on the edge of their community, partly out of necessity, partly out of circumstance, but partly also because they somehow differ from the other members of the community. "These protagonists all suffer in a sense an ontological and epistemological displacement from the world: they are in the world, but do not live according to its rules; they think they understand the world, but they are using the wrong interpretative parameters" (Lane 2003, 27). It is precisely the combination of a rich imaginative landscape and the individual's irreversible fate and profound moral dilemma that invites readings and interpretations that reach beyond the scope of the actual story. His character and landscape construction are thus two sides of the same coin as the former is determined by the latter, and the latter becomes meaningful through its interconnectedness with the former.

19 Parts of this chapter were published in Petr Chalupský's articles "A Parable of Humanity – Character and Landscape Construction in Jim Crace's *Signals of Distress*" in *Ostrava Journal of English Philology* 4, no. 1 (2012) and "'Siblings to the empty spaces in the heart': Space, Place and Landscape in Jim Crace's *Quarantine*" in *Atlantis: Journal of the Spanish Association of Anglo--American Studies* 44, no. 1 (2022).

4.1.1 Of Words and Deeds: Aymer Smith

The cast of characters Crace creates to inhabit the world of *Signals of Distress* is rich and varied in order to embody the different aspects of humanity the story needs to confront, from grave seriousness to obscure eccentricity. "Generally, the characters represent traditional (recognisably Shakespearean) archetypes: a radical male virginal puritan, an unsympathetic ambitious brother, two young lovers brought together by fate, a Rabelaisian female innkeeper, and a grasping merchant" (Tew 2006, 95). However stereotypical they may appear, the characters are brought to life and made vivid and plausible through the various situations in which they find themselves and their encounters with one another. What connects most of these characters is their feeling of or need for dislocation, whether willing and voluntary or not. As Crace notes, "most of the main players are out of place. They're either waiting to be dislocated entirely – they're going to the New World as emigrants – or they are dislocated because they are washed up on the shores of this place where their culture, and their attitudes and their responses don't really gel" (quoted in Tew 2006, 97). It is this feeling of displacement and unbelonging that brings together individuals who, under normal circumstances, would be unlikely to ever meet, and which thus forms the backbone of the novel's compelling plot.

Aymer Smith, the protagonist of the novel, is in many respects the inverse of Victor from *Arcadia*, in that the only thing they have in common is their isolation due to a lack of basic social competences. However, even their isolation differs in nature and cause: while Victor likes to be left alone and spends most of his time fortified in his "Big Vic" tower overlooking the city, Aymer wants to be a respectable member of society, and so he constantly tries to socialise with everyone he encounters, but these attempts could be described as desperate or even disastrous since other people regard him as ridiculously odd at best and arrogant at worst. Compared to the cold, calculating, self-centred, and businesslike Victor, Aymer is a humanist character with a sincere persuasion that his destiny is to make the world a better place for those less fortunate than himself. Victor was forced to live in the city as a child and eventually became a multimillionaire entrepreneur, but he is still a country boy at heart with a dream of leaving his mark on the city by building a pastoral oasis in its very bustling centre. Aymer, on the other hand, is a prototypical city person with urban habits and manners who foolishly believes that he will be able to impress the rural community of Wherrytown and even find himself a wife there.

Aymer Smith is one of Crace's most vivid and tragicomic characters, an illustration that high-quality ingredients do not automatically make a tasty meal, and that the best intentions do not always achieve good results. Despite all his admirable character traits – he is kind, helpful, charitable, generous, altruistic, well-mannered, educated, and well-read – he rarely makes the desired impression on those he would like to befriend. Due to his lack of empathy, his naivety, inexperience, and ultimate inability to communicate, he comes across to the ordinary villagers of Wherrytown as aloof, conceited, pompous, self-important, and annoyingly verbose. They are especially put off by his rousing speeches, in which he ponders and preaches on countless more or less serious issues, be it slavery, botany or sea storms, and which he mistakes for evidence of his eloquence. "He liked to think of himself as a plain man, plainly spoken. He didn't care for adjectives, or anything that was too ornamented. He liked the force of facts and objects, and he endeavoured to make his conversation instructional" (Crace 1995, 25). Aymer is both a ridiculous and a miserable character, simultaneously deserving to be mocked, pitied and liked, and Crace repeatedly treats him with a mixture of irony and sympathy. On the one hand, he presents his "hero" as being aware of his limitations, yet still eager to please and make a good companion: "[Aymer] knew he would never have a reputation for vivacity, and that he was more comfortable with documents than company, but still he'd meant to be amusing and relaxed" (Crace 1995, 17). On the other hand, he ironically comments on almost all of Aymer's attempts to gain the respect and sympathy of the locals, the sailors or his fellow lodgers. When he is explaining to George why the only inn in the village should still have a distinguished name, the narrator interrupts his lecturing monologue by calling it a "Comedy of Wisdoms" (Crace 1995, 15); the description of his failure to make a decent impression on the innkeeper and the parlourman is concluded with the sentence that "George the parlourman had seemed to find his conversation comic, except when [Aymer] attempted jokes" (Crace 1995, 17); and when he desperately seeks out the Norrises' company, which he greatly enjoys, the narrator readily compares him to the dog Whip chasing sea creatures on the seashore: "So while the dog played in the surf or made life difficult for crabs and sander-lings, Aymer joined the Norrises and made life difficult for them" (Crace 1995, 196–7). Aymer seems condemned to inhabit a social void outside of any conceivable community, where he will forever experience an inexplicable clash between his theoretical mastery of the principles of humanism and the mockery, bullying, and ostracism he is exposed to in reality.

The character Aymer most closely resembles is the eccentric preacher Phipps, the spiritual leader of the local congregation. Although Aymer's attitude of Radical Sceptic Amender differs greatly from the religious view of the preacher, their personalities are remarkably similar. Both men pride themselves on being unorthodox, educated, and well-spoken and are ambitious to be taken as a moral authority, with a strong tendency to patronise people and tell them how to behave, while simultaneously being unable to put most of their ideas into practice, thus remaining on the theoretical level of abstract ideas. Like Aymer, Phipps is a "man who loved debate, who took his pleasures from a book – for Mr Phipps was Aymer's twin in many ways. Both were prisoners of priggishness, and dogma, and vocabulary. Both had Latin. Both were smitten by Katie Norris. They were two peas, except they disagreed on everything they had in common" (Crace 1995, 159). Despite their being potential intellectual allies, Aymer and Phipps can hardly stand each other precisely because they recognise in each other what they really are like, a mirror image too unbearably different from how they wish to be seen. As the story unfolds, by letting the reader know their dreams, it discloses that the two men's aloofness, verbosity, and obstinate argumentation are mere protective mechanisms they employ in order to conceal their unhappiness at being lonely. After his zealous sermon aimed at the Sabbath-breakers, Phipps is haunted by his fierce words, devoid of all kindness and Christian charity, and drowns his self-pity in secretly kept brandy, dreaming up "better times in Wherrytown" (Crace 1995, 205), when he spends pleasant evenings in the friendly company of Aymer Smith and the Norrises. Similarly, when the *Belle of Wilmington* eventually departs for America, the once again desolate Aymer dreams of Miggy and Katie being happy in their new homes, welcoming him warmly as a guest and showing him much gratitude for what he has done for them, while in reality the former finds him disagreeable and the latter views him as a difficult yet vulnerable child. He even tries to dream of Otto's bright future, trying to "find a happy ending for the African as well" (Crace 1995, 252). What the two men fail to see, however, is the real reason for their social isolation.

Unable to imagine or understand that other people need not necessarily share his view of the world, Aymer becomes a desperate solipsist whose declared altruism and helpfulness easily transform into a self-centered obsession to prove that his actions are valid and beneficial. With his mission a failure and his reputation tainted, Aymer finds himself the only person in the village who is of no use during the catching and loading of the pilchards, realising that "even greeting enemies was better than the desolation of being the only person on the beach without a job" (Crace 1995, 139). However, even though everything suggests that it would be wiser for him to leave Wherrytown as soon as he can, Aymer decides to stay in order to show the locals and the sailors how mistaken they have been in judging him a show-off and a nuisance. "He had to put the world to rights. *His* world, that is. He wanted to be liked. He wanted to regain his dignity before he left" (Crace 1995, 157). His problem is that he persistently tries to project his idealised world onto the real one around him, ignoring the fact that there is almost no overlap between the two, and that the rules and values of the former are incomprehensible or even unacceptable for those inhabiting the latter. Therefore, although he wants to believe that his new Duty is to provide financial support to the Bowes, the fact that he plans to do it "in public view" so that others "would see who was charitable and who was not" (Crace 1995, 196) makes it rather an egotistical Duty to himself, one no longer motivated by a sincere desire to help those in need.

"Words have power, George. Words are deeds. [...] words and deeds should be the same. You make a promise, you should keep it. You hold a view, then you should stand by it. You should say what you do: you should do what you say" (Crace 1995, 141), says Aymer, explaining why he revels in long speeches, to which George replies with his typical common-sense turn of phrase: "People in these parts in't impressed by words. They don't mean what they say. They only mean what they do. And that, I think, makes better sense" (Crace 1995, 141). What Aymer gradually reveals is that his flawless theory about words and deeds does not tally with what he does in practice. Long before he does, however, Crace provides the reader with several, more or less ironic, examples of this discrepancy: as soon as Aymer decides to travel to Wherrytown in order to perform what he sees as the moral Duty, he realises that he has "no appetite for such a long and testing journey" and that he is not "suited to the countryside" (Crace 1995, 22), and what helps him to endure his unease is not so much the idea of ethical responsibility for the fate of the poor kelpers as the prospect of finding himself "a loving country wife" (22) there; he sets Otto free, "a greater duty to a greater Brotherhood" (Crace 1995, 41) as he calls it in his letter to his brother Matthias, without thinking about the consequences of his act, namely the immediate fate of the illiterate slave who cannot even speak English, and thus spends much of his waking hours searching for the African and daydreaming foolishly about secretly bringing him home "disguised in a dress and bonnet" (Crace 1995, 164), and giving him a job at Hector Smith & Sons: "The plan was not preposterous. He'd dress him well. He'd mould him into shape. Otto would learn to read, write, cipher, be a gentleman, and enjoy the status of emancipation that otherwise could flourish only in his dreams" (Crace 1995, 164); when he makes up his mind to marry Miggy Bowe, he does not think of her as a human being but as a project that he has a moral duty to accomplish, similar to that concerning Otto, since in his visions Aymer plans to "*liberate* the girl" and "break her chains of poverty" (Crace 1995, 76), with the aim of turning her into a lady. Crace ironically makes his protagonist use almost identical rhetoric as with the slave: "The thought was not preposterous. He'd dress her well. He'd mould her into shape. She'd learn to read and write and cipher. She'd pick up the proprieties of city life and adopt a more womanly demeanour" (Crace 1995, 73). Despite his noble words, Aymer's acts run contrary to the very essence of humanism as he is unable to acknowledge other people's desires, needs, and wishes, imposing on them exclusively his own, and he is thus "revealed to be a pompous prig out of touch with the world he wants to save" (Lane 2003, 27). The selfishness and pettiness behind Aymer's words and acts are only more clearly demonstrated when he looks forward to his brother's jealousy of his new young wife.

Another example of the lack of concordance between words and deeds in Aymer's life can be seen in the book he is reading – *Truismes* by Emile dell'Ova, both the text and its author invented by Crace, namely the passage about the benefits of solitude: "The solitary Traveller has better company than those that voyage in the multitude, for he has Nature as his best Companion and no man can be lonely in its Assemblies of sky and earth and water, nor want of Friends" (Crace 1995, 159). Aymer likes to see himself as such a destined solitary traveller, a "Radical, an aesthete and a bachelor" (Crace 1995, 160), whose noble mission is higher than the life of an ordinary person and thus transcends and inevitably excludes most earthly pleasures. However, after all the troubles and injustice in Wherrytown, the book offers little solace for Aymer's loneliness as he comes to understand the stark truth of his deprivation: "He couldn't fool himself. He'd rather be some cheerful low-jack, welcome at an inn, than the emperor of all this landscape" (Crace 1995, 160). This painful realisation of what human needs actually are in everyday life, and that words alone offer little consolation when divorced from reality, is the most useful lesson Aymer learns in Wherrytown, one that makes him throw the book in the fire, watching as "[t]he fire grew strong on aphorisms, epigrams and teasing ambiguities" (Crace 1995, 176), a mocking commentary on the connection between his bookish erudition and genuine emotional warmth.

Thus, ironically but understandably, the only instance of Aymer doing something that another person finds beneficial or desirable occurs when he is not the initiator of the act and is actually unaware of its effect – the sexual intercourse with Rosie Bowe during which her second child is conceived. The situation that precedes the act makes Aymer very ill at ease, as neither his speeches nor his wisdoms prove helpful in handling it – he is alone with a woman with whom he has nothing in common, and this woman is strong, independent and self-sufficient, which makes him realise his uselessness:

> Nothing that he valued in himself had any value there. His modest wealth, his manners and his education – what did they count for? His charity? His Scepticism? His love of conversation and debate? His unexpected sympathy for dogs? His democratic spirit? His prodigious memory for Latin names? Which among these attributes should Rosie Bowe admire? Which of his parts and virtues could she burn for candle wax, and which would stew well with a turnip root? What use were manners for catching fish? Would Scepticism make a sauce? Would education batten down the roof against a lifting wind? (Crace 1995, 233)

It is only when he gives up being useful in his terms and lets Rosie take the initiative that Aymer is finally depicted as a proper human being. Without words, without handing out soap or coins, he performs what he has been preaching about since he arrived in Wherrytown and makes someone's life better. His late loss of virginity thus becomes symbolic because it transforms him mentally more than physically, making him learn that in order to help another person it is essential to get to know what they are like and what they want and feel, even though he might not fully understand or identify with it. This simple lesson in the necessity of empathy for any humanistic project appears to be the central moral of Crace's parable.

4.1.2 Symbolic Topography – Landscapes of Distress

Crace admits to a keen interest in imaginative landscape construction. In his novels, the landscape always serves as a mediator between the characters and the happenings of the external world. "Places lend themselves readily to symbolical extension because there is so little that is inherently affective in their physical properties" (Lutwack 1984, 35). Aware of this attribute of physical environments, Crace makes the setting a crucial component of the stories of his novels, creating a distinctly unique landscape in each and implementing it in the novel's symbolic meaning. It is so closely linked with the consciousness of the characters that it forms a kind of a "mental space that is both cognitive and emotional [...], both free floating and yet time-bound and situated, both inward-facing to the habits of pure thought yet also compromised by the circumstances of the corporeal self" (Menigan 2008, 19). Moreover, the very act of imaginatively constructing a "verbal space endowed with psychological, ideational, and aesthetic dimensions" and "retreating to the neutral territory fashioned by the imagination" gives the author a measure of freedom, as it liberates him or her from the "constrictions of the ordinary time/space matrix of 'reality'" (Malmgren 1985, 25). Place in literature evokes numerous connotations – both positive, such as "security, stability and meaningfulness", and negative, for instance "oppression, repression and the related desire to escape from the place in question" (Hardy 2008, 7). If place is rather fixed and limited, "space is more suggestive of openness and freedom to move, but also of emptiness and lack of meaning and orientation" (Hardy 2008, 7). It is obvious, then, that if the setting of a story is to fit into its framework of meaning, there must be a correlation between the place and the space in the narrative. It is precisely the profound complex of geographic place with physical and mental space that generates the unique atmosphere of Crace's novels.

From the geographic point of view, *Signals of Distress* can be understood as a counterpart to *Arcadia*, which is set almost exclusively in a city and deals with urban themes. The fictional landscape of *Signals of Distress* is substantially different: not only is it that of a village, countryside, and seashore, but Wherrytown, the setting of a large part of the story, was a genuinely existing small settlement in west Cornwall until it was destroyed by a storm in 1962. However, although both the location and the time are precisely specified, the whole story, including the shipwreck of the *Belle of Wilmington,* is completely invented, which renders its actual year and place subsidiary in terms of the novel's structure of meaning, and enables the plot, characters, and landscape to be interwoven in a way similar to its predecessor. What the two novels have in common is the relationship between the protagonist and the environment in which he finds himself. Unlike Victor, Aymer is a townie born and bred, with no notion of what life in the countryside is like, and so he is also a stranger and loner in Wherrytown, where "[t]here wasn't any city etiquette" (Crace 1995, 151), and is perplexed by the realisation that the locals are not in the least "paralysed by such a visitor" (Crace 1995, 65). Both protagonists are determined to set things right by making their mark, thus showing other people their worth and, consequently, earning deserved respect and gratitude. But while Victor uses the means that are natural to him – his money and his managerial skills – and remains safe in his wished-for isolation, Aymer enters unfamiliar territory, socialising with people whose values he can never fully comprehend, and inevitably ends up in an isolation that brings him only despair and confusion.

Crace's construction of the landscape in which Aymer finds himself perfectly reflects the relationship between the place and its uninvited intruder. That he will not feel comfortable there is already foreshadowed by the description of the inn, which becomes a metaphor for the whole local community and its attitude to strangers, though in terms of social background and frame of mind rather than geographic origin – wary, reticent, distrustful, and suspicious. The effect is even intensified by the fact that the inn has no name, which Aymer is unwilling to accept because, in his view, all things must have names (which he is so proud of being good at remembering), which points to the irrelevance of words in this world. "The inn was ideal for hide-and-seek. It was a warren, untouched by architects. [...] There wasn't any logic to the place nor, even, any regimental regularity to the shapes and sizes of the building's bricks and stones" (Crace 1995, 16). It is a place where the logic, rules, and values of Aymer's life do not apply, a place where more is hidden than laid bare and which will therefore forever remain a mystery to him, a place that will at best brush him away, but which also has the potential to destroy him. As with Aymer's attempts at "liberating" Otto and Miggy, Crace uses a doubling image when he describes the inn and the village: Wherrytown, "just like the inn, was made for ambushes and hide and seek. It was a warren, with perplexing levels [...] There weren't streets or civic places, just a lattice of steep intersecting alleyways and lanes, some no wider than a horse and none with any compass sense or geometric logic" (Crace 1995, 89). The settlement symbolically lacks all the traditional characteristics of a small town, suggesting no overlap with Aymer's experience, and he feels as if he is in a maze, a "reckless labyrinth" (Crace 1995, 90) in which he soon loses his way and himself, and which toys with him in a manner he neither likes nor is able to restrain and resist.

Another territory essential to the story is the coastal beach around Wherrytown. The beach, along with the inn and the chapel, is a significant public place for the Wherrytowners, their "agora" of sorts, where they repeatedly gather for various occasions of common duty and pleasure. As an area that links the village with the source of its primary income – the sea – the beach is a site of both communal work and festivity. The narration portrays the beach as an important meeting place on a number of occasions: it is where the villagers heartily welcome the sailors from the *Belle of Wilmington*, where they help the sailors to collect and process the drowned cattle from the ship, and where they make their living from fishing. So, one moment they are rejoicing in the rare snow on the beach, treading in it and snowballing each another, only to transform the beach into a busy place of work a few hours later with their pilchard catching and kelp gathering. But even this hard work is an opportunity for them to enjoy togetherness and the community-binding values of helpfulness, selflessness, and cooperation, which is why the shore looks "like a winter carnival" (Crace 1995, 134) to the unacquainted observer. However, there is one more aspect that all these scenes on the beach have in common – the absolute exclusion of Aymer Smith. While the locals are hugging and shaking hands with the sailors, Aymer suffers a much cooler reception at the inn; unable to help the villagers pull the dead cow carcasses from the sea, he is pushed aside to hold the dog, passing the time by recalling the Latin names of fish and seaweed; and he also gets sidelined during the fishing, not so much because of his injured arm and shoulder but because he is seen as a good-for-nothing when it comes to manual work and physical enterprise. Though equipped with the maxim that a "traveller should leave himself exposed to humankind, not art or landscape" (Crace 1995, 138), he once again retreats into his detached, distanced position of a theorising observer who feels desolate in his exclusion, but at the same time does not dare to do more than look down condescendingly on the human-imbued landscape with "this live pageant", "the spectacle of one small, single-minded, unremitting town at its busiest" (Crace 1995, 138).

However, there is one specific place on the coast, further away from the village, whose role in the story differs substantially from that of the beach: the Cradle Rock, a massive boulder that can be swung on its pivot stone like a cradle or seesaw. The rock assumes a symbolic meaning in the novel: if the beach is a bustling and often chaotic workplace for the kelp gatherers and fishermen or a site of spontaneous communal merriment, the Cradle Rock is a peaceful and tranquil place, the only fixed point in the lives of the local people, a natural monument whose remarkable quality gives it an aura of solemnity and a profound spiritual, almost religious, dimension:

> It was a perfect paradise of rocks, much loved, in summer, by watercolourists and lizards. But in the winter, with so much grey about and so little light, the dull pinks of the exposed stone were warm and beckoning. [...] If it was natural masonry, then it had been weathered by a geometric wind and shaped by architectural frosts. This topmost block – the shape and size of a small stone cottage – rested with solid poise on the nipple of a flat but slightly rounded rock. If anyone sat [...] on the bench and stared for long enough it could seem the block was hovering an inch above the world. It had a tarred cross on its side. (Crace 1995, 81)

The swinging of the rock can be taken as a barometer of events and changes happening in Wherrytown and its surroundings, an indicator of the social equilibrium within the local community. At the beginning of the novel, a storm makes it seesaw in the gale as the sea brings in two ships with people on board who will affect the life of the small and quiet port – Aymer, Otto and the crew of the *Belle of Wilmington*. Symptomatically, they all have something to do with the rock in the course of the story, which illustratively reflects their position in the local community.

For Otto, the Cradle Rock becomes a hiding place, a refuge where he hopes to be at least temporarily safe from those hunting him for a financial reward, the sacred place thus ironically playing the role of sanctuary for the community's greatest imaginable outsider. For Aymer, the rock becomes a source of momentary happiness when he and the young sailor Ralph set it swinging on their way back from the Bowes to Wherrytown. Thrilled that he managed to do something so astonishing, Aymer "had seldom felt such unselfish pleasure" (Crace 1995, 82). But when the brief moment passes, they set out on an unpleasant and tiring journey to the village through the ice and snow, only to find the inn empty and cold. Aymer soon forgets his exhilarating experience with the rock when he first discovers that his clothes are gone, and later even has to face an embarrassing and painful confrontation with Shipmaster Comstock. The scene shows how unwelcome Aymer is in Wherrytown, and that it is only when he is far away from the settlement and its inhabitants that he is able to do something he would be satisfied with. At the same time, it suggests that even such an act will be rather irrational, stemming from outside the realm of his manners and erudition, and therefore short-term and consequently accompanied by confusion and unease, thus anticipating his lovemaking with Rosie Bowe.

The characters who most markedly change the life and events in Wherrytown are the crew of the *Belle of Wilmington*. These sailors are typical representatives of their kind – restless, mischievous, "becalmed and idle and, almost, bored" while ashore, unable to amuse themselves and therefore looking for a "chin they'd like to punch, a silver time-piece or a pair of boots they'd like to lift, a mouth they'd like to kiss" (Crace 1995, 46). Nevertheless, they still manage to affect the lives of several people from the local community, such as Rosie Bowe, Palmer Dolly, Walter Howells, Alice Yapp, and Lotty Kyte. Feeling stuck in the dull village of hard work, sober mores, and strict religious morality, they more than appreciate the opportunity to leave Wherrytown for the coast to drive a herd of cattle back to Howells, equipped moreover with bottles of spirits. Predictably, they get drunk and decide not only to swing the Cradle Rock but to "displace it from its pivot stone" (Crace 1995, 217), causing the massive rock to lose its centre and fall from its platform into the sea. Palmer Dolly, the only local person in the group, does not take part and only watches the scene superstitiously, believing that destroying the rock will bring bad luck, and when he later hears "the distant impact of the Rock" he "trembled in his bed. The Rock was down. The coast would never be the same" (Crace 1995, 218). The bringing down of the rock could have several interpretations within the symbolic meaning of the story: it suggests that the very core of the local community's livelihood, kelping, and catching pilchards might soon give way to other, possibly more industrial and mercantile activities; it can also reflect the transformation of the community as many of its young members are to leave it in hope of finding a better future overseas; but it can also indicate the future fate of the ship, which sinks on its voyage to Canada. The Cradle Rock, much like the simple rural community of Wherrytown, which has survived all the blows of the forces of nature, thus symbolically succumbs to the social and economic pressures of the rapidly developing capitalist world outside.

The penultimate chapter, symptomatically entitled "The Lands of Promise", finds Aymer as the only remaining guest at the inn, everyone else having left Wherrytown on the *Belle of Wilmington* earlier that day. Lonely, tired of reading his books, haunted by the confusing memory of his sexual experience with Rosie Bowe, and worried that he might fall fast asleep and miss his early morning ship, he devotes himself to daydreaming about the people he encountered "in all propriety" and who, in his view, were exposed to his exceptional courtesy and benevolence. In reality, as he "could put right in his mind's eye things that might go wrong in life. That was his major skill" (Crace 1995, 245), the true purpose of this imaginative exercise is to compensate for all the failures he has suffered and all the misconceptions he has fallen prey to. And so he conjures up the landscapes of their happiness – the pregnant Miggy in America, the landowning Norrises in Canada – only to reveal that the essential element of these imaginings is his self-projection so that these people can express their gratitude for what he has done for them and for the fact that they have had the chance to benefit from his kind and magnanimous friendship. Crace's ironic treatment of his protagonist is only underscored by the terse note at the end of the novel that the *Belle of Wilmington* sank not far from the Canadian shore and none of its human passengers survived the incident.

In the end, however, when Aymer resolves to include Otto in these imaginary landscapes and "find a happy ending for the African as well" (Crace 1995, 252), they do not provide the desired solace and relief. Unlike with Miggy and the Norrises, who are aboard a ship that is taking them towards their dream on the North American continent, the harsh reality of Otto's dismal situation, a poorly dressed black man left alone in the frosty countryside without money, food or knowledge of English, prevents Aymer's imagination from conceiving a plausible way in which the unfortunate African could be saved and transported back home, still less one in which Aymer would play the role of rescuer. Even though he tries hard to relocate Otto from the white and grey winter seaside to a landscape of brighter colours and a gentler climate, his mind begets no such miraculous twist of fate: "No matter what he improvised, the landscape wouldn't change" (Crace 1995, 254). And so, eventually, Aymer's escapist fantasy must settle for the improbable possibility that he would encounter Otto on the streets of some English town, imagining the enervated and starving man's joyful reaction upon seeing his "good old friend," who would then use his means, connections, and wisdom to make the African a respectable and contented citizen.

In order to complete the novel's irony, in the last chapter Crace moves the story to the city where Aymer lives. Although he seems to be a different person now, "less preacherly, and more resigned" (Crace 1995, 258) as his brother points out, deep inside he has remained the same self-deluded fool and idealist, which can be seen from the very first lines of the chapter: "City air makes free? Well, yes. It was a liberation to be home again amongst the soft civilities of city life, and free from the embarrassments of Wherrytown. But Aymer Smith affected not to like the taste of city air that much. He was a travelled man now, amphibious between the country and the town" (Crace 1995, 256). Based solely on his short and, to a large extent, unfortunate stay in Wherrytown, Aymer already considers himself a well-travelled man with a newly acquired capacity to feel at home in both the country and the city, while in reality he will always be a stranger in both, though in the latter it is easier for him to sink into the anonymity and refined manners of the crowd. Therefore, although the city is the milieu in which he should be happy and safe, the opposite is in fact the case. When, in search of adventure and education, he decides to visit the poorest area of the city, dressed "democratically" in plain clothes because "[o]ne ought to know the city of one's birth, including those parts that were not well furbished" (Crace 1995, 264), so as to prove that "[i]t would be wrong to regard as low and mean in character those people whose homes are low and mean in built" (Crace 1995, 264), he gets severely beaten, not only because Howells has asked for it, but also because his appearance enrages the rogues, especially the apparent discrepancy between his shabby dress and "that bony, educated face, those soft and fussy hands, that self-esteem" (Crace 1995, 265). Once again, his inability to empathise with other people turns his theoretical humanism into pompous conceitedness in the eyes of those who should supposedly benefit from it. The fact that he is attacked in his own city but on the orders of someone from Wherrytown, symbolically demonstrates that he will never fit into either of these two environments, for his truly natural milieu is that of his books and his dreamt-up world, his "childish landscape" where he can always "put the world to rights again" (Crace 1995, 276).

4.1.3 The Old, the New, and the Unchanging

Signals of Distress fits perfectly into the complex framework of the idiosyncrasies of Jim Crace's fictional world. Like his other novels, it portrays a community in transition, an establishment facing inevitable transformations and losses due to external social and economic developments; its fictional landscape becomes an inseparable component of the story; it explores the essential human moral concerns through allegorical meanings; and despite the serious issues it deals with, it bears distinctive elements of social satire, with a surprisingly intense employment of irony directed at the fracturing between the naivety of a character and the world that has always moved on (Lane 2003, 28). The novel also demonstrates its author's remarkable descriptive powers, his gift of making fictional place and events look realistic and authentic: the characters and settings are vivid, sharply observed, convincing, authentic, and agreeably unpredictable, and through them he creates unique imaginary microcosms in which his uncomplicated stories assume a larger symbolic or even mythic dimension.

The novel can be read, above all, as a parable of the passing of the old establishments, whether antiquated, obstructive, or redundant, and their replacement by new, dynamic, and progressive social and economic forces. Set shortly before the beginning of Queen Victoria's reign, in the winter of 1836 and 1837, the novel depicts the community of Wherrytown, enclosed, rural, and self-sufficient, at the dawn of a new era in which it will be forced to open itself up to fresh impulses and become part of the surrounding industrial and commercial world. Aymer becomes aware of this immediate progress when watching the coastal steam packet *Ha'porth of Tar* passing the sailing boat the *Belle of Wilmington*: "It seemed to Aymer that the tussling spirits of the age were passing on the sea; the old, the new, the wind, the steam, the modest and the brash. The future would be driven by steam, he was sure. It was a more compliant slave than wind" (Crace 1995, 228). Being an anachronism himself, he sees the coming changes as dangerous if not downright shameful but, as in *Arcadia,* with the rainbow that symbolically connects the old and the new at the end of the story, pointing to "urban renewal, and the human possibility of a city that retains its pastoral symbolism" (Head 2002, 210), *Signals of Distress* is rather muted in terms of any conclusive interpretation of the scene. When read as a parable, the novel has a strong moral dimension, which, however, does not side with either party of the conflict; Walter Howells and Matthias Smith, the two men who represent the spirit of the new era, are shown to be inconsiderate and immoral, while Aymer, an advocate of the good old days, is depicted as an impractical and hapless dreamer. As is characteristic of Crace's writing, the key moral focus of *Signals of Distress* is on the universal, unchanging, and timeless human and humanist values that constitute any functioning social paradigm, regardless of particular historical circumstances, and whose implementation can never be achieved through self-centered idealisation or mere theoreticising.

4.2 Quarantine

Crace admits that his novels are often variations on other stories, and their aim is to reinvent the original narrations. *Quarantine* (1997) imagines Jesus Christ's forty-day sojourn in the desert, as described in *The*

New Testament. It does so in accordance with Magdalena Mączyńska's claim that rather than destroying iconic literary texts, "contemporary iconoclasts appropriate and transform them" (2015, 1), which in the case of scriptural material results in "an ambivalent but productive relationship between sacred originals, now wholly or partially emptied of their traditional authority, and their novelistic correctives" (2015, 3). The atheist[20] Crace notes that he merely proposed a new story instead of the old one by the "retelling of a narrative [he] thought was harmful, and replac[ing] it with a version which [he] thought was more relevant in the 21st century" (Lawless)[21], his intention being to offer an unorthodox revision from the perspective of a contemporary agnostic or unbeliever.[22] And so, Crace's Jesus is an untutored yet pious Galilean boy[23] who is neither of divine origin, nor seems to possess any exceptional capacities. The devilish role of the tempter is assigned to Musa, an ordinary human being, and the story's Jesus dies of starvation and dehydration after thirty days.[24]

As Crace believes ambiguity to be the "lifeblood of fiction" (Proctor 2000), *Quarantine*'s conception of spirituality to a large extent counters that of the Bible[25], and the story features a number of paradoxical

---

20 Although an atheist, he acknowledges the human impulse for consolatory "narrative[s] of recovery" (Lane 2003, 37). It is in this need for stories of consolation that he sees himself and religious belief related since, as he notes, "we both embrace the power of narrative" (Proctor 2000).

21 This approach accords with Mączyńska's delineation of post-secular fiction as texts that "openly question or destabilize the religious/secular dichotomy on the mimetic, formal, or metafictional levels by juxtaposing religious and secular discourses within the economy of the fictional construct", by which they "engage the reader in an open, often irreverent, reevaluation of the very concepts of the secular and the religious" (2009, 76).

22 Crace claims that the immediate impulse for the story came not from Scripture but from his visit to a care-in-the-community hostel near Moseley (Wroe 2013).

23 Crace admits that originally Jesus was not meant to be a fully-fledged character in the novel, only an historical reference, but as the story unfolded it called for his sustained presence (Mahmood 2015).

24 David Jasper, however, describes Crace as a "religious writer" whose stories have much in common with some aspects of the ancient spiritual tradition of writing where "the sacred is found and felt everywhere in rocks and landscape, and especially when 'religion' itself is either abandoned or else, and more often, it abandons us", which is why his characters "can only be accessed, if at all, through story, built up in the imagination and by the willing suspension of disbelief" (2018, 167).

25 The story, however, though written by a scientific atheist and neo-Darwinist (Bookgroup.info 2007), does contain uncanny elements that strongly echo those of the Gospels, particularly the resurrection of Jesus. *Quarantine*'s ambiguous and ambivalent blending of the natural and the supernatural is discussed at length in Graham Holderness's article "Jim Crace, *Quarantine*, and the Dawkins Delusion".

and ironic events and twists of fate that blur the borderline between good and evil, right and wrong: Jesus inadvertently cures Musa, in consequence of which the cynical self-seeker recovers, while the Galilean devotee dies helpless, without receiving any celestial solace. Musa exploits and bullies everyone around him, yet the unused hole his wife Miri digs for his corpse fills with water overnight to become a life-saving cistern. Moreover, it eventually becomes the grave where Jesus is buried prior to his resurrection, an act fitting into the symbolic cycle of extinction and regeneration. Musa brutally rapes another quarantiner, Marta, while unknowingly "curing" her by making her pregnant, which gives her and Miri the courage to flee his control. And, when the spiritual body of Jesus comes back to life, the first person to benefit from the miracle is Musa, who immediately makes it into "his merchandise" (Crace 1998b, 242).

A determining factor behind all these incidents is the environment in which they take place. Deborah Lilley demonstrates how Crace experiments with pastoral settings in his novels "to represent and reflect critically upon the relationship between people and place, highlighting the blind spots in their characters' visions, and the imperative to account for what lies beyond their fields of view" (2018, 36). His employment of wilderness in *Quarantine* is analogous to this. The scrubland is depicted with the utmost precision and sense of minute detail of a natural historian: Crace presents the geological profile of the region, paying attention to its rocks, sediments, and minerals with their shades, shapes, and crevices; he examines the rare desert vegetation, and is observant of its natural inhabitants in terms of their appearance, behaviour, and instincts. However, this rock-bound area in the middle of the Judean desert assumes further and more meaning-making functions with regard to the plot and character development, which are only amplified by the absence of scriptural spiritual authority. Referring to selected theoretical conceptions of space and its representation, the aim of this section is to discuss and analyse the diverse ways in which Crace uses the landscape of the novel to generate and exemplify meanings reaching beyond its physical presence, with a particular emphasis on its ethical role as a superior principle controlling its occupants' fates.

4.2.1 The Haggard, Incautious, and Rewarding Land of *Quarantine*

Quarantine's spatial representation is based on the space-landscape-place triad defined above. The fictional space of the novel is that of the Judean desert, but the most significant role is actually attributed to just one specific site in this desert – a scrubland located up in a hilly area amidst steep rocks and cliffs in which there are eleven caves. It is a true wilderness, absolutely unsuitable for any long-term habitation, and so, even within the sparsely populated desert, it is a territory of its own as it is simultaneously close and distant for settlers and travellers: close because it is within walking distance of one of the major trade routes, but distant because it is difficult to access and inhospitable. The narrative stresses that this area is often unsafe for its animal dwellers, not to speak of humans, for example, after a heavy storm:

> The storm had lifted stones to show their hidden faces. It had made firewood from bushes, and pulled up roots and soil. Lice and termites tumbled in the daylight where the earth was scarred, busy with repairs. The birds were feeding everywhere. Their nests and eggs had been destroyed, but they could fret on insects until their stomachs burst. [...] A layer of dust and grit was spread across the ground, like seeds and flour sprinkled on a loaf. This was the way the world had been before mankind, the childhood of the earth when it was innocent and undisturbed. This was the way the world would be when all mankind had gone, when the cleansing wind of prophecy had swept all sins and virtues from the earth and the wilderness was strewn with fallen and abandoned faiths. (Crace 1998b, 201)

The scrubland rises above the desert valley – serene, undisturbed, ominous, and inscrutable – which is also reflected in the novel's portrayal of its environment: the narrator describes the wilderness of "avalanches of dry scree, and a threatening conspiracy of rocks, wind and heat" as "treacherous and unpredictable" (Crace 1998b, 13), "large and inexplicable" (Crace 1998b, 75), and as such a "lazy and malicious host" that it is "undiscriminating in its cruelties" (Crace 1998b, 8) towards all creatures from a foreign habitat.

What transforms the character of this uncivilised locale, however, is the fact that the caves are customarily used as refuges by quarantiners who go there to spend some time in complete isolation, with very limited food and drink supplies, or even fasting completely, believing that this time spent on their own with their god(s) will change their lives for the better. The motives of these people may vary from the material and personal to the spiritual, such as trying to cure a disease, seeking good luck, or achieving some transcendental experience, but the pattern is always the same: they arrive, occupy the caves, and, at the end of their quarantine period, they leave for home filled with new prospects as "the scrub sen[ds] all of them away enriched and dryly irrigated" (Crace 1998b, 219). These pilgrims do not only provisionally inhabit the scrubland, but they also endow it with meanings derived primarily from their hopes and expectations, by which they personalise this environment and get attached to it. As a result, the presence of the quarantiners makes the severe and impersonal space into a place bestowed with imaginary and symbolic patterns of human projections and interpretations, and, in consequence, a factor in their identity formation. Also, as they are individuals of different kinds, with diverse personal histories and wishes, the character of the site is, to use Prieto's words, inherently one of dialogue and contestation, which infuses the place with a number of contending projections of meaning. Moreover, as they tend to be rather isolated and occupy only a small area of the caves and their immediate vicinity, it is justifiable to speak of the concept of landscape to denote the specific environment in which several socially and emotionally charged places are located and reconciled within a larger geographic unit.

The desert scrubland as portrayed by Crace meets the parameters that Prieto sets for *entre-deux*, in-between places. It is innately heterogeneous because its rough landscape, with its harsh and changeable climate, defies control from outside and thwarts all attempts at imposing any kind of regularity, order or hierarchy on it, including that of temporal linearity.[26] The individuals who come to settle there are subjected to natural forces so hostile that mere survival becomes their principal ambition. With regard to human culture, it is positioned both inside and outside: outside because it lies far away from settlements and the desert travel routes, and it also lacks any permanent connection, physical, or imaginary, with society and its daily functioning; but it turns into an "inside" when, every now and then, irregularly and unforeseeably, a member of this culture decides to undertake his or her quarantine there. In either case, the scrubland liberates its incomers from the requirements and restrictions of their home cultures and communities. The interstitial and peripheral

26 David Jasper notes that in the wilderness of the desert "time ceases to be [...] and so the narratives that operate only within the narratives of temporality cease to be effective" (2004, 92-93) in rendering its true character.

character of this place is also underscored by the fact that the people who seek hope and solace in the caves themselves tend to be outsiders or people who are not highly regarded in their home milieu, such as the ill, the adolescent, the elderly, and the disabled. It is also transitional as the quarantiners go through their respective rituals, rites of passage, fasting, praying, and meditations in order to walk from the scrubland "improved" and, in most cases, hoping to be more fit for re-inclusion into their communities.[27] And sporadically, they actually do feel transformed upon their departure,

> rewarded for their quarantines with sacred revelations. The scrub allowed them its steep and narrow tracks, and through the softened silhouettes of hills, to their attending gods. And there it stretched its grey horizons to reveal what far-off armies were approaching with their spangling phalanxes of spears, what distant kings and preachers came with gifts and prophecies, how slow and never-ceasing was the world. And there it gave its voyagers their glimpse of paradise. (Crace 1998b, 220)

The transitional dimension of the place is thus given by the fact that the pilgrims come and go, only to be replaced by newcomers, and it is also considered by these transitory residents as a vehicle of transformation, a stepping stone to a more bearable destiny. Last but not least, it meets Prieto's criterion of possessing a dynamic creative property, being an intermittently vigorous site intersected with a number of lines of force, as each resident's interference with the environment disturbs its natural equilibrium and stirs up its undercurrent energies to new incidents and stories.

The novel's scrubland, with its caves used as quarantine shelters, also falls within Foucault's delineation of heterotopia. It simultaneously mirrors and contradicts other sites from the culture by receiving and "rectifying" individuals who are somewhat incompatible with these official places and the institutions embedded in them. It is a counter-site that differs entirely from all the other places within this culture. In terms of its temporality, it is heterochronous, operating across the linear timeline

27 Stephen Palmer argues that Crace's novels use marginal landscapes – liminal spaces on the "cusp between nature and culture", "in and out of time" (2012, 52) – as both a symbol and a setting. Such liminality "suspends the dominant conventional organisation of human relationships and ties, and allows another, destabilising mode of organisation briefly to be glimpsed" (2012, 52-53), enabling the writer to explore "moments of extremity and transformation" (2012, 56).

by means of circularity and layering: its time arrangement is circular, as newly arriving pilgrims recurrently succeed those who have departed, but these temporary stays do not affect the peculiar character of the place; this arrangement is also one of layering of spatiotemporal experience since the pilgrims do not know one another and have different socio-cultural backgrounds, which is why the accumulation of this experience is palimpsestic rather than that of a continuum. Moreover, although secluded, it is potentially accessible to everyone, but the few who wish to reach it need to make a gesture in the form of undergoing the lengthy and arduous journey into the hills. From the point of view of the heterotopia typology, the scrubland represents a perfect example of crisis heterotopia as the quarantiners are precisely those individuals that Foucault associates with this type, for instance, an elderly man with cancer, an infertile woman, and a zealously pious youth. But it is also a heterotopia of fleeting, transitory temporality which, in spite of its provisionality, aims at a kind of eternity through the cyclical recurrence of its temporary residents and the incessant layering of new experiences and the accumulation of new energies. Thanks to this, it is a place that opens itself to the pilgrims' imaginary projections, a place that propels their innermost hopes, wishes, and dreams, even those which may not comply with the demands of the cultures whose pressure had prompted them to quarantine themselves.

Crace's treatment of his fictional environment corresponds with Tally's, and, in particular, with Prieto's ego-centred and phenomenological approaches, both in terms of examining how it affects the characters' states of mind, and in terms of how he makes the reader experience that environment through his distinctive rendering. The scrubland is, primarily, a place of disparate human experiences, whose clashing lines of force *Quarantine*'s narrative tries to map. Jasper observes that in *Quarantine*, just as in Crace's other stories, a "deep yearning" can be found "within and beneath the teeming, external stuff of his worlds" where the human condition "is always located in the particularities of place" (2018, 176). A significant part of the novel focuses on the spatial experience and awareness of some of the protagonists, particularly on how these are reflected in their consciousness and how they affect their mental processes. The ultimate otherness of the landscape forces these visitors into a heightened awareness of and alertness towards the peculiarities and perils of the place from the moment of their arrival: "They were so concentrated on the land which would be their host for the next forty days, and so fearful of it, that hardly a beetle could move without them knowing it" (Crace 1998b, 16). The environment's impact on the quarantiners' psyches is instant as they have to restructure and simplify their values to prioritise those related to their immediate survival, especially enduring the disheartening discomfort of their provisional lodgings and the cold "unity of damp and sleeplessness inside the caves" (Crace 1998b, 41). For them, the scrubland is both real and imaginary – real because they are exposed to it in its unembellished essence, imaginary because they have previously imagined it and projected their expectations onto it. Crace pays attention to how they experience and perceive this environment, and the characters given prominence are Jesus, Marta, and Miri.

Jesus's problem is that he is not able to respond adequately to the discrepancy between the real place and his imagined preconception of it, based on his intention to get closer to his God since in the wilderness he will not be distracted from his sacred communion. And indeed, in this regard, his vision is fulfilled as the barren and unwelcoming scrubland, with its "valleys waiting for their rivers, the browns and yellows waiting for their green" (Crace 1998b, 22), looks to him as if it were still to be completed, and as such an ideal place "to find his god at work" (Crace 1998b, 22). He is at first appalled that this "edge of god's unfinished universe" (Crace 1998b, 77) is no longer to be worked on by the Creator since it is in fact a limbo, but eventually consoles himself with the idea that God, in his generosity, left it incomplete in order to provide Jesus with "a place opposed to sin and nourishment" where he "could starve himself of both without distraction" (Crace 1998b, 126), a true battleground for the chosen one to be "eased to freedom from the devil's grasp" (Crace 1998b, 149). Believing that a harsh and uncomfortable journey and shelter will appeal to God, he deliberately chooses the most remote and inaccessible of the caves, an uncomfortable one most exposed to the workings of the elements, and recklessly decides to make it to the cave barefooted, lightly dressed and with nothing to eat and drink, relying only on "god's provision" (Crace 1998b, 75). His displacement is thus voluntarily undertaken, though on the basis of a fallacious assumption.

His withdrawal into the cave is indicative of his "retreat into the mind" and "stands for the search for a heightened connection with consciousness" (Groes, 2018, 156). In fact, the heterotopic site of the inaccessible cave becomes, for a time, the shell of his consciousness, a sanctuary for his dematerialised existence. But after a few days, dispirited and frightened, Jesus is filled with disappointment that the land would not offer greater hospitality to someone like him – humble, modest, and devout. Exhausted, thirsty, and sore, Jesus finds it increasingly hard to concentrate on his unearthly communion, and when his prayers do not result in any divine intervention, he gradually abandons them to find a more feasible scheme for his survival. By then, however, he is too frail and listless to climb down the precipice that separates his cave from the ground, thus doomed to become a captive of the place and the landscape whose harshness he believed would make him free. And so, he dies, taken in by the scrubland, his body symptomatically having "the colour of the land behind" (Crace 1998b, 205), only to have his wish to be a healer at God's command fully granted through his resurrection and transcendence.

Marta's hopes for the scrubland are also high as she believes that it can cure her infertility. However, unlike Jesus, her encounter with reality is not so desolating or shocking, though its severity takes her by surprise. She is not as young and naïve as he is, and her expectations of the landscape are far more sober, and this, combined with her optimistic nature, means that she feels respect for the wilderness and is able to discern its charm:

> [Marta] stepped into the damp earth and the bushes at the foot of the cliff. She was surprised how sombre it was, and how blustery the wind had become. [...] But the night was beautiful, nevertheless, more beautiful than any night she had known at Sawiya [...]. This scrubland was the roof. From where she stood, the moon was level with her eyes. (Crace 1998b, 46)

On the one hand, the menacing authority of the landscape makes her slightly fearful, but on the other, its discreet grandeur fills her with confidence that her troubles can be overcome there. Although she often feels uneasy there, imagining all the living creatures hidden in the dark outside her cave, she gradually gets used to the place's myriad sounds and even mildly enjoys listening to "the conversation of the gnats, the dry remarks of crumbling soil" and "the living rocks around the healer's cave, breathing, humming to themselves, praying even" (Crace 1998b, 115). She takes her stay in this inhospitable place as a test of her determination to change her destiny. Through a combination of her tenaciousness and her sensitivity towards the landscape, she keeps on with her quarantine despite the vagaries of fate, assuming that "[a]nything was possible, in that haggard and incautious land" where "[i]f anything could happen, then it would" (Crace 1998b, 114), as if subconsciously relying on the fact that "there are always miracles in the desert, as it suspends normal categories of human experience" (Jasper, 2004, 100). While Jesus's encounter with the unforeseen reality makes his formerly unwavering faith falter, Marta's already strong will strengthens even more when faced with the scrubland's harshness. In the moral dimension of the narrative, however, the landscape not only mirrors the characters' states of mind and mental properties, but also actively responds to them. And so, it is as if Marta is rewarded for her perseverance and her belief that overcoming hardships bestows recompense: having endured Musa's sexual assault right in her cave, she is granted the pregnancy she so longed for.

A special case in this regard is Miri. Unlike the quarantiners, she finds herself in the place not by choice but by circumstance, when, having been left behind by the rest of her caravan, she looks for a suitable spot to dig a grave for her dying husband. This, however, does not mean that she suffers less than her quarantining companions: as a young girl, she was given to Musa as a wife by her family, only to find that her husband was an egocentric opportunist and an irredeemable brute who soon makes her married life a continuous nightmare by treating her like a servant, and not even the fact that she is pregnant with his baby tempers his bullying behaviour. For her, Musa's terminal illness actually represents a hope of liberation from such a miserable existence. As with Marta, it is as if the scrubland knew about her persistence and fortitude, and, in an attempt to alleviate her undeserved suffering, showed her its less hostile face:

> Yet the scrubland welcomed Miri there, to its dead hills. It gave its hospitality to her. It would use what little skills it had to make her life more comfortable, to keep her bedding free from scorpions, her skin unsnagged by thorns [...] The earth was showing kindness to the flesh. It let her pull its stones quite readily out of the ground, so that her husband's grave grew waist-deep without exhausting her or causing any strains. (Crace 1998b, 8–9)

Indeed, the narration emphasises Miri's exceptionality as a person by likening her character to that of the scrubland:

> She had bewitched the scrub on her first day. They were equals in their plainness and their endurance. Usually it was a less forgiving, more dogmatic host, despising doubt and mocking faith at once, and favouring the predatory, whatever their beliefs. It was even-handed in its cruelties. [...] The scrub required its passengers to take care of themselves or go without. The scrub was economical, as well, and boundless in its bareness and poverty. (Crace 1998b, 219)

Although not a predator but a victim of one, she wins the favour of the scrubland through her straightforwardness, stamina, and covert strength – undisguised in her diffidence, defiant in her subjugation, knowing in her reticence, alert in her inertia – which actually parallel the distinctive attributes of the landscape. *Quarantine*'s phenomenological spatial rendering, which rests in the concord between the properties of the scrubland and the psyches of its occupants, thus prepares the ground for Crace to elevate the environment into a moral agent of superhuman intervention. The landscape as portrayed in the novel is more responsive to those who are worthy of its helpfulness, which is to say to those who are free of pretence, self-delusion, and self-pity, and who, against all odds, keep on struggling with their fate. And Miri proves to be such a person, which is why she happens to become a beneficiary of its meagre magnanimity, unlike the male quarantiners, who tend to blame the place's stinginess for their misfortunes and disappointments.

Marta and Miri endured their stay in the wilderness because they were able to both respect its otherness and confront it when their brighter prospects were at stake. Once they have received their "gifts", that is, the conception of a child for the former and the confidence to leave her despotic husband for the latter, they realise that it is time to leave the place that, despite its apparent sternness, has shown its generosity to them. Once again, the description of their daring but successful flight from Musa's oppression and, as Nicola Allen (2018, 120–21) observes, the constraints of the religion that has allowed their subjugation, down into the desert valley to take the route to Marta's place, is full of polysensory landscape imagery:

> Marta and Miri hurried on in silence down the landfall [...] The scree grew softer as the temperatures increased, closer to the valley floor. The earth was gypsum, spiced with salt. It smelled of eggs. But by the middle of the afternoon – already covered in a yellow film of salt – they'd reached more gently sloping and more sweetly smelling ground, a landscape of soft chalk and which a child could pull apart in its hands as easily as breaking bread. The land was more reliable, at last, and they could walk side by side towards the trading road. (Crace 1998b, 236)

Having been trained to move on the treacherous and unpredictable terrain of the scrubland, they find their hasty descent into the desert valley almost effortless. As the land grows more temperate and yielding, so the outlines of their new future – a life more temperate and yielding than their previous experience – start to emerge. Strengthened and invigorated by their (mis)fortunes in the scrubland, the two women can enjoy the unaccustomed comfort of their journey towards "the uneventful world" (Crace 1998b, 238) of their days to come.

However, it is not only agreeable characters who depart from the wilderness "rewarded" for their tenacity and/or endowed with new prospects. At the beginning of the story, Musa, the story's central antagonist, miraculously recovers from his deadly fever. At its end, though deserted by his pregnant wife, he is far from devastated and downcast since "the scrub would not return him empty-handed to his market-places" (Crace 1998b, 220). The fact that the character of the scrubland actually suits Musa had already been noted by his wife, who deemed it a perfect spot for his grave because the "world from there would seem large and borderless [...] and that would be appropriate for a traveller like [him]" (Crace 1998b, 6–7), a person of boundless self-assurance, self-complacency, appetites, but also vigour and perseverance. Some traits of Musa's character thus comply with what the wilderness demands from its inhabitants if they are to survive – adaptability, self-reliance, resourcefulness, and a will to live, and the way he gets away with his tricks, abuse, and misbehaviour resonates perfectly with the above-quoted observation that the place favours the predatory: as soon as he recuperates, he reveals his rapacious self and, displaying little if any fear of the scrubland, takes control of the immediate situation and exploits it, claiming the landscape as his property and, subsequently, making the docile quarantiners pay him rent.

As well as enriching himself by cheating the pilgrims of their money, Musa also finds among the caves a new commodity he can trade: the great news of a saviour's rebirth. Of all the occupants of the scrub, it is Musa who is "blessed" to catch sight of the apparition of the resurrected Jesus, an ethereal experience he, as an exceptionally inventive and persuasive storyteller, will turn into unearthly profit. And so, although his last glance is directed at the distant scree down which the naked, thin Galilean is painfully making his descent, his mind is already preoccupied with townscapes – the squares and marketplaces where he will barter the story of his new identity as a zealous quarantiner turned prophet for the favour and money of the rich and powerful. Thus, one of the results of Crace's replacement of biblical spiritual authority with that of the natural world is that this ethical system also values those whose ability to surmount difficulties does not always stem from honest and unselfish impulses.

4.2.2 The Landscape as a Moral Agent

Quarantine's employment and rendering of space and place comply with the analytical and interpretive paradigm of phenomenologically focused geocriticism as developed by Tally and Prieto. Indeed, the novel, "like the desert itself, [...] confuses interior and exterior" (Jasper, 2004, 100), particularly the minds and souls of its characters on the one hand, and their struggles for survival and redemption in the desert wilderness on the other. Although its story takes place some two thousand years ago, its setting is appropriate for geocritical scrutiny: it is inherently heterogeneous, volatile, and transitory, prone to permanent movement. It occupies an extreme periphery from the point of view of the quarantiners' home communities, and this remoteness from the centre displaces its human visitors, contesting the very fundamentals of their identity, by which it corresponds to Prieto's *entre-deux* places. Its temporality is cyclical and isotopic, which is why the manner in which it is experienced assumes the form of cumulative, palimpsestic layering rather than continuous succession. It also meets the criteria of Foucault's crisis heterotopia and heterotopia of fleeting, transitory temporality. Consequently, the novel's wilderness evinces a latent potential to enhance its occupants' sense of independence, confidence, and belief that a welcome change in their lives is attainable.

Sebastian Groes points out that Crace's fiction argues for "a form of cognition that includes landscape, nature, inanimate objects, and animals of every kind (including humans) that exist outside a human timeframe" (2018, 162). Accordingly, *Quarantine's* location crucially determines the protagonists' sense of self and their place in the world. Crace puts focus on the mental reflections of these individuals' spatial experiences, examining the ways in which they condition and influence their daily existence, their feeling of displacement and belonging. The immediate trigger for this process is the tension between the actual place and the quarantiners' expectations based on their imaginary projections onto it prior to their arrival. Only the unaffected and persistent prove able to grasp the in-between place's ominous properties and reconcile the imaginary and the real into an experience that is meaningful and productive in the sense of helping them to adjust to the established places of their culture. The narrative thus maps the spaces of the protagonists' experience, allowing the reader to simultaneously map the fictitious spaces within the narrative by means of apprehension and interpretation. Crace's phenomenological treatment consists of a consistent examination of the mirroring correlation between the space/landscape and the characters' psyches:

> But there was also something rich, at times, about the scrub, despite itself. Something sustaining, unselfish, fertile even. Perhaps this was because it made no claims. It did not promise anything, except, maybe, to replicate through its arrays of absences the body's solitude and to free its tenants and its guests from their addictions and their vanities. The empty lands [...] were siblings to the empty spaces in the heart. (Crace 1998b, 219)

Crace goes further, however, in suggesting that the scrubland's dynamics rest in its potential to facilitate a transformation in the lives of those individuals who "deserve" such assistance – those who may suffer or feel miserable but still display a sufficient degree of self-reliance, tenacity, and forward thinking. However, a combination of these qualities may not inevitably make such a person likeable, as is the case of Musa, who, despite his pathological self-assertion and boastfulness, benefits from his stay, albeit at the cost of losing his wife and unborn child.

Quarantine confirms the legitimacy of its author's reputation as a landscape writer by offering a physical and mental topography of a real-and-imagined place, possessing properties customarily attributed to human beings. The scrubland thus operates as the setting, while also being one of the crucial initiators and movers of the action, almost like a character in the story. Moreover, it is endowed with a capacity surpassing human possibilities, allowing it to assume the role of a higher principle controlling the forces that determine destinies. Therefore, the narration does not conclude with any of the protagonists, but with an image of

> the endless movements on the trading road, the floods, the rifts, the troops, the ever-caravans, the evening peace that's brokered not by a god but by the rocks and clays themselves, *shalom*, *shalom*, the one-time, all time truces of the land. (Crace 1998b, 243)

In its complexity of meanings, the environment serves as a figurative device for reflecting, anticipating, and modifying the protagonists' mental processes and states of mind. Moreover, the landscape not only absorbs and mirrors the workings of the human element, but, within the novel's ethical framework, given by the absence of both societal and divine authorities, it also claims the right to establish justice and to rectify what contradicts "its" notion of the natural order, a legitimate strategy for an atheist and self-proclaimed moralistic writer.

5. Jim Crace's Cityscape: Spatial Hybridisations, Transgressiveness, and Transmodern Critique in *Arcadia* (and *The Melody*)[28]

5.1 *Arcadia*

Although there have been numerous attempts to identify the unnamed city in *Arcadia* (1992), most frequently as Birmingham[29], its universality allows it to be compared to almost any modern Western city, since it embodies the very essence of the urban condition rather than any specific concretisation. Crace's imaginary cityscape, a kind of Craceopolis, is a generalised concept based on two essential properties of any modern city – appropriation and coincidence. The first relates to the city's capacity to appropriate assorted influences, ideas, and tendencies, to take hold of them, transform, and adapt them to its ends, and incorporate them as if they have always been part of its existence, be it country people with their folklore, beliefs, and aspirations or various architectural styles and systems of urban planning. However, this tendency is not all-encompassing, and the city always carefully scrutinises whether the particular object of appropriation is worth the effort, whether it disposes of the potential to contribute to and survive in the diversity and heterogeneity of the city. That is why neither Joseph's dreams nor Victor's orderly shopping mall can ever succeed in this process, because both suffer from a symptom that is largely incompatible with the city – self-delusional idealisation. The sec-

28 Parts of this chapter were published in Petr Chalupský's articles "The Urban Pastoral – Hybridisations in Jim Crace's *Arcadia*" in *Litteraria Pragensia* 20, no. 40 (2010) and "Transgressive Spatiality and Multiple Temporality in Jim Crace's *Arcadia*" in *American and British Studies Annual* 15, (2022).

29 Crace has lived in Birmingham most of his adult life. See, for example, John Williams's review (1992) of *Arcadia*, at the beginning of which he looks for signs that could identify the novel's city with Moseley or Birmingham.

ond property – coincidence – refers to the ultimate randomness and contingency with which the individual aspects of city life encounter and clash with each other, only to be reconciled in a juxtapositional symbiosis, as in *Arcadia* where "the rural world coincides with the urban extreme" (Williams 1992). It is only the perpetual concurrence of these two tendencies that ensures the vital social, cultural, and aesthetic hybridity of the city.

Begley suggests that Crace's novels "are about communities in transition", caused by change that "comes suddenly, irrevocably, and the human response to it is captured with wonderfully uncluttered intensity" (Begley 2002). In *Arcadia*, this transition is closely connected with the changes in the cityscape, which is depicted in a condensed form as an evolvement from the preindustrial to the modern and postmodern. Such a transition is always accompanied with anxieties and fatal losses for the individual, who is suddenly forced by circumstances to cope with often conflicting demands in order to survive or preserve the community. It is unsurprising that these people feel the need to create the myth of an escapist, alternative world devoid of their everyday pressures and feelings of displacement, a fundamentally anti-urban vision of communal rural peace and harmony. Crace's narrative captures the tension between the seductive illusion and the immediacy of reality. Such an illusion is helpful only as long as one is able to keep their distance from it, as long as it does not become a simulacrum of a reality nourished by unrealisable dreams. Crace takes the motif of the pastoral, which is defined by its opposition to the urban, and places it in the centre of the city milieu, in the focus of its lines of force. Once uprooted from its original location, the arcadia is immediately modified by the host environment, thus losing some of its fundamental properties while gaining several new ones. As nothing retains its original structure once imbedded in the city's fabric, becoming hybridised for the sake of its further functionality, so Crace's *Arcadia* challenges the genre of the urban novel by putting to use the pastoral myth in a satirical form.[30]

5.1.1 The Urban Pastoral

Arcadia tells the story of Victor, a self-made, rags-to-riches multimillionaire, who, although born in the countryside, becomes a city dweller as a baby because his tragically widowed mother leaves her village for the

30 *Arcadia* thus follows the tradition of the early eighteenth-century satirical London poem, namely Jonathan Swift's "A Description of a City Shower" (1710) and John Gay's *Trivia: or, the Art of Walking the Streets of London* (1716), by adapting it for the genre of the novel.

city, hoping to find better opportunities to make a living there. Her fate, however, is quite unfortunate, as she ends up begging in the fruit and vegetable market, nicknamed the Soap Market, and seven years later she dies in a fire, leaving her orphaned son in the care of her sister. Having experienced a childhood of poverty and emotional hardship, young Victor makes a resolution to always rely only on himself and, by means of relentless hard work, become a wealthy person. His enterprise is so successful that he is able to buy the marketplace and make himself into a fruit and vegetable tycoon, not only by charging rent for the stalls, but also by running a chain of countryside farms that supply the stallholders with fresh merchandise every day. The novel's plotline starts when he is celebrating his eightieth birthday, on which he decides to "make his lasting, monumental mark upon the city" (*A* 47) by demolishing the Soap Market and replacing it with a modern, steel and glass shopping mall, and it ends some ten years later when the mall, named "Arcadia", is already in operation and Victor is planning the final step in his successful life: having his memoirs written.

Yet, in spite of this seemingly straightforward storyline, the interpretation of the novel is far from obvious and unequivocal, in keeping with Crace's belief that ambiguity is "the lifeblood of fiction" (Proctor 2000). Consequently, it can be read, for instance, as a psychological novel, a sociological study of modern urban life, a mock-pastoral, or an ethical contemplation on the shortcomings of late modern capitalism. It also evidences its author's claim that ideas matter more than individuals in his stories, since neither Victor nor any of the other characters can be described as the novel's undisputed leading protagonist. Although Victor's life story determines the novel's plotline, his role in the "present-day" happenings is more subdued and shadowy, as he actually leaves the premises of the tower block in which he lives and works only once, for a short while. Rook, Victor's go-between in terms of organisation and supervision of the market and collecting rents from the vendors, occupies a larger space in the story, but even he, who gradually transforms from a confident and spirited man of action into an almost pitiable "Martyr for the Cause" of the market (Crace 1998a, 274), leaves the stage before the plotline reaches its climax. Similarly, Anna, once Rook's colleague and lover, who later replaces him in his position after his dismissal, and Joseph, initially Rook's antagonist but ultimately his accomplice out of necessity, are characters who are rather instrumental within the novel's overall thematic framework. And, finally, the narrator of the story – a journalist with the pen-name of The Burgher – is occasionally actively involved in the story, but fulfils the role of a detached, and at times ironic or even sardonic, observer and commentator of the action.

The diversity of the city in *Arcadia* is most manifest in the fruit and vegetable market, which metonymically stands for the whole of Craceopolis. The figurative role of the market-place is further reinforced by the fact that the city cannot boast any other source of wealth than money from trade. Within the thematic and narrative framework of the novel, the market is significant not only because it is a place of trade and money, but also because it represents the fusion of the urban and the rural, the site of the perpetual encounter of these seemingly contradictory principles, which in fact jointly drive the very dynamics of the development of modern civilisation. As early as 1973, in his seminal study of literary and social history, *The Country and the City*, Raymond Williams undermined the traditional binary opposition between the two environments. Instead of presenting the country from a nostalgic perspective and the city from a critical one, Williams sees them as changing historical realities, inextricably related to each other and to various social developments. Therefore, he warns against the dangerous temptation "to reduce the historical variety of the forms of interpretation to what are loosely called symbols or archetypes" (Williams 1973, 289). It is, above all, this challenge that contemporary city novels like *Arcadia* attempt to meet. Rather than being considered as two mutually exclusive forms of life, the country and the city should be understood as differentially connected moments on a continuum that includes numerous other possible variations. By using the market as the central locus of the story, Crace's novel dramatises Williams' concept and shows some of the negative consequences of adhering to the binary opposition he critiqued.

Far from being a manifestation of country life implemented intact into the city centre, the market, though it originated as the country brought to the city, has since been appropriated by the city, transformed, and adapted to its purposes. At the same time, however, the original spirit of the countryside proves difficult to subjugate as it finds its voice in the polyphonic market discourse. It is therefore a place where the continuity between the two forms of civilisation is most apparent, a territory that is no longer rural but not yet wholly urban. The products and the marketeers might come from the country, but the rules of sale, its processual and spatial organisation, have been supplied by the city: Crace's detailed description of the market captures precisely the unique fusion of these two principles: the earthiness and directness of the country people and the multitudinous chaos of city life:

> The marketeers parked where they chose, or where the Man in the Cellophane (who took it madly on himself to block and beckon traffic) directed them. [...] It was safe haven for a sprinting criminal pursued by police in cars. The odours here were less opaque than those which spilled out, windborne, into the streets beyond. [...] No gallery of modern art could match the colours there, the tones, the shapes, the harmonies and conflicts on the stalls. [...] Every knife, and every traders tongue, was sharp as limes. (Crace 1998a, 15–16)

The result is a space in permanent transition, unstable and transient in many respects, yet somehow insisting on its permanence both for and in spite of the city. It is a space impossible to discipline, one that defies any imposed shape or outward control, which is exactly what Victor dislikes and wishes to put right. It is as if the market echoed the very nature of the city, while satisfying some of the atavistic rural cravings of its citizens. The market gets even more urban and rampant at night, when the awnings and the stalls are taken down and the city's dark side takes over, turning it into a refuge for the homeless and other unfortunate city misfits. Once again, the market asserts its intermediate position, beyond any control – if by day it represents a battlefield on which the country defies the machinations of the city, by night the raw, and in principle non-urban, existence of the vagrants threatens the city's self-confidence.

5.1.2 In Search of Hope: The Townies

The novel's fictional milieu is meant to be archetypal and, as such, "its inhabitants as prototypes of citizens present different approaches to the city" (Teske 2002). Crace thus peoples his story with several typical representatives of postmodern city dwellers. The first is Victor, whom Teske sees as "the isolated urban ruler who defines the city by mapping or 'reading' it from above and by creating buildings that manifest his urban vision" (Teske 2002). He thus carries out what Michel de Certeau describes as perceiving the city from above, as a whole, an entire world complete in itself yet unlike the actual one below as it "is transformed into a texturology in which extremes coincide" (de Certeau 1988, 91). Seeing the city from such a perspective is a source of pleasure, which is caused by feeling the power of totalising this otherwise immensely diverse human text. In doing so, one experiences the freedom of being untouched by the anxieties of the hectic city life, and one can change from being a compelled, alert walker into either a confident voyeur or a distanced, godlike figure in whose omniscient eyes the disordered world transforms into a lucid, readable text (de Certeau 1988, 92). Victor exemplifies the latter case, which is associated with a position of wealth and power and based on a detachment from the urban practices of everyday life. The problem with such an omniscient, god-like perspective is that what one sees is no longer the actual city but its mere representation, a fictional narrative created through the viewer's projection of his or her own wishes, illusions, and needs. It is a dehumanised, theoretical city, a simulacrum. Victor's attachment to the city does not rest in his liking its cityscape and *genius loci*, but in his reshaping of it into an idealised setting for his emotive life story.

Even though he has spent almost his whole life in the city, Victor has never identified with it, seeing it merely as an instrument for achieving his goals, as a source of his wealth. He in fact represents a kind of forerunner of the global market elites, supranational financial tycoons whose mobile capital enables them to be free of ties to any locality or fixed institution, and controls his realm via virtual money flows. Yet sentimentality about his own life, one of his dominant character traits, prevents him from enjoying the freedom of his financial situation. Fortified in his Big Vic ivory tower, his living space is an artificial one, devoid of direct contact with outside reality. He is, therefore, most content when overlooking the immediate yet distant city while imposing on it his sentimental self-projections. The city as he views it is of his own making, reflecting his greatness and, as such, deserving of his lasting architectural imprint. Victor resembles another literary self-deluded megalomaniac, Sir Jack Pitman from Julian Barnes' *England, England* (1998), who believes the world needs his "one last great idea" (Barnes 1998, 34), a historical England theme park, also based on a nostalgic, wished-for illusion. Unlike Victor, however, Pitman understands that such a thing cannot be realised within the already existing reality but only in the form of its more enticing alternative. Victor is a pseudo-townie, having never lost his fixation on his mother's recollections of the pastoral countryside, resulting in his sentimental plan to implant such an arcadia into the city's heart.

Rook, on the contrary, feels most at ease in the city's bustling streets and thus represents a detached insider, a spy or detective who, on his walks, tries to uncover the power structures of the city (Teske 2002). He is, with all his aptitudes and misconceptions, portrayed as an exemplary product of the city. On the one hand, he sees himself as a city predator, a confident walker whose sharp city instincts make him alert to all the pitfalls of the streets, while at the same time allowing him to exploit the freedom of passing unrecognised, securely hidden in the anonymity and democracy of the crowd. Having successfully defended himself against an inept mugger, Rook expresses his conviction that Joseph's lack of the right instincts will always doom him to failure when confronted with a city-wise person like himself. These instincts cannot be learnt, they must be acquired in the course of one's life, as in the case of the rhythm of the city streets. In terms of Zygmunt Bauman's typology of postmodern identities, Rook is a mixture of "the player" and "the stroller".[31] Like the player, he likes to take his life as a slightly but not too risky game in which things might, but do not have to, happen. It is a game he enjoys as long as he sets the rules, and as long as nothing personal or private is at stake. So, when he is dismissed by Victor and left by Anna, his life loses all its comfort and dispassion, as the identity of the player only fits a winner. What Rook shares with the stroller is his taste for taking advantage of the anonymity of the crowd in order to observe other people and, in his imagination, project their lives and identities, while simultaneously constructing a self-deceptive image of his own almost limitless power and invulnerability. Yet this illusion always proves to be a fragile one, as Rook realises after an attack of asthma renders him helpless right in the midst of the marketers, and his only feeling is a longing to be in the safety of Victor's palace.

Rook, moreover, to a certain extent embodies one of the central concepts of what Guy Debord identifies as the postmodern *flâneur*, or the *flâneur* within the postmodern city: "the spectacle" (Debord quoted in Jenks 1995, 153–156). Unlike de Certeau, who claims that everyday practices resist spectacularity in favour of the routines by which ordinary people create an autonomous life space, an urban text they write without being able to read, a network of intersecting and manifold stories that has neither actor nor spectator (de Certeau 1988, 93), Debord considers the spectacle as one of the principal means of relating to city life. Rook is the character in the novel who is able to enjoy the thorough spectacularity of the streets, the "cabaret, with mime, and all the spoken badinage delivered stagily, in a whisper or a shout" (Crace 1998a, 12). Watching the spectacle is the most natural way in which city people can approach the otherness of the ever-changing urban reality and strangers in the crowd. As Debord puts it, "the spectacle is the dominant mode through which people relate to each other. It is only through the spectacle that

31 For a more detailed analysis of the four postmodern identity patterns – the stroller, the player, the vagabond, and the tourist – see Zygmunt Bauman, *Life in Fragments. Essays In Postmodern Morality*, 72-104.

people acquire a (falsified) knowledge of certain general aspects of social life [...] It answers perfectly the needs of a reified and alienated culture" (Debord quoted in Jenks 1995, 155). What distinguishes the postmodern *flâneur* from Bauman's unfortunate stroller is the ability to resist the temptation to impose an interpretative framework on what is seen. The *flâneur* accepts that no complete knowledge of the city spectacle can be obtained and thus exposes himself[32] to it without any preconceptions or self-projected expectations. Only when he is able to assume such a detachment does Rook feel truly happy in the streets, and it is his lack of this ability that means Joseph can never become a proper townie.

Finally, there is the narrator, "the Burgher", whom Teske describes as "the nineteenth-century flâneur who renders his individual urban experience in a satirical tone changing from humour to bitterness" (Teske 2002). A satirical tone, however, is not the only one the Burgher assumes: his voice is the voice of the city, which satirises and mocks, but also celebrates and shows sympathy. The narrative voice thus not only comments bitterly on the story, it also guides the reader through the city's individual layers of meaning. It becomes most celebratory and poetic when it elucidates the potential and appeal of cities in general:

> This is the sorcery of cities. We do not chase down country roads for fame or wealth or liberty. Or romance even. [...] The conspiracy is this, that we – the seemly citizens – obey the traffic lights, observe timetables, endure the shadows and the din. We do not cross, or park, or push, or jump the queue, or trespass, except where we are ordered to. [...] We ebb and flow with as much free will as salt in sea. Yet we count ourselves more blessed, more liberated than the country dwellers And why? Because we townies are the only creatures in the universe to benefit from chains, to make our fortunes from constraint, to wear the chafing, daily harnesses of city life as if they are the livery of plutocrats. [...] We flock in to the city because we wish to dwell in hope. (Crace 1998a, 237–38)

Although essentially unpredictable, variable, and sometimes hostile, the city's environment still attracts many with its countless opportunities, anonymous privacy, and the chance to realise dreams. It is the most natural human living space in the postmodern era, where hope combined with pragmatism and hard work can accomplish almost anything. A significant

32 The *flâneur* is traditionally being depicted as a male figure (as opposed to "passante/flâneuse"), hence the use of masculine pronouns in this text.

level of meaning in *Arcadia* is that the story of each city is the story of its dwellers' fulfilled and unfulfilled dreams, their successes, and failures.

The prevailing tone of the novel, however, is satirical and sardonic, and thus the Baudelairean *flâneur*, combined with the genre of the parable, is a perfect device for presenting the narrative and performative nature of urban life. The *flâneur* is far from being a simple stroller of the streets – for him, city life in all its possible forms can always be constructed as a kind of artistic creation or expression. He is impossible to pin down, as walking and looking are the only aims of his strolls, which makes him an incognito observer whose walks seemingly lack purpose. Although the *flâneur*'s strolling takes place in the midst of everyday reality, his perspective is detached, as if uncommitted, which always makes his account of the streets an artefact in itself. The *flâneur* represents not a person but "a narrative device, an attitude towards knowledge and its social context" (Jenks 1995, 148). His vision is an alternative one because it does not come from a position of power, but from curiosity and amazement, motivated not by a desire to totalise by imposing an interpretation, but by an interest in the mutability of the multitudes. Therefore, the *flâneur* embodies a useful perspective on (post)modern city life, a very democratic one, as can be seen from the Burgher's confession:

> I would not wish to be too grand for streets. It's said that great men have the grandest tombstones, too, and throw the longest shadow even after death. The cemeteries prove the truth in that. But I prefer to think that worms and damp and degradation are open-minded democrats which treat us all the same. We are all citizens at last. At least until we are all soil. (Crace 1998a, 311–12)

However smug or elitist the Burgher's flâneurie may appear to many, he exemplifies one of the great truths of cities: although grand monuments and pompous buildings often become their useful symbols, cities in reality do not live on through them, their *genius loci* does not perpetuate itself in gleaming grandiosity but in the shadowy everydayness of the multiplicity of the streets' narratives and spectacles.

5.1.3 Agora vs. Arcadia

Victor's illusory visions of his architectonic imprint on the city finally materialise in Signor Busi's idea of a shopping mall called, symptomatically, "Arcadia". More or less unconsciously and intuitively, Busi presents a project that exactly fulfils Victor's dream, already partly realised in Big Vic – a rural oasis in the heart of the city. The project appeals to him mainly because it deliberately ignores and rejects the city's fundamental condition in favour of overt regulation. The mall's ironic name is more than apt, as it is based on the implementation of an illusion into the texture of the cityscape that is unrelated to any historical time or geographic location. Although Busi proudly introduces the mall as "building as event", it is an event displaced from any historical or spatial continuum, a fortress of glass and concrete hysterically protected from the possible intrusion of the city outside it.

In true postmodern spirit, "Arcadia" replaces the former market exchange with a conception of consumption as entertainment and entertainment as lifestyle, a homogenised universe of regulated space, topography, and climate. Above all, it attempts what Teske calls "the imaginative appropriation of the public space of the city" (Teske 2002) through which the urban elites redefine the cityscape in their image. The desire to control the architectonic reshaping of the city centre thus becomes a manifestation of political influence and economic power through the commodification of public space. The Soap Market in the novel can also be understood as the archetypal agora of the ancient Greek city-states, a public social space where citizens meet for various purposes, from selling and buying, via the everyday exchange of opinions and ideas, to political gatherings: in *Arcadia* it develops from a place of undisturbed market exchange into a site of violent riots. The agora, as a concretisation of its democratic potential, thus contains the essence of city life. No matter how kitschy and incongruous the architecture of places like "Arcadia" is, the greatest danger they represent in cities is the commodification of multifunctional and heterogeneous public spaces, where activity is always on the side of the people, and their replacement by the sterile yet manipulative designs of commercial malls and arcades, where the independence of shoppers is only illusory.

However, although these places attack urban public life, they never subdue the independent spirit of the agora, for the atavistic forces of the city will always refuse to be contained by structures that disdain the nature of the city. John Fiske, for instance, sees shopping malls not as cathedrals of consumption but as an effect of crises of consumerism, since they represent contested arenas of struggle in which shoppers "can inflict most damage on, and exert most power over, the strategic interests of the powerful" (1991, 14) by using numerous strategies such as window-shopping with no intention of buying, consuming images and space rather than commodities, and exploiting the malls as meeting places and shelters in extreme weather. Just as the mall's aviary for exotic birds was invaded by city sparrows, so "Arcadia" cannot resist the city's need for an uncontrolled public space, which eventually transforms into the new market, which wages its guerrilla war just behind the mall's rear gates. The contrasting perceptions of the mall and the new market can be seen in the narrator's response to them. Although he knows that, as Victor's official biographer, he should praise "Arcadia", his attitude is rather ambivalent and unconvincing, and does not lack the typical ironic bitterness of the previous pages. For the Burgher, "Arcadia" is a commercially successful yet ultimately artificial social space, a shopping theme park that can keep its visitors entertained but can never satisfy the human need for spontaneous communication and socialising, a place where blatant spectacularity simulates a sense of community. Soap Two, in contrast, with its "haphazard evolution", offers him precicely this public spontaneity, "for despite its apparent chaos and disorder, Crace's narrator finds a congruity where a sense of community clearly emerges" (Tew 2006, 93). It is Crace's humanistic approach to the exploitation of public spaces that crucially shapes the perspective that permeates the whole of the novel.

5.1.4 Straightforward Complexity

A characteristic feature of *Arcadia* is its striking formal and thematic simplicity. Its language is clear and straightforward, the informative journalistic style of short sentences presenting the novel's ideas in an intelligible and distinct way. The narration, although at times the narrator attempts to establish complicity with the reader, is rather a traditionally detached one that does not attempt to obscure or conceal the presented message. The novel's playfulness is more or less confined to the final part, in which the reader learns that what he or she has been reading are notes for early drafts of Victor's memoirs that the Burgher is supposed to complete. However, as we already know this evasive attitude towards the mall's functional grandiosity, we can only speculate what the final version of the book will look like and how successful it will be with Victor. What makes *Arcadia* a complex work, open to multiple readings, is the fact that it incorporates and juxtaposes a great variety of genres.

Tew's prevalent reading of the novel is that it presents a disturbing parable of modern city life, in which "conciliating various marginalities renders a thematic and structural unity, where different individuals, opposing fields of vision, different forms of expressiveness, and a sense of *mythos* and place intersect" (Tew 2006, 83). Jakub Stemporowski (2002) concentrates on the novel's mythological structure, namely on the mythology of the Arcadian countryside as a retreat from stressful city life, and explores how Crace systematically demystifies the mechanics of the myth. Teske (2002) shows that *Arcadia* can be read as a fictional version of a sociological and urban study of selected modern urban phenomena and their impact on people, such as the destruction of the agora and disrespectful and context-free architecture and city planning. Another perspective sees the novel as a sociological exploration of distinctive prototypical postmodern city inhabitants, from the economic elites to those whose actions are seldom motivated by material gain. A related genre within the novel is a reflection on the machinery of commercial and consumer culture and its consequences for the commodification of public space. *Arcadia* also contains a mixture of psychological probes into the lives of its main protagonists and the motives behind their acts. Moreover, the overall generic framework of the novel is one of social satire, which crucially determines the way in which the individual genres incorporated "talk" to one another.

Arcadia represents an interesting enterprise in the transformation of the British urban novel in the 1990s, primarily because it attempts to hybridise the form through mixing diverse genres, some of which were originally considered mutually exclusive, namely the pastoral myth and the social urban satire. The result defies an unequivocal labelling, some version of the urban quasi-pastoral or mock-pastoral that challenges traditional novel narratives and invites multiple readings. Although he does not indulge in ostentatious postmodernist experimentation, Crace is a writer who acknowledges the significance of the hybridisation of the genre of the urban novel as one of the crucial means of retaining its vitality. The genre's authenticity largely depends on the degree to which it succeeds in capturing the particular *genius loci*, which is what *Arcadia* succeeds in above all – through its employment of various genres and discourses, the novel reverberates with the polyphony of voices and narratives that constitutes the very essence of the texture of every city.

5.1.5 The Transmodern Paradigm Shift

According to a number of thinkers, since the 1980s, a socio-cultural paradigm shift from Postmodernity to what has been called "Transmodernity"[33] has been taking place. This new perception and understanding of reality stems from the specific character of the social, political, economic, technological, cultural, and environmental circumstances in which we have been living. Susana Onega speaks of a "fragmentary, polycentric, multicultural and chaotically arranged" (2014, 496) decentralised yet interconnected information society evincing multiple parallel occurrences of events and phenomena in different places. Transmodernity is thus more ambitious than Postmodernity in that it not only challenges the centre/margin binary, but also replaces it with a concept in which the centre no longer exists. Theoreticians of Transmodernity agree that we live in an era of volatility and interconnectedness, but they differ in their evaluation of this transformation.

The pessimistic attitude, forcefully voiced by Rodríguez Magda, claims that postmodernism, despite its proclaimed contestation of grand narratives and acknowledgement of pluralisation, facilitated the opposite tendency by creating yet another totalising Grand Narrative of Globalization (2017). For her, ours is a "period of transformation, transience, and accelerated time" (2017) which favours the virtual over the genuine, instantaneity over permanency, exteriority over interiority, exclusion over inclusion, nationalism over cosmopolitanism, populism over democratic dialogue, fundamentalism over multiculturalism, and economic pragmatism over environmental awareness. She thus calls for recovering the above-mentioned suppressed concepts and argues for the necessity of what she calls "narratives of fracture" or "narratives of the limit" (as opposed to "narratives of celebration") which, by undermining current totalising mechanisms and transgressing established rules, will enable us to come up with new realities and values.

The optimistic perspective interprets the transmodern paradigm shift as evidence of a major shift in thinking in the context of the post 9/11 world. For Irena Ateljevic, it is a geopolitical move to "biosphere politics" (2013, 203) promoting values such as solidarity, interrelatedness, and respect for the other.[34] She also argues that the development of human society is a process of oscillation between two antagonistic systems:

---

33 Rosa María Rodríguez Magda coined the term in 1987.

34 In a similar vein, Fritjof Capra ascribes to the transmodern shift the potential for "[d]eep ecological awareness [which] recognizes the fundamental interdependence of all phenomena", and,

partnership and domination. From early Modernity, the latter system held the reins in the name of reason and progress, but with the advent of Transmodernity, a reverse "partnership shift" has taken place (Ganteau and Onega 2020, 4–5). Similarly, Jeremy Rifkin believes that human beings are essentially empathetic, and Transmodernity is the "Age of Empathy" (Ganteau and Onega 2020, 7), a hopeful cultural shift generated by the global reawakening of communal, spiritual, and environmental values of the partnership system.

In either case, Transmodernity's task is to harmonise the purportedly antagonistic global and local tendencies into what Roland Robertson has called the "glocal" (Aliaga-Lavrijsen and Yebra-Pertusa 2019, 7). This requires "anti-dialectic theoretical frames" (Ganteau and Onega 2020, 9) that would equip us with anti-linear models of such key concepts as memory and history, which privilege the horizontal over the vertical and operate on the principles of dialogue, cooperation, and interdependence. Transmodernism's indisputable stimulus was the so-called "ethical turn", which originated in the 1980s as a response to the extremes and excesses of postmodernist sensibility and found its point of departure in Emmanuel Levinas's ethic of alterity. Hence, Kwame Anthony Appiah defines the "poetics of cosmopolitanism" (Aliaga-Lavrijsen and Yebra-Pertusa 2019, 243), which rests not in the search for universals, but in the recognition of what interacting participants share, seeing moral values as relational and connective, and postulating a continuum between all living and non-living beings, interconnected in what Luyckx Ghisi terms "shared vulnerability" (Ganteau and Onega 2020, 16).

One of the cardinal side-effects of globalised (post)modernity has been a widespread relinquishment of the communal and a consequent redefinition of human happiness and progress as personalised and privatised. However, in the long run, such a tendency results in frustration, not only from an underlying fear of inadequacy in the face of the omnipresent glitter of visual culture, but also from the absence of a hopeful vision towards which one's existence might be directed. With an unsatisfactory present and an untrustworthy future, it is only a step away from a dangerous reinvestment of one's prospects in a reinvented past. This is why Zygmunt Bauman (2017) speaks of the age of nostalgia and the emerging "retrotopias", quasi-communal, desperate longings for a wished-for history. Likewise, Rodríguez Magda (2017) warns that such

based on it, Marc Luyckx Ghisi proposes a "policy of 'genuine sustainability'" while Enrique Dussel has the idea of a world-system (Aliaga-Lavrijsen and Yebra-Pertusa 2019, 8, 240).

a fixation on an illusory past that suits our present-day desires can easily lead to a dangerous "melancholy loop", destined to produce only new (semi-)fictitious narratives.

5.1.6 Transmodern and Transgressive Craceland

Literature written in English has been responding to anxieties of the present-day world "by generating new stylistic, generic and/or modal forms that would correspond to a transmodern culture" (Ganteau and Onega 2020, 13). By contesting the established thematic and narrative conventions, these works exemplify Rodríguez Magda's belief that transgression represents a way out of the ethical crisis brought about by the Age of Globalisation (2017). Such literature attempts to eliminate the gulf between the self and the other by means of approaching rather than assimilating differences, to de-abstract the "imaginary stranger" by being "imaginative enough to reach the other [...] and break with otherness" (Aliaga-Lavrijsen and Yebra-Pertusa 2019, 239). In doing so, these texts address the values promoted by the new paradigm, such as connectivity, relationality, empathy, and environmental sustainability.

Crace's novels can be subsumed under the umbrella term of transmodern fiction for a number of reasons: throughout his career, he has eschewed postmodernist themes and narrative strategies in favour of what he calls traditional or imaginative writing, which relies on a clear storyline and pure invention (Begley 2002); therefore, his novels, though set in different historical periods, can hardly be described as historical metafiction because, rather than questioning the knowability of history and the trustworthiness of memory, they make use of diverse historical and geographical settings in order to build their metaphorical stories on a more attractive and thought-provoking background; his novels, regardless of the time in which they are set, are always meant, by means of "provocative and complicated parallels with our own world" (Shaw and Aughterson 2018, 4), to address acute contemporary issues, to be "drenched in [present-day] sensibilities" (Guidarini 2013); his stories always revolve around serious ethical concerns of direct relevance to his readers, especially the relationship to the other, be that to human beings, to animals, or to the environment; and, last but not least, hand in hand with his moral focus goes his political engagement and criticism of the inauspicious impacts of capitalism and globalisation.

Crace's novels depict transitional moments in the life of human communities through the fates of individual characters who are directly afflicted by these changes. However, because he is more interested in timeless moral questions than in individuals (Mahmood 2015), he must use other devices to effectively convey the allegorical meanings of his deceptively uncomplicated stories. Central among these are his representations of spaces, places, and landscapes/cityscapes – his Cracelands – which serve as figurative mediators of and communicative vehicles for the depiction of the characters' feelings and states of mind, as well as of the larger mechanisms and implications of the transformative processes. As such, these environments always simultaneously reflect and actively interfere in the protagonists' struggle with the ongoing vagaries of fate, namely their often futile attempts to resist impending changes through disparate acts of transgression and defiance. Crace's narratives thus feature various places that are in some way caught between the old and the new worlds. Yet, just as his protagonists are far from heroic, not uncompromising rebels and activists, but ordinary, more or less unexceptional, people with admirable traits as well as flaws and weaknesses, who find themselves incapable of warding off the coming state of affairs and eventually succumb to it, retaining their dissatisfaction and disapproval only privately in their minds, so these *entre-deux* places follow a parallel trajectory of transition: from transgression and resistance to submission and transformation. At the same time, Crace also shows that the loss of one such place does not mean that the forces of dissent are suppressed for good, as new, different liminal places emerge, ready to take up the transgressive agenda.

5.1.7 *Arcadia's* Spatial Representations

Symptomatically, alongside the actual action, Crace expresses his ideas and concerns through spatial representations, which is why the novel's central locations – Big Vic, the Soap Market, Soap Two, and Arcadia – are closely interconnected and assume their meanings in relation to one another. Big Vic is the nickname of Victor's modern, twenty-eight-storey tower block, which is close enough to the city centre to overlook the Soap Market, but high enough to provide a view of the city's outskirts. The top floor is reserved exclusively for Victor, who has his penthouse and boardroom there, while the rest of the building is occupied by his company offices. For him, it is a place of utmost and longed-for security and privacy, but also of self-imposed isolation, as, partly due to his age, he only very rarely leaves it in order to be in direct contact with the outside world. It is a perfect materialisation of his childhood dream of making enough money to build "a fortress shield of wealth, beyond which the dramas of the world can run their courses unobserved", in which he would be "protected from the city by what his wallet held" (Crace 1998a, 151). Although the city, and its market in particular, have enabled him to gain wealth and influence, Victor has never really identified with their landscape, atmosphere, and values; he has never really got used to "the clutter and the hardness of the streets" (Crace 1998a, 121). Crace describes him as a "townie almost through and through" (Crace 1998a, 67), caught between the two realms – the city and the country. Deep inside, he still considers himself a countryperson, although he has never actually lived in the country and would not have become so rich and powerful there. His attitude to the city is therefore pragmatically instrumental; he does not see it as his environment or natural habitat, but rather as a means to achieve his goals, which, once exploited, must be kept at bay.

Having been deprived of his childhood and sustained parental care and having been forced by circumstance to rely on himself from an early age, Victor has come to believe that there is nothing valuable that money cannot buy, and that there is no one who can be entirely trusted but himself. Lacking in social skills and affability, he ends up a person who belongs nowhere: he does not feel at home in the city and its market and thus employs the "market-wise" (Crace 1998a, 183) Rook to walk the streets for him, but he is not a villager either, and his attempt to celebrate his birthday in hearty country style with the senior Soapies proves to be an embarrassing situation due to his insurmountable haughtiness, aloofness, and discomfort in company. Victor therefore prefers to spend his time fortified on the twenty-eighth floor of his homogeneous – rectangular, air-conditioned, sanitised, and heavily guarded – ivory tower, safely detached from the city's turmoil, watching it "like a hawk" (Crace 1998a, 44) almost unconcernedly from above, as only from this height and through "tinted, toughened glass" (Crace 1998a, 4) does the city appear orderly, lucid, and controllable. The city of his mind is an abstracted, topographic one, devoid of most of its heterogeneous manifestations, which only partially corresponds to the actual reality. That is why, paradoxically, given that he has spent his whole life in the town, what he still cherishes most is the remote Arcadian view beyond its limits, "the blue-green hills, the grey-green woods" (Crace 1998a, 54), which he considers the true source of his mental balance and well-being.

Victor may not like the city much, but he detests the Soap Market because, with its clamorous hustle and bustle, it embodies precisely those urban properties he has never been able to tolerate, seeing it as a "garish blockage at the centre of the city which spurned both logic and geometry" (Crace 1998a, 45). Moreover, the place is an intrusive reminder of his unhappy childhood and humiliating destitution, which is why Claudio Busi's Arcadia project appeals to him particularly strongly. The experienced and seasoned architect perfectly understands the elderly millionaire's mind-set and sentiments and, in his presentation, denounces the market as "a tumour at the city's heart" (Crace 1998a, 185) that needs to be removed, modernised, and regulated by the imposition of "geometric harmony into the ancient centre of the town where legibility and graciousness are out of fashion" (Crace 1998a, 190). Although he flatters Victor by calling him "a man of now" (Crace 1998a, 190), with his mind set in the present and directed into the future of the city, he is aware that the opposite is the case, which is why the central premise behind his project is to bring the intact, idealised countryside right into the heart of the town. The places in which Victor lives and feels good thus reflect his character and values – they are pragmatic, designed, costly, comfortable, yet dehumanised and emotionless, essentially urban yet out of touch with the day-to-day life of the city.

The Soap Market is a completely different kind of place – lively, colourful, and disharmonious – a place in which life is pulsing day and night. With its ambiguous character, it represents an apt example of an *entre-deux*, in-between, place: on the one hand, it evinces certain features of the countryside, since it engulfs the area of the city park and garden and provides a compound where country people can trade in products from country farms. On the other hand, the market is not as spontaneous and unrestricted as it might seem, as the sellers must comply with Victor's requirements and principally sell goods from his farms. However, the marketplace is very popular with the town's residents, attracting them not only with its fruit and vegetables, but also with its inexpensive refreshment stalls, snack bars, and cafés. Moreover, due to its relatively unrestrained and carefree atmosphere, it becomes a popular refuge for the dispossessed, the vagrant, and the homeless, "the closest citizens in town to the earth's enduring elements" (Crace 1998a, 179), particularly after dusk when the stalls are dismantled. This heterogeneous area is thus made up of all kinds of people – the sellers and waitpersons, their customers, the needy beggars, the layabouts, but also the archetypal urban strollers who, like Rook, like "the city at full pelt" (Crace 1998a, 12), relishing the democracy and privacy of the crowds and watching the cabaret of the streets. It is a limitlessly productive place in terms of the multiplicity of stories and narratives generated by the incessant encounters between these diverse individuals, as well as the imaginative creativity of those who offer their services or display their misery. At the same time, however, it is a latent site of transgression and resistance to the forcible homogenising measures exercised by the rich and powerful to appropriate and commercialise this territory. Both these faces of the market are revealed in the events of the last day before it is closed and pulled down to make way for the construction of Arcadia: while in the daytime, the place is frolicsome in its exuberant celebration of life, despite its approaching demise, with buskers, musicians, and dancers, at night it transforms into a place of riot and revenge in a violent, spectacular but short-lived defiance of the official authorities.

Arcadia also dramatises how the disappearance of one in-between place gives way to the emergence of a new one, which may or may not be of the same nature and have the same function as the original. Not long after Arcadia opens on the site of the former Soap Market, supposedly fulfilling Busi's promise to replace the chaos of the old marketplace "with the harmony and dignity of a modern one" (Crace 1998a, 228), a new open fruit market spontaneously establishes itself in the shopping mall's vicinity. This much smaller "Soap Two", as it is known to the townspeople, gains strength and makes the once uneventful district in which it is located "as noisy and congested, lively and unsafe, as the Soap Market used to be" (Crace 1998a, 309). The novel makes the point that heterogeneous, transgressive, and resistant forces/spaces can never be silenced and suppressed completely as they are an inherent quality of any human society, and the urban condition only amplifies them. Thus, as the narrator notes, they leave their vigorous mark upon the city(scape), albeit intangible and immaterial:

> So now we see that it's not true that 'cities swallow up the small', that soufflés only rise the once'. The pygmies flourish on the street. I used to think that buildings were all that could endure in cities. But people, it would seem, endure as well. They hang on by their nails. They improvise. They kick. They leave a legacy which is not brick or stone. (Crace 1998a, 308–309)

This emergent interstitial place demonstrates that the need for various forms of communal, socio-cultural, and spatial organisation is in fact a persistent and invigorating aspect of any city's life, no matter how alternative, inferior, or even dangerous it may be in the eyes of Victor and his ilk.

The last pivotal space in the novel is the eponymous shopping mall that Signor Busi designs for Victor to supersede the ancient marketplace. Although Arcadia does not really play an active part in the storyline, the building teems with meanings that are fundamental to the interpretation of the novel. The construction accomplishes the project's promise to bring the country and its landscape to the city centre, just like its open-air predecessor, but by different means – through its architectural design, based on horizontal curving lines of glass and steel, reminiscent of a "country greenhouse" (Crace 1998a, 192), which is not only efficiently consumer-friendly, but also deliberately exclusive. The market's productive multifariousness is replaced by spectacular uniformity: the goods traded are polished and arranged in standardised wicker baskets and, when sold, wrapped in bags with the mall's coloured logo, the sellers are all dressed in the same folkloric costume, their shouts have given way to recorded music, the customers are all from similar social backgrounds, the vagaries of the seasons have been flattened into a permanent absence of the elements. It is a climate-controlled and defended "fortress [...] to keep out drunks and tramps and demonstrators and people who do not come to spend" (Crace 1998a, 193), in other words, those with whom the Soap Market was always teeming.

Snobbish, haughty, and pompous, rather than a spontaneous extension of the city, Arcadia, nicknamed "Fat Vic", is seen as complementing Victor's business centre, "Big Vic's plumper sibling. One stands, one squats. They are the city's strangest twins" (Crace 1998a, 306). Profitwise, it is a triumph, "the perfect cash machine" (Crace 1998a, 304), a union of "art and industry and arrogance" (Crace 1998a, 302), but although the narrator admits that the latter properties are idiosyncratic to urban life, his sarcastic tone suggests that in his view, the mall's calculating homogeneity represents a dead end in the city's evolutionary trajectory. The irony of the shopping mall is that although it is meant to be modern, advanced, and progressive, for Victor, the key person behind its construction and profits, it is first and foremost a monument to the past, symbolised by the bronze statue "The Beggar Woman and her Child". Victor enforces the placement of this old-fashioned sculpture, a thorn in Busi's younger fellow-architects' side, right behind the mall's doorway to memorialise his mother and, more importantly, his dismal childhood, thus highlighting his own life achievements. The aim of making the artwork an item of reverent commemoration could not be achieved, however, even in such a monitored and fancy location, as, due to human nosiness, light-fingeredness, and vandalism, it was eventually railed off, and subsequently derisively dubbed "The Cage".

In all three of these major places, their spatiality is inseparably intertwined with their temporal dimension. Interestingly, each of them evinces a tendency towards a multiplicity of temporalities. The most straightforward in this regard is Big Vic: it is an embodiment of the present and of the future, of tough business, rational pragmatism, and unrestrained money-making, in which the past is taken as something to be outdone and surpassed. It is no surprise, then, that any attempt by Victor to bring the past into his workplace/home, such as restoring his former stallholder self, is inevitably destined to fail. Arcadia is a more complicated case, because it is necessary to distinguish between the project's promotional ideas and its actual reality: the former presented the mall as essentially a contemporary place, yet one in which the heritage is maintained in an updated form so that it can continue into the future. In reality, however, the standardised indoor stalls have nothing to do with the Soap Market tradition, and the mental history connoted by "The Beggar Woman and her Child" statue is meaningful to no one but Victor. Moreover, Arcadia is not even very related to the present – just as it is neither countryside nor city but their artificial crossbreed, so its temporal coordinates are also impossible to pin down, its marketing strategies working most efficiently in a perpetual timelessness that promises no change for the future. Geocritically speaking, it is a no-place without any spatiotemporal identity and thus without any productive evolutionary capacities.

The Soap Market, on the other hand, actively incorporates diverse temporalities. With its long and rich tradition, it represents a unique site of historical continuity that has affected the atmosphere and development of the city for centuries. It has always been the city's *agora*, an openly accessible public meeting place whose larger role – social, political, and cultural – far exceeds its manifest economic activities. Its position has been conditioned by its liminality: an official marketplace and leisure district on the one hand, and a locus of the outcast, the derelict, and the disaffected on the other. And so, while retaining the customs and wisdom of its ancestors, it is also a place of the here-and-now, and, in consequence, of the future, in which acute contemporary issues resonate powerfully. It is a transgressive area, always only a step away from becoming a tempestuous battlefield where the city's underdogs struggle to assert their claims against the authority of the powerful, who consider it inconvenient and strive to reduce it to a relic of the past by means of restriction or destruction. However, due to its miscellaneous spatio-temporality, the market is imbued with a particularly strong communal identity and attachment, so that, once demolished, its social and emotional drive facilitates the emergence of another such place, one with the potential to become a platform for dissenting voices, just as the novel suggests with Soap Two.

5.1.8 *Arcadia's* Transmodernist Critique

Arcadia touches upon several concerns that theoreticians of Transmodernity have identified as determining. First, it satirically depicts a highly centralised world of rigid binary hierarchies in which power is concentrated in the hands of a small affluent elite, here embodied by Victor. The story is set shortly after the onset of globalised capitalism and, through the selfish and complacent Victor, with his hunger for profit and power and his utilitarian thinking, shows why this process would have generated a totalising and hegemonic discursive formation. Victor's is indeed an era of transition, transformation, and a growing demand for immediate gratification of one's needs and desires, which, to echo Rodríguez Magda's words, prefers inauthenticity, external appearance, transience, exclusion, autocratic decision-making, mercantile pragmatism, and extreme individualism over their binary opposites. Victor's method exemplifies the system of domination rooted in "the legitimation of violence and greed, the justification of capitalism, colonial domination, the subjugation of the other and the exploitative annihilation of the earth, unrestrained by belief in transcendence and in the spiritual dimension of life-giving and sustaining powers" (Ganteau and Onega 2020, 5).

Victor's successful trading company is built on his idea of happiness and achievement as highly individual and privatised, and therefore ultimately self-centred, and so he wants Arcadia to be a monument to himself, "a market like a cathedral, grand and memorable, worthy of a millionaire" (Crace 1998a, 63). At the same time, however, he comes to realise that no such thing can ever be accomplished completely, since it is impossible to make other people fully recognise the connotations that he himself sees as most significant. Moreover, with its implicit referencing to and honouring of an idealised history, the Arcadia project also exemplifies Bauman's concept of retrotopia, which, under the guise of present-day needs, mentally preserves itself nostalgically in a bygone past. In spite of his business-oriented disposition and liking for modern architecture, Victor's mind is stuck in a self-deceptive "melancholy loop", so that the discourse he uses to explain and justify his intentions towards both the Soap Market and its people, and Arcadia and its true purpose, are actually (semi-)fictitious narratives nourished by his covert self-pity, insecurity, and need to come to terms with his traumatic childhood experience.

The Soap Market (and potentially Soap Two), on the other hand, represents a set of contrary values, namely communality, solidarity, and interdependence. The Soapies, though personally driven by profit, in fact compose an independent community of stallholders, sellers, pub and bar owners, waiting staff, street artists, and buskers, in which the success of one can bring benefits rather than ruin to the others. They are united not only by a common workplace and clientele, but also by the common goal of attracting as many people as possible to the marketplace. Theirs is a partnership system requiring cooperation, dialogue, and mutual support, based on the ability of participants to recognise the values and interests they share, which in most cases outweigh their trading competition. The market is also a forerunner of a local environment, primarily serving locals but offering products, services, and entertainment imported from other parts of the country/world. In Victor's business empire and the Soap Market, *Arcadia* presents two almost antagonistic environments with different principles and ethics, which can only coexist when the former respects the autonomy of the latter, a condition that is violated in the novel. The incompatibility of the two systems is illustrated in the character of Rook, a person who believes he can be a double agent. Though essentially a "Soapie through and through" (Crace 1998a, 14) who loves the market and feels at home there, his "pimpish" nature has alienated him from the stallholders as he charges them extra fees for representing and defending their interests with Victor. His prospects are ruined when his employer hears about his private income and dismisses him on the spot, and the Soapies, considering him a traitor, also refuse to take him in, which is why he ends up as a zealous but rather unfortunate campaigner for the Market's cause and its only victim.

Whereas the world of Big Vic and Arcadia embodies a strictly vertical structure, with the main centre at the top and a linear time concept running straightforwardly from the present to the future, the Soap Market's spatio-temporal model is different and more convoluted. In terms of distribution of power, it is organised horizontally, with a number of partial, lesser centres that need to communicate with one another in order to keep the whole operational. Timewise, it follows a combined pattern in which the linearity of past-present-future is disrupted by the circular character of the market, derived from the cycle of the year, both in the seasons of the products and in the life of the city. At the same time, these cycles are not entirely identical, and every year some innovations have to be made if the market is to remain attractive, which makes its developmental arrangement not only spiral, but also multidirectional, as these innovations draw inspiration from diversely dated (and located) sources – past, present, and future-situated, and palimpsestic, as each new year's temporal arrangement is layered onto the preceding ones, which still retain their visibility, at least in part.[35] The market is therefore a composite temporal structure of miscellaneously connected and interconnected historical moments that resists any imposition of linearity. In other words, it is a place where the present, the past, and the future unceasingly interact, without one dominating the others.

In its first plan, *Arcadia* depicts the supremacy of mercantile forces over what appears to be an outdated remnant of early capitalist social organisation. However, its tone is mostly ironic or even sarcastic towards Victor and his "monumental" architecture, and the real target of Crace's satire is the winning side in this conflict, or more precisely, its psychological, social, and moral deficiencies, due to which its victory may be taken as rather Pyrrhic. As the novel can be read as a paean to cities and city life, with all its flaws and pitfalls, the implicit critique of Victor and his visions principally rests in their being at odds with the very essence and ethics of the urban condition, which is seen as communal and cooperative. While Victor is an unsociable loner who believes that the streets are paved with gold, the narrator suggests that other values are at the core of the city's dynamic viability: he claims that the true magic of cities lies in their inhabitants' instinctive seeking out of crowds (Crace 1998a, 237), and that it is "hope – not gold – what they pave the cities with" (Crace 1998a, 238). Paradoxically, the Burgher makes his most crucial critical comment after acknowledging Arcadia's economic triumph, when he observes that retaining Victor's grand bird's-eye position would mean losing the vital touch of the streets as

> [t]o be removed from them is to lose the blessing of the multitude. The tallest buildings throw the longest shadows, it is said, by those who spend

35 The multidirectional and palimpsestic concepts of memory and history are discussed at length in Michael Rothberg's *Multidirectional Memory: Remembering the Holocaust in the Age of Decolonization* and Max Silverman's *Palimpsestic Memory: The Holocaust and Colonialism in French and Francophone Fiction and Film*.

> their lives in contemplation of their monuments, and for whom the shadow life is better than the real. But most of us who live in the cities die and take our shadows to the grave. We don't outlive the masonry or glass. [...] I make my mark upon the city, too. My living mark. [...] My rainy footprints on the pavement will soon dry, but footprints and the thousand sodden paper bags which held a thousand pears, the eyes, the cores, the stalks, the rinds of daily life, are more substantial [...] than shadows. They swell the middens of the town. (Crace 1998a, 311–312)

The narrator implies that Victor, and others like him, may be rich and successful in realising their professional ambitions, but they can never be happy as people and residents because they do not really understand the city and its mechanisms. Having exploited its opportunities and landscape for his own, personal and self-centred, ends, Victor willingly alienates himself from the environment and fabricates for himself a comfortable virtual reality in which he is the absolutist ruler. The true spirit of the city, however, is to be found in its day-to-day, commonplace community happenings, which favour those qualities that Victor most lacks.

5.1.9 *Arcadia's* Transmodern Spatio-temporality

With its overt critique of globalised capitalism and its totalising discourse, its rigid hierarchical power structure, and its lack of empathy, tolerance and respect for the other, and its promotion of opposing values and social arrangements, *Arcadia* represents an example of Rodríguez Magda's narrative of the limit/fracture. The story points to some of the detrimental impacts and consequences of what it sees as an antisocial, alienating, and unethical establishment that produces flocks of deeply unhappy, anxious, and lonely individuals – some of them successful and content on the outside – their only coping strategy resting in fabricating a soothing alternative reality built on illusory consolatory narratives. Against the atomisation of an individualist society, *Arcadia* implicitly argues in favour of the principles that allow the formation of strong community bonds. Moreover, it portrays a clash between the domination and partnership systems in which the former temporarily prevails, but in which the latter, despite its innate vulnerability, is shown to be more viable, since it is much more in accord with the variability and mutability of contemporary city life. The novel thus falls into the category of transmodern literature, not only because of its subject matter, but also because of the generic and narrative form of its seemingly simple plotline that, when read carefully, offers a variety of voices, perspectives, and interpretations.

Characteristically, Crace makes use of various spatial representations to render and communicate his principal ideas. The novel's meaningful cityscape consists of two different kinds of places – Big Vic and Arcadia on the one hand, and the Soap Market and Soap Two on the other. While the first kind – homogeneous and carefully designed – are depicted, despite their modern architecture, as being almost unproductive in terms of their contribution to the city's wholesome development, the second – varied, volatile, and liminal – prove to be the vital bearers of its *genius loci*. The heterogeneous and transgressive marketplaces, with their assorted social metamorphoses, countless narratives, and potent evolutionary energies, are shown to be the enduring and invincible constituent of the city's essence. Importantly, the novel's spatiality is imbued with a convoluted temporal dimension, particularly in the second group, which evinces a compound and non-linear time arrangement that undermines the straightforward consequentiality of the chronological model in favour of multidirectional and palimpsestic variants in which the relationship between past, present, and future is one of interaction, circulation, and transposition. Thus, by combining transmodern critique and spatio-temporal metaphorical representations, *Arcadia* provides an ingenious, multi-layered, and thought-provoking commentary on some of the determining aspects of the present-day urban and civic condition.

5.2 Transmodern Concerns and Transgressive Spatiality in *The Melody*

Arcadia is not Crace's only urban novel to address transmodern critique with the aid of spatial representations. Through both its subject matter and its narrative mode, *The Melody* (2018) also reflects some of the underlying concerns voiced by the transmodern paradigm shift. The first of these is the pernicious effect of translating progress and development into purely materialistic and mercantile terms. In the character of Joseph Pencillon, a calculating developer with political ambitions, the novel shows how the town's modern redevelopment, though ostensibly made in the name of continuity and community, is motivated solely by profit and selfish pragmatism. Hand in hand with this is the theme of the vulnerability of those who are negatively affected by the consequences of Pencillon's demolition and (re)construction projects, both human as well as other members of the natural world. The story aptly demonstrates how easily victims as diverse as Alfred Busi, the celebrated singer, the town's homeless people, and the animals and plants of the bosk, can become equal in terms of their powerlessness and vulnerability when threatened by the inconsiderate actions of official, power-holding authorities.

In examining this shared vulnerability, Crace not only touches on the theme of the inherent interdependence of all the constituents of the environment, but also proposes the values of solidarity, empathy, and relationality as the most available means of resisting and/or surviving within a domination system, even though their effect is often far from immediate, lasting, and guaranteed. Through the fates of selected individuals and their personal crises caused by the pressures of such a system, he portrays how the whole community is endangered when the defining principles of humanity and communality are at stake and the essential bonds between humans and the natural world are severed.

Like *Arcadia*, *The Melody* employs representations of space and place, particularly the interconnectedness of the urban and the natural, to articulate its pivotal ethical concerns. The places and spaces that prove most meaningful within the novel's thematic, or transmodern, framework are the town's heterogeneous green areas – the Mendicant Gardens occupied by the homeless and vagrants, and the bosk, with its wilderness-like character – Busi's villa, which is transformed from a once distinguished symbol of its owner's status into a redundant, semi-derelict relic of the past, and the Poverty Park, a forest on the outskirts of the town that is gradually being commodified into a tourist attraction through the "urban legend" of mysterious and rare neanderthal humans who are said to inhabit its more remote nooks and occasionally venture out into the streets at night to feed on leftover food in dustbins. They are all examples of in-between, emergent, or transgressive places/spaces that allow Crace to render through them the various facets of the transitional process the novel depicts.

With each of the multiple layers of the plotline – Busi's, Pencillon's, Terina's, Soubriquet's, the homeless', the bosk's – and their respective spatial representations, *The Melody* foregrounds the values and principles that theorists of Transmodernity proclaim as fundamental to the conception and promotion of alternate systems to those generated by totalising narratives and discourses, namely partnership values, universal empathy for the other, concern for the environment and its sustainability, and relationality and solidarity in the face of the imperatives of the liberal capitalist market economy. Thus, like *Arcadia*, it exemplifies Rodríguez Magda's "narrative of the limit" (2017) in its immediate critical response to some of the principal tensions of today's homogenised, but ultimately alienated and disparate, globalised world.[36]

36 For a more in-depth analysis of transmodern and spatial concerns in Crace's *The Melody*, see the chapter "Spatialising the Transmodern in Jim Crace's *The Melody*."

6. Literary Cartography in Jim Crace's *The Pesthouse* and *Harvest*[37]

6.1 *The Pesthouse*

The overriding story of Crace's novels is one of fateful loss as his protagonists are exposed to the consequences of the process by which one era gives way to another. Forced by circumstance, they have to learn to cope with an uncommon, liminal situation defined by the collapse, transformation or even eradication of existing values, norms, and beliefs before new ones are fully determined and established. The power of his novels lies in the fact that they present a recovering narrative of hope – his protagonists, though initially distressed and confused, never give up and keep on struggling to restore their shattered identities and adapt to the transformed reality. This section focuses on Crace's 2007 novel, *The Pesthouse,* and explores the ways in which he links his protagonists' mental, emotional, and spiritual worlds to the geography and topography of the territories they journey through and, consequently, how the novel's fictional space-time transforms from one of pain, despair, and confusion to one of hope, consolation, and promise. By tracing the protagonists' progress in space and time, their physical as well as mental movement on the "map" of its fictitious world, the novel represents an example of a literary cartographic narrative.

37 Parts of this chapter were published in Petr Chalupský's articles "The Landscape of Trauma, Pain and Hope in Jim Crace's *The Pesthouse*" in *Ars Aeterna* 10, no. 1 (2018) and "'Something Odd and Beautiful': Literary Cartography in Jim Crace's *Harvest*" in *Brno Studies in English* 45, no. 1 (2019).

6.1.1 The Heterogeneous Space of Crace's Imagined America

The Pesthouse presents a dystopian vision of America's imagined future. Once the safest and most prosperous place on earth, Crace's America has regressed and deteriorated into a quasi-medieval, pre-modern, and pre-industrial state. It has turned into a devastated, disorderly wasteland: the soil is barely fertile, the technologies are almost forgotten and no longer used, the communities have fallen apart. The country is slowly being deserted as most of its inhabitants have found it uninhabitable and have made the decision to pack up their essential belongings and travel eastward to board a ship sailing for Europe in the hope of making a new start there. This America is a dismal, sparsely populated place as only those settlements and villages that can profit from providing board and lodging to the refugees survive, though their social structure and relations are far from unaffected by the larger historical circumstances. Living in despair and destitution and having lost all certainty, the people's lives are dominated by superstition and irrational beliefs. Life has taught them selfishness, distrust, prejudice, and suspiciousness, which is true of both the emigrants and the few who still reside in their semi-derelict homes. Moreover, they live in constant fear as the main roads are raided by gangs of merciless rustlers and highwaymen who take advantage of the anarchy to rob the travelling families, rape the women, and take the men who are fit for work as captives and slaves.

Even in this extreme context, Franklin and Margaret are a curious-looking pair of refugees. Under normal circumstances, they would have probably never met or got together because of their age difference. Franklin and his older brother Jackson are heading towards the east coast before the winter comes when the younger's inflamed and swollen knee necessitates an unwelcome stop in their hasty journey. As he cannot walk, the brothers agree to leave Franklin on a hill overlooking the village of Ferrytown to rest his knee while Jackson goes down to see what the place is like. The previous day, the thirty-one-year-old and still unmarried Margaret, who is ill with a contagious disease called "the flux", is taken by her grandfather from Ferrytown to spend time in quarantine in the pesthouse, a boulder hut located on Butter Hill, which rises above the village. Driven to seek shelter by heavy night rain, Franklin finds the older and, despite her weak frame and shorn head, beautiful woman sleeping in the hut and, against all reason, stays there with her and even massages the soles of her feet the way his mother used to do for him when he was ill, which Margaret later comes to believe saved her life. When she gets better and his brother does not come back as he promised, Franklin decides to resume walking and the two lonely strangers, drawn to each other by mutual sympathies bordering on affection, out of necessity become a particularly unusual couple: a tall, limping young man carrying on his back a woman with a shaven head who is eight years his senior.

The world in which the story is set is an example of a heterogeneous space as it lacks all the crucial properties of a homogeneous, or striated, space that is determined and kept under surveillance by the state apparatus, which makes it "the space of the polis, politics, the policed, and the police" (Westphal 2011, 39), an orderly and ordered space of parallel verticals and layers. America in *The Pesthouse* is the opposite – a place in which the government has collapsed and no longer has any control over the country's communal and political functioning. As there is no single site of power, the distinction between centre and periphery has become meaningless, as has the concept of a border or any other geographic or social delineation. As a result, the prevailing state of affairs is that of chaos and anarchy in which rules and laws are observed habitually and instinctively rather than enforced by an external, institutional authority. This America has transformed into a decentred no man's land whose inhabitants have lost much of their sense of belonging and territorial identity as it is dominated by strong deterritorialising forces making life for its people one of permanent uprootedness, movement, and exile. These people, forced to be on the move rather than moving by choice, roam this space, crossing what little has remained of the former boundaries of territorial units and social hierarchies as well as of universal human morality and decency.

In terms of spatiotemporality, it is a space simultaneously in and out of time. On the one hand, the overall condition is that of some sort of timelessness, of time stopped still or even turned backwards, as the country is being depopulated and the existing communities or settlements are surviving in a state of stasis rather than evolving in time. On the other hand, the sense of temporal chronology has not diminished completely; people have a notion of the past, the present, and the future, nostalgically missing the past, fleeing the present, and fixing their hopes on the future, which is for most of them the only way in which they can cope with the fluid world of permanent instability. The state of this space-time is that of a non-equilibrium whose principal operating forces are bifurcation and entropy. Although the migrants' progress seems to observe a linear timeline of going directly to the east, in reality this line is crucially violated: first of all, it disintegrates into isolated, disparate points as the travellers are forced by various unforeseen circumstances to make unplanned stops and breaks. Subsequently, their journey becomes rather labyrinthine as they have to change their pace and direction; some of them have to stay in one place and cannot move further on, ceasing in their effort, the fit ones settle down, others choose alternate paths to the main and shortest one. Moreover, most of those who reach the coast get stuck, oscillating between the encampment and the shore as they are repeatedly denied access to the ships, which makes the camp an ambiguous place of order and disorder, of great hope yet where "[a]nger and impatience were in the air" and "[w]orry was a full-time job" (Crace 2007, 262, 264).

The whole space in the novel is thus teeming with entropic disorder, turbulence, and isotropy. This entropy is still in its early phase when the energy necessary to allow evolution is slowly accumulated, but its amount is not yet sufficient to power such a transformation. Crace provides a small-scale picture of such a world in the opening chapter of the novel when he describes an image from the wayside to the coast:

> The wayside going east was already littered with melancholy camps and shallow graves – soon to be torn by wolves – of those whose bodies couldn't take the journey, those who had been fatally chilled by wading through rivers, those who had starved and weakened, those who had been thrown by their horses or poisoned by their suppers, those who had been crushed between the fears of going forward and the dread of going back. (Crace 2007, 9)

From the geocritical perspective, however, this entropy, no matter how devastating its immediate consequences may be for the lives of individuals, is a temporary and largely positive state as, infused with pulsing flows and motions, it has the potential to generate energy to drive the system forward and, as such, it contains complex stories to be told. All the protean forces of restlessness and transgression that govern such a space and its dwellers are therefore to be understood as salutary evolutionary impulses with the capacity to gradually transform it into a new, and potentially better, one. Symptomatically, out of the multiplicity of stories that his imagined America offers, Crace presents that of Franklin and Margaret, as it exemplifies precisely this trajectory from displacement to renewal within a determining set of spatiotemporal coordinates.

Crace's treatment and rendering of place and space adheres to Tally's and Prieto's concepts of geocriticism rather than to Westphal's as he is not much interested in the geographical referent. In other words, the countryside and places he describes are not truly inspired by any real-life model and the author does not strive to achieve verisimilitude with the actual landscapes of the United States. Instead, Crace's America is a universal, imaginary construct loosely based on the referent, yet the story's location is more significant for the novel's thematic composition, that is, on the symbolic, allegorical or mythical rather than representational level. Although he pays great attention to space and place in his narrative, they always exist in relation to the human element, both interior, in the form of characters, and exterior, in the form of readers. As a result, his narrative has a substantial evocative and aesthetic dimension, often polysensoral and multifocal, which enables the reader to picture the rendered spaces/places and experience them within their imagination, but also the psychological dimension which examines how the protagonists experience, interpret, and project these spaces/places and how this spatial perception affects their psyches and mental states. And, counter-wise, it also explores these protagonists' lived experience in relation to the spaces/places they occupy or pass through as well as within a wider socio-spatial context. With its refugee and emigrant protagonists journeying across the States in search of a better future, *The Pesthouse* has the ground plan of an adventure story, yet, more importantly, it works like Tally's mapping narrative and focuses on landscape, and in consequence place, rather than on space.

6.1.2 The Volatile Real-and-Imagined Landscapes

As the world around offers little comfort and few prospects, the inhabitants and travellers often resort to imagination as a device that can most effectively compensate for their deprived and frustrated existence. They make up stories of imaginary spaces and places of hope and consolation that may exist somewhere beyond the borders of America, diverse versions of a promised land of safety and bounty, a place "where the encouragements held out to strangers were a good climate, fertile soil, wholesome air and water, plenty of provisions, good pay for labor, kind neighbors, good laws, a free government and a hearty welcome" (Crace 2007, 42). As they are exchanged during the communal evening gatherings, these stories, passed from generation to generation, have become a folk mythology, an inherent part of these people's lives, an ultimate motivation that propels them on their travels and in their daily routines. However, not all the stories of distant lands are reassuring as those too fearful, weak or lazy to set out on the troublesome journey need to come up with counter-narratives of places of danger and despair – "of rivers and swamps too wild and wide to cross, impenetrable and gloomy forests, dusty and waterless plains, and ridges sharper than a knife" (Crace 2007, 43) – to justify their inertia. Even the rational and realistic Jackson and Franklin pin their hopes on finding a friendlier and more welcoming place to live, though Jackson, after hearing all their fellow travellers' stories, sceptically notes that there must be "at least a hundred different lands beyond the river. And none of them strikes [him] as likely" (Crace 2007, 44).

No matter how important these stories of perfect places are for their tellers, Crace also shows that they are primarily constructed by men, and as such they tend to emphasise exterior aspects, such as physical effort, work, and material provisions. As the societies in *The Pesthouse* are strictly patriarchal, the women's narratives are not heard in public, yet the reader can learn of one when Margaret, terrified and hiding from rapists in a forest, pictures her own imaginary place:

> ... a place of greater safety, but not outside America. There were no salt-water boats or any gulls. There was no Promised Land. Her place of greater safety was a soddy on a hill. She could envisage dying there, an ancient girl, her hair as long as the bed beneath her, with hands – more hands than she could count – in touch with her, and faces she could recognize and name, all saying *Margaret, sweet Margaret, you loved us and we loved you in return*. (Crace 2007, 167, emphasis original)

Her imaginary place is much more interior, permeated with human intimacy. It is not a place of stark contrast to the world she comes from, but one of simple familiarity and continuity, somewhere that may not exist too far away. In fact, the distance to such a place is not physically measurable as it involves the otherness of another person and calls for a resurgence of the basic human values of kindness, tolerance, and compassion. It is only when Franklin adopts this vision as his own that the couple can truly embark on their journey towards happiness and freedom.

Crace shows how the landscape gets infused with volatile and changeable meanings that the travellers ascribe to it on the basis of their current prospects and expectations. Overlooking Ferrytown from Butter Hill, Franklin sees it as a place of comfort and rest, its river and lake as a grand gateway to a brighter future, glinting like a pendant on a silver chain. However, this changes overnight when the poisonous fumes from the slip in the lake turn the village and its surroundings into "the habitation of the dead" (Crace 2007, 70), and when Franklin and Margaret descend the hill they find themselves in a place of pain and misery as they come across one corpse after another, including the whole of Margaret's family. The narration depicts this walk in silence, with careful descriptions of the dead bodies found, the exact positions of their limbs and bodies, and their facial expressions. Franklin does not find his brother's corpse, and the whole experience is particularly devastating for Margaret, who is left with no hope of finding any surviving relative; moreover, because of the fear that what killed the people of Ferrytown could be contagious, she has only very little time to come to terms with the situation and just manages to close the eyes and mouths of the dead and say a few "simple words of the burial lament to herself" (Crace 2007, 73). Such an experience can easily provoke trauma, which "is not locatable as a single, healable event" (Letissier 2009, 211) in an individual's past, but stems from "the *missing* of this experience", from not being experienced *in time*" (Caruth 1996, 62, emphasis original). The traumatic event is too abrupt and overwhelming for Margaret to even weep and mourn, and the only emotion she feels is that of misguided guilt that it was her flux that caused this catastrophe. Fleeing the land of ghosts, the once comfortingly glittering river and lake are now a mere inconvenience in their way, to be passed over as quickly as possible.

The novel also shows that the perception of a space/place may be substantially different for an observer than it is for a traveller. Once they get to the eastern shore of the lake, a natural scenery so splendid opens up before them that Franklin admits he has "never seen a spot more beautiful" (Crace 2007, 93). However, this enthusiasm soon falters as they discover that, in practical terms, its terrain is very difficult to navigate for a person with a heavy barrow who struggles to wheel it through the slushy mix of mud and leaves. And so despite the undeniable charm of the landscape portrayed by Crace,

> [t]hese wetlands, silt-rich forests – a mixture of chestnuts, marsh oaks, maples and hickories, which at this time of the year were exchanging green for oranges and reds – were distended with water and, therefore, so fertile and tightly undergrowthed in places that not even a mule could pass. What might look from a distance like startled outstretched hands were antlers of pink lichen, a breathtaking and a magical sight, especially in this dusk, with the sun finding angles through the hammock to pick out strips of foliage and blaze its reflection in puddles. (Crace 2007, 94–95)

The two mournful pilgrims are indifferent to the beauty around them: frail Margaret, overwhelmed with sorrow and fatigue, and Franklin, preoccupied with pulling the barrow through the dense forests, and wishing for more open countryside that would allow more speedy progress. The combination of his grief for a lost brother, compassion for Margaret's family, and exhaustion from labouring with the cargo weighs on Franklin and makes him weep secretly, an indisposition he immediately associates with the place, feeling "as inundated as the landscape he was pushing through" (Crace 2007, 96).

The situation changes when they reach what is known among the emigrants as the Dreaming Highway – a wide and straight road leading to the coast. The narration then presents an ultimately different kind of landscape, a man-made construct built with a clear purpose:

> ... an unnaturally shallow, flat valley without a river but flanked by parallel mounds as regular as the best-plowed furrow – except that no plow was big enough [...] to throw aside so great a swath of earth. Initially, they were merely baffled. This was no escarpment provided by nature, unless nature had on this one occasion broken its own rules and failed to twist and bend, but had instead hurtled forward, all symmetry and parallels. (Crace 2007, 110–111)

Ironically for Franklin, the spacious road in effect brings them the opposite of what he hoped for. Lured by the thought of easier progression, he dismisses Margaret's legitimate worries that such open ground will leave them exposed and vulnerable. When a gang of bandits rob them and take Franklin away as a captive, Margaret is left alone to continue along the highway with complete strangers. Once again, the landscape she passes through is one of pain and desperation: first, the deserted road scattered with dreadful evidence of the highwaymen's violent raids – abandoned overthrown carts, the bodies of raped and murdered women, the carcasses of cattle and domestic animals; later, the camp at the outskirts of Tidewater, transformed out of necessity into a makeshift market where the journeymen waiting desperately to board a ship are trying to make a living to survive the impending winter; and, finally, the Tidewater estuary where a vast majority of the refugees are rejected as passengers for an overseas voyage. Margaret's disappointment and frustration is thus naturally projected into the seascape, and so is Franklin's after they reunite – the ocean is no longer viewed as a longed-for pathway to freedom and prosperity, but as a hostile, unpredictable amorphous mass – ungenerous, wearying, leaden, hard-surfaced, lacking in expression (Crace, 2007, pp. 236–246) – an obstacle, safe and promising only when imagined, and therefore "best as a memory or as a prospect" (Crace 2007, 284).

The fact that a traveller's mind maps and simultaneously is mapped by the landscape is shown on their way back west. Having learnt from their past mistakes, Franklin and Margaret avoid the main routes and contact with the homesteaders, keeping to the unpeopled back ways. Their pace may be slower, but they in fact feel more comfortable as the landscape and places they journey through are infused with positive meanings for them: since they are no longer fleeing misery and devastation but heading towards renewal and happiness, all the difficulties they have to cope with this time seem "natural and inevitable" because they "no longer fe[el] defeated by America" (Crace 2007, 287). And so, although they travel through forests and marches as impassable as on the way eastwards, their perception of the landscape is very different:

> Otherwise, the journey back proved kinder than their journey out had done. It was as if the country that had once been hostile to them was regretful for it, and was now providing recompense – fewer dangers, warmer nights, softer going in a season that was opening up rather than closing down. It even decorated the way with early flowers. (Crace 2007, 290)

Their feeling of security and confidence is further reinforced by the familiarity of the places beyond the river. What once was a landscape of trauma and pain is now one of reconciliation. Even though Ferrytown is still a destroyed place, Margaret has enough time to mourn and weep over the cremation of her family and remember the most precious intimate moments from her childhood, an essential act to enable a successful coming to terms with her traumatic experience and prevent the recurrence of its most obtrusive haunting symptoms, such as hallucinations and nightmares.

6.1.3 The Doomed Turned Blessed – Heterotopic Places

In the heterogeneous space of the novel's American landscape, Franklin and Margaret stop at and inhabit a number of places, which are mostly unrelated in character, as what only randomly connects them is that they are situated on the two pilgrims' trajectory to the sea and then back homewards. Some of these places are experienced only fleetingly and are abandoned before they can become part of the protagonists' mental space, such as the derelict factory where they are assaulted by the bandits or the refugee camp at Tidewater. Others are suffused with more positive meanings and emotions, namely the off-track cabin they stay in after Franklin is freed from slavery and they have escaped their pursuers. However, two places in the novel are particularly noteworthy as they are essentially heterotopic in nature and prove crucial for the protagonists' good fortune – the Blessed Ark and the Pesthouse.

The Blessed Ark is a typical example of a heterotopia as it is a place which reflects outside places by contesting them and inverting them. Although it is located in Tidewater, it is in fact an isolated social and geographic unit other than the rest of the town, a place in its own right, self-sustaining and self-governing, with its own strict rules, laws, and hierarchies established by the religious community of the Finger Baptists, a highly ordered sanctuary in the chaotic and lawless world. It also stands outside of conventional time as its temporal rhythms are determined by observing the regular duties of communal work and religious practices and rituals. The Ark is thus a heterotopia of accumulated temporal mass, layering new slices of time onto ancient ones to which they bear strong structural resemblance. To be allowed in, one needs to undergo an entry procedure, a cleansing ritual of a kind, in the form of giving up all metallic objects, as the Baptists believe that metal is the devil's work and causes greed and violence. Within the novel's narrative framework, the Ark functions as a "space of compensation", a healing oasis which proves crucial for the restoration of Margaret's trauma-stricken, destabilised identity manifested in a feeling of "disconnection and isolation as bonds are broken and relationships and personal safety are put into question", which can undermine or even destroy "important beliefs: in one's own safety or competence to act or live in the world, one's perception of the world as meaningful and orderly, and one's view of oneself as decent, strong and autonomous" (Vickroy 2002, 23). She finds in the Ark not only a place where she can last out the winter, but also a safe and comfortable refuge from the ruthless and opportunist outside world where she can experience what she has most missed in her life: a sense of belonging, identity, and neighbourliness. It is a place of peace and routine, which enables Margaret to find out who she is and what she really desires in her life.

The central heterotopic place in the novel, however, is the eponymous Pesthouse. Crace was inspired by the stone quarantine station on the island of St. Helens, one of the Isles of Scilly, which lie about thirty miles off the coast of Cornwall, where all ships approaching the British Isles were obliged to abandon passengers with any sign of contagion by an Act of Parliament in the 1760s (Biblio Blog 2007). In the novel, the Pesthouse, located on Butter Hill above Ferrytown, is the place where any villager who is ill with a contagious disease is supposed to be taken by their relatives and left to the mercy of fate. Like the Ark, it is a site in and outside of time and place: a timeless shelter in which the past and the future lose their relevance and only the present matters; a place that technically belongs to the village but is deliberately isolated from it, a self-contained unit detached from the community's physical and mental space. It is also a place of the accumulated history of the individual fates and stories of those quarantined there, heaped one upon another. Although the boulder hut can be accessed freely, the outsider, that is, a healthy person, is in the position of an uninvolved visitor who cannot utilise its proper purpose. Although Margaret is taken there by her grandfather to get rid of her flux at the beginning of the story, in the inverted world of the novel, the function and meaning of the Pesthouse get inverted as well.

The process of this inversion begins when Franklin peeps into the hut and catches sight of a young woman with a shaven head lying asleep on the bed. He interprets this not as a horror story whose threat must be avoided by taking immediate flight, but almost as a fairy tale in which the prince finds his sleeping beauty and brings her back to life through the magic of his fingers. The fact that Franklin refuses to take the Pesthouse as what it is supposed to be – a house of contagion, suffering, and isolation – opens this originally enclosed site to new meanings, and it gradually becomes a place of restoration for both Margaret and Franklin. They attribute these positive meanings to the Pesthouse on their way back home as the place is already infused with pleasant memories of Margaret's recuperation, surviving the disaster that afflicted Ferrytown, and the earliest moments of their affection, and these are further intensified by the place's soothing familiarity:

> It hadn't changed, despite the bare branches and blanched-out colors of the undergrowth. It was still a little warmer than the hillside path, its dips and hollows protected from the worst of the wind. It still appeared the safest acre in America, a place of remedy and recovery where, surely, they could at least spend the night, or spend the month or spend eternity. (Crace 2007, 306)

Although they use the boulder hut for a completely new purpose, the month they stay there may actually be understood as a kind of quarantine for them in the sense that they can shake off the disagreeable germs of the world they have returned from and its dominating values: callousness, self-interest, and indifference. After this symbolic purification, they are ready to move on in search of their new home "in some old place, some territory begging to be used" (Crace 2007, 309), begging to become the real-and-imagined place of their common future.

6.1.4 Mapping the Landscape of Trauma, Pain, and Hope

The world portrayed in *The Pesthouse* offers fruitful material for a spatial critical approach, in particular a geocritical one. First of all, it represents a highly heterogeneous space in which all regulations, regularities, and hierarchies have collapsed and been replaced by lawlessness, disorder and displacement, and in which the vector-like, arranged lines of force and operation have broken down into a profusion of disparate points that can only be connected by unpredictable and contingent convoluted patterns. It is an entropic system that is teeming with diverse stories and narratives as meanings in such a turbulent state are not firmly tied to material realities, spatial ones included, but are unstable and rather float free of their potential referents. Accordingly, representation of this transgressive space in permanent motion is far from stable, is essentially fluid as it is determined by the volatility of meanings and perceptions. As Crace's America lacks any specific, real-life geographical referent it is the novel's discourse, or, more precisely, its narrative, that establishes the "more-imaginary-than-real" spaces/places whose correlation with the real is rather loose and indirect, as in the case of the pesthouse: what correlates is the function and perhaps the size of the hut, but the fictional quarantine station differs in all other respects, particularly in its location and appearance. Crace's depiction of the landscape and places also endorses the principles of multifocalisation, though only two points of view are offered, and polysensorality, since he likes to employ a combination of visual, auditory, olfactory, and tactile images.

Because the protagonists progress across the country and experience various kinds of spaces, the novel is an example of a threefold mapping narrative: the characters map the terrain both physically, through their movement, and mentally, through the processes of its apprehension, interpretation, and appropriation; the narration maps their progress by situating their lived experience of place and space in the larger, and more abstract, spatiotemporal network of the novel's socio-historical context of a dystopian, regressed America; and, finally, readers are invited to map these mapped fictitious places and make them part of their interpretive and experiential frameworks. In its literary cartographic approach, *The Pesthouse* pays specific attention to the interconnectedness of physical landscapes and how these are reflected by and projected in the human psyche, namely with regard to Franklin and Margaret. It shows how the same spatial environment can enter different kinds of relationship with the travellers' mental universe depending on their state of mind – their feelings, emotions, and moods – and how real-and-imagined landscapes of trauma and pain can change, along with the recipients' inner transformation, into those of hope and consolation. Moreover, it also demonstrates how the distorted world of inverted norms and values allows certain heterotopic places, the Pesthouse especially, to assume meanings and interpretations different from and even contrary to their original ones. This can be taken as part of the entropic process of gaining momentum that would enable the society's evolvement into a new, better functioning organism. Within this transformation Franklin, Margaret, and their adopted child, Jackie, thus turn from being "the final family on earth" (Crace 2007, 300) into its first, founding one.

6.2 *Harvest*

Harvest (2013) is a complex example of the typical aspects of its author's writing: it is set in an elaborately conceived landscape and explores a painful transition, both individual and communal. Moreover, the interconnectedness between the space and its dwellers' psyches is reinforced by the motif and theme of mapping and map-making. Using primarily the geocritical perspective of literary cartography, this section argues that the novel represents a unique mapping narrative whose fictional space-time is constructed not only through description, but also by means of figurative topography, which reconciles in itself the subjectivist and objectivist approaches to textual representation of space. *Harvest* thus fulfils Tally's proposition that mapping narratives "make possible novel spaces" (2014a, 12) and the geocritical explorations of these literary cartographies can help us better understand our own spatial experience.

6.2.1 Delusive Idyll

Harvest presents a very homogeneous milieu at the beginning of the story: a small agrarian English village of some sixty people, which in reality is a large homestead owned and governed by the landowner, Master Kent, on whose land the villagers live and in whose fields they work throughout the year. It is a remote place – a three-day ride on horseback to the nearest market town – and it is also a strongly autonomous unit as it has no magistrate, constable, or clergyman to assist the landowner with administration, guidance, and surveillance. The village is, in effect, self-sufficient and sealed off: it produces just enough crops to feed its people, and the people produce just enough offspring to keep their numbers more or less stable. With the exception of the landowner, the inhabitants do not leave the boundaries of their village, living in and for their community, their existence fully conducted and measured by the events and requirements of the year's natural circle.

As a result, there is virtually no contact between the villagers and the world outside as they do not partake in trade and feel no need to welcome and accept newcomers. Walter Thirsk, the narrator and main protagonist of the novel, was the last newcomer to settle in the village, and that was twelve years earlier. Moreover, he was not a true outsider asking to be let in as he was brought in by Master Kent as his clerk, and only later, by marrying a local woman, was he gradually accepted as one of the villagers. The community, "ditched and fenced against the outside world" (Crace 2013, 21), is unused to hospitality, suspicious of and prejudiced against all forms of otherness, other people in particular. Any reminder of the world beyond the limits of their familiar territory is unnerving and potentially threatening for them. They believe that by keeping troublesome strangers *ante portas* they can preserve the status quo, but they are too blinded by their xenophobic narrow-mindedness to notice that the intruding elements are already *in portis*.

Having been sealed off from larger socio-economic changes, the villagers cannot see that they are about to be faced with forces of modernity too mighty to be fended off. A family tragedy – that Master Kent's wife dies while giving birth to their child, which also dies – triggers consequences that far transcend the limits of the serene pastoral seclusion. The manor house and the land ownership are not passed on to the widower but to the wife's kin, her cousin Edmund Jordan who becomes the single heir of the property. Unlike Kent, Jordan has no personal interest in the place and its community and, being a man with business instincts, intends to transform the self-sustained settlement into one that generates profit. Following an Enclosure Act, the cousin decides to fence the common lands in and around the village – the fields, the meadows, and the woods – to make pastures for sheep, as marketable sheep farming is to replace the existing unproductive tillage. To this end, "economies" will be made, that is the number of hands needs to be reduced, which is why Jordan and his crew arrive to "persuade" some of the villagers, by any means necessary, to leave their homes and seek their fortune elsewhere. However, a few days before Jordan and his cohorts appear, some other disturbing harbingers of impending changes appear in the village. The first is Philip Earle, or Mr Quill as he is nicknamed by the villagers, the chartmaker whose task is to make a map of Jordan's new property. His arrival is soon followed by that of three strangers who build a provisional hut with an open fire on the outskirts of the village estates. As Mr Earle is officially appointed by Master Jordan, the villagers have to put up with his presence, though unwillingly, and so they all the more strongly vent their unease and confusion on the nameless vagrants by driving them away by force.

Although the new, capitalist forces are portrayed rather negatively, especially when personified by Edmund Jordan, as ones that value pragmatic materialism over elementary humanity and age-old values and traditions, the deluded and hypocritical villagers are also not spared critical treatment. The central irony is that the three newcomers that the villagers assault, capture, and torture by placing in the pillory, the young man with his wife and his father, are in fact "fugitives from sheep" (Crace 2013, 228) from another part of the country, which makes the villagers' acts a sinister foreshadowing of the harsh treatment they themselves may suffer in the near future when looking for a new place to live. Moreover, they accuse the strangers of crimes they know they did not commit only because at that moment the end justifies the means, but the end soon turns against them when the young man's wife slaughters Master Kent's beloved horse. Jordan believes such an act could have only been carried out by a man, which is why an investigation is started, houses are searched, interrogations carried out, charges brought, including those of witchcraft, as a result of which the community, governed by fear and mistrust, disintegrates and one by one the villagers flee their homeland to avoid further persecution. The despised and mocked Mr Quill is the person who, in spite of his physical defect of a stiff left arm, repeatedly shows the most bravery, fairness, composure, and kindness: he is the one who prevents physical violence between the villagers and the fugitives, who secretly attends to the men in the pillory, and who publicly opposes Jordan's harsh measures. For his moral superiority he "deserves" nothing else than being falsely reported as being the true disseminator of witchcraft, a pretext for Jordan to get rid of this inconvenient individual.

The narrator is not spared critical treatment either. Though once a townsperson like Mr Earle, Walter Thirsk is now much more like his fellow country people and feels like one of them. Ironically, they have never accepted him completely and after his wife's death he is once again perceived as a semi-naturalised outsider closer to the manorial men about town than to the earthy peasantry. Although we see most of the action through his perspective, it is often hard to sympathise and identify with him as he is a person prone to a number of vices, such as cowardice, self-deception, vanity, egotism, jealousy, and envy. He is comfortable and dependable when part of a crowd, but rather untrustworthy and erratic when he acts on his own, particularly in critical situations. In many respects, he functions as a counterpart to the man of integrity, Mr Earle: when the chartmaker is trying to make peace in the heated atmosphere between the villagers and the fugitives the narrator is trying to find excuses to avoid taking part in what he knows is going to be an unpleasant encounter; when the crowd falsely accuses the strangers of arson he connives in it though he knows that in reality they are all "conspirators" with "good cause to blame" themselves (Crace 2013, 33, 87); while Mr Earle speaks his mind in front of Edmund Jordan, Walter Thirsk nods at anything the cousin says to avoid the aggressive whims of his temper; when Earle is looking for Mrs Bedlam to offer her shelter on a stormy night Thirsk is ridiculously consumed with jealousy that the two are making love somewhere in the dark; and when he eventually sets the young man free from the pillory to join his wife, he feels self-pityingly wronged that the couple, who have not only lost their father and father-in-law but who have also been deprived of their freedom and dignity, do not show enough gratitude to him by asking him to join them for dinner.

6.2.2 The Narrator

No matter how fallible and weak-minded Walter Thirsk may be, he is an ideal guide to the space and place he inhabits. This is in part due to his exceptionally observant nature, and in part because as an outsider who spent most of his life in a completely different environment, he is much more sensitive to the particularities of the landscape of and around the settlement than its natives. This is made apparent from the very beginning of the story when he reports the two alarming events that violate the habitual practices of the village – the ominous arrival of the strangers and the fire in the manor barn – through their immediate impact on its landscape:

> Our land is topped and tailed with flames. Beyond the frontier ditches of our fields and in the shelter of our woods, on common ground [...] some newcomers [...] have put up their hut – four rough and ready walls, a bit of roof – and lit the more outlying of these fires. [...] It rises in a column that hardly bends or thins until it clears the canopies. (Crace 2013, 1)

Due to his spatial sensitivity and perceptiveness, Walter always associates people and their interpersonal relationships with the physical environment they inhabit, and he often demonstrates deep understanding for the intrinsic interconnectedness of the social and spatial coordinates of human existence. He presents his own twelve-year residence in the village as inseparable from its landscape: how as a townish cub he was mesmerised by the paradisal scenery, liberty, and scope of "such giving land" (Crace 2013, 63); how he soon found out that it is like that only for a passing visitor and that in reality the countryside is "argumentative, inflexible, stern and impatient" (Crace 2013, 63, 75) in that it requires unceasing and strenuous labour from those who want to live off it; how he grew to like even these hardships after he fell in love with his wife to be, yet how he felt more and more alienated from it again after her sudden death.

The loss of his wife makes Walter realise how infused with social and emotional meanings the landscape of his recent life has been. Without her he becomes aware that he has in fact never been "woven to the fabric of the place" as he is "not a product of these commons but just a visitor who's stayed" (Crace 2013, 63). More and more frequently he experiences moments when he misses the greater world of his past, all the more so as his neighbours let him know that, under the current troublesome circumstances, they see him as a master's man who is hard to trust. Philip Earle, with his townsman's appearance, his politeness, and pleasant manners, his body "not well suited to the balks and bumpy edges of a field" (Crace 2013, 5), and his innocent excitement about the place's natural beauties, thus reminds him of his younger and by now lost self. At the same time, he feels relaxed – respected and appreciated – in Earle's company and cherishes a dream of resuming the once abandoned city life should he "escape the fleecy prospects of our fields by leaving here in his employ" (Crace 2013, 124). It is only when assisting Earle in the topographic measurements that he finally utilises his liminal status: on the one hand, he can boast of possessing almost intimate familiarity with the landscape, like the old residents, while, on the other hand, he can display his ability to assume the detached and objective perspective of a worldly person, complacently enjoying the knowledgeable authority of someone who can name local places and plants to an uninformed outsider, though at times he must invent some of the names to cover up his own ignorance.

The narrator offers a contrary perspective on the nature of his fellow villagers and makes use of spatial tropes to characterise them, calling them his "land-born neighbours" who are "too rooted in their soil, too planched and thicketed" (Crace 2013, 21), as argumentative, inflexible, and stern as the land on which they live and work. As such, they have difficulties when encountering some form of otherness, especially in human conduct, and so they are all taken aback by the "unwomanly", audacious, and impudent behaviour of the young stranger's wife, who not only dares to talk back disrespectfully to Master Kent but even spits in contempt on his horse. The velvet shawl around her shoulders is thus not the only object of the onlooking women's envy. Constrained by their patriarchal world, they can hardly believe in a female creature so free-spirited and unbridled. Again, Walter resorts to a spatial simile and parallels their enforced docility to how the males approach their estates: "The local women were like land – fenced in, assigned and spoken for, the freehold of their fathers, then their husbands, then their sons. You could not cross their boundaries, or step beyond your portion" (Crace 2013, 29). Bound geographically by the limits of their homeland, the villagers' mindset and responsiveness are shown to be equally confined.

After all the neighbours have fled and Jordan and Kent are also about to leave the village, Walter takes refuge at the top end of the landscape, on a little hillock from which he can see the whole place. He remembers Kent's words, that their land "has always been much older than ourselves" but "[n]ot any more" (Crace 2013, 196), meaning that the community to come will exploit and have command of the land rather than humbly live in accordance with its demands. Watching the procession of the landowners and the captives fading from sight, Walter no longer sees the hillock as a promising vantage point of opportunity as he used to when he was a newcomer there, but "a friendless place, and capped in cloud" (Crace 2013, 202). The prospect of the empty village makes him feel desperate and panicked, and although even after the harvest the land has not "lost its open-handedness", he knows that the "summer's in retreat" and the "year is leaving us" (Crace 2013, 205). Once again, he draws a parallel between himself and the landscape in that no matter how vitalising and giving it might be, without a social dimension it is too foreign and dismal for him to face. All he is capable of is a little personal, and rather harmlessly symbolic, sabotage of the lost land – "a noble and an honest scar" (Crace 2013, 229) made by sowing a strip of barley on the future pasture.

Upon his own departure from the village, Walter symptomatically cannot help but return in his thoughts to the landscape. Even though the transformation of the place from a still, secluded, and enclosed settlement into one ready for opening itself to dynamic social, economic, and spatial changes drives him away, when looking back at it from its edge, he realises that even in its seemingly pristine, homogeneous form it was always "too precarious a place" (Crace 2013, 270). Having confined everything within its hermetic bounds, the place fostered an illusion of permanence and safety, thus managing to conceal how fragile and prone to disintegration such a socio-spatial system is when challenged by an intrusion that is impossible to deflect by conventional means. And so, rather than making sentimental farewells to the village, Walter turns his hopeful eye to what awaits him, once more metaphorically represented by the land. Although the land appears wild and unpredictable, he somehow subconsciously feels that setting out on a journey through it is the right thing to do:

> If anything, the views ahead, beyond our bounds, are more rewarding to the eye. They are more savage, certainly. And more formless and more void. The hedges there have not been cut and trimmed for many years, if ever. They spread across the lane with their great arms as if to send all travellers back, or at best to make their passage forward troublesome. [...] The lane is telling me I should not fear the futures that it holds. (Crace 2013, 272–273)

Paradoxically, to some extent, the previously unwelcome changeability and heterogeneity fill him with unwonted vigour and mettle "to take this first step out of bounds" (Crace 2013, 273) of both the landscape of the irreversible past, but perhaps also of his small-mindedness and complacency.

6.2.3 Mapping and Being Mapped

The unique achievement of *Harvest* within the body of Crace's work with regard to literary cartography rests in its theme of map-making, which makes it a kind of meta-mapping narrative that not only maps the real-and-imagined places and their perception, but also enriches this by elaborating on the process of creating an actual map of these territories. The chief role in this regard is assigned to Mr Earle, who is hired by Master Kent to map out the village, but his position is tricky from the very beginning: as soon as he embarks on his work – pacing the area, measuring, and taking notes – he is being "mapped" by the mistrustful villagers. They watch every step of this unusual and odd-looking disabled gentleman with his elegant clothes, polite manners, kindness, helpfulness, and sociability, as they suspect that what "Mr Quill" is doing will bring them much more harm than good. As a result, the more affability and courage he shows, the more the villagers convince themselves that these are just the cunning ruses of a dangerous person who deserves nothing but hatred, which is further fuelled by the fact that Earle's principled behaviour highlights their own moral failures. Mr Earle thus plays an ambiguous role within the novel's plot: he is a likeable character who shows respect and sympathy to the local people, yet the "Domesday" outcome of his activity seals their fate as it is going to serve as the groundwork for Edmund Jordan's sheep-farming plans.

When Walter, who is not able to take part in the harvesting because of his burnt arm, is asked by Master Kent to assist Mr Earle he is excited by the prospect of having the chance to witness the familiar landscape being charted. As Earle is drawing the preliminary sketches and mixing the appropriate shades of colour, Walter is eager to see how the map is going to "make the story of [their] farmscape – and our sheepscape – easy to decipher" (Crace 2013, 129). While the professional Earle is working on his task, Walter abandons all reserve and tells this stranger the whole story of his life in the village and his engagement and disengagement with its landscape. Absorbed in his own misfortune, the aroused narrator approaches the early draft of the map with misguided and impossible to meet expectations of verisimilitude and narrativeness, which is why his first impressions are ambivalent, viewing the draft as both "odd and beautiful":

> There is no lettering as yet. Just shapes and lines and colouring. I recognise their intrigue and their sorcery. I've seen equally compound patterns, no less ineffable than these, when I've peeled back bark on dying trees, or torn away

> the papering on birches. [...] I've found these ordinary abstracts in the least expected place hereabouts: I have only to lift a stone, or turn some fallen timber in the wood, or reverse a leaf. [...] But none of these compare for patterned vividness with Mr Quill's designs. His endeavours are tidier and more wildly colourful [...] than anything that nature can provide. They're rewarding in themselves. (Crace 2013, 133)

Unable to distinguish between the imaginative realism of a landscape painting and the scientific abstraction of a map, Walter foolishly assesses the draft according to how it corresponds with the physical, social, and even emotional reality of the settlement. He is fascinated by seeing the shape of the village from a bird's eye view, which reminds him of "a profile of a brawny-headed man" (Crace 2013, 135). But examining the map carefully and looking for where the actual places are graphically represented is rather unsettling for him as he misses many small points of orientation – a solitary tree, a pebblestone gap between fields, a lane of thorns, a short slope – which he considers inherent in and defining of the landscape as he is used to experiencing it. Therefore, he comes to the conclusion that, beautiful though it looks, it is not "as honest as [Earle] hopes. He's coloured and he's flattened us. [...] The land is effortless: a lie. He hasn't captured time: how long a walk might take; [...] how long the seasons or the nights must last" (Crace 2013, 136). Walter's misapprehension of the map reflects his inability to cut himself loose emotionally from a landscape into which he has projected many personal and intimate meanings so as to make it a coping device to alleviate his feelings of anxiety and frustration.[38]

It is only with Earle's help that the chart starts to make sense to him, and he can match its geometrical patterns with their real-life referents. Yet the map still disquiets him, as if its detached matter-of-factedness and present-time motionlessness tried to keep from him the naked truth of what is to happen with the village, and himself, in years to come. His anxious mind finds little solace in the conceptual landscape as he feels "[t]here's something in these shapes and lines, in these casual, undirected blues and greens, that, for all their liveliness, seems desolate" (Crace 2013, 137), obsessively focusing on what cannot be charted. And so, before he leaves the village for good, he decides to burn all the charts, together with the corpse of their maker, as a symbolic gesture of breaking

38 Walter's mind, however, is never so distorted so as to project into the landscape purely imagined, dream-like, or supernatural elements, and as such, he does not stop being a relatively credible narrator.

free from the place and all its connotations. At the same time, he keeps one unused vellum for himself, believing it to be "an unmarked sheet" which "could be anywhere" (Crace 2013, 271), just like his future and the place where he will eventually settle down. However, the vellum will probably remain blank as, given the narrator's unstable and unprepossessing personality and his difficulties in assuming an emotionally unbiased point of view, it is unlikely that the mental mapping of landscapes he is to encounter will ever transform into a cartographic chart.

6.2.4 Cartography of Insecurity and Wonder

Unlike *The Pesthouse*, *Harvest* unfolds a geocritical mapping narrative without depicting the actual act of characters' physical journeying. It portrays how a strictly homogeneous place gets heterogenised by exterior socio-economic forces so powerful that they overwhelm the place's capacity to fend them off. In Westphal's terms, the village at the beginning of the story is in a state of equilibrium, which, in its orderliness and regular, unvarying cyclicality, is deprived of history and as such is equivalent to a nonstory. Dynamic and turbulent capitalist forces undermine this state by breaking down the customary timelines and causalities, which throws the system into a disorder that generates new energies and possesses the potential for a complex story. The novel shows how the seemingly stable and permanent lines that delineate the existence and functioning of a homogeneous system are in fact fragile and vulnerable. This is true all the more so if the system is deliberately closed off and obstinately insists on its principles and values being the only correct and permissible ones. From their self-absorbed, worm's-eye view, the villagers are unable to perceive any larger historical context for their settlement and thus to distinguish between a cause and an effect. Therefore, they mistake a side effect – the arrival of refugees from another village – for a real threat, and instead of using the incomers' knowledge and experience to their advantage, they assault and humiliate them. As a result, the convoluted story triggered by this intrusion soon gets out of their control and is anything but advantageous for them.

Within a few days, the village changes into an in-between, transitory place, no longer secluded land under crops, but not a sheep farming homestead either, with its former values and hierarchies violated and distorted, but with new ones yet not fully established. The rigid and inadaptable villagers, however, find themselves at a loss in such a situation and are not able to grasp the place's subversive potential and look for a way in which they could fit themselves into the newly evolving establishment. They thus lose a chance to affect its final form and are left with no other option than to flee their homes. Though a perceptive observer with a developed sense of space and, moreover, a liminal, in-between character himself, Walter also fails to recognise and take advantage of the transforming landscape's productive potential. The main reason in his case, however, is that his perception of space is always filtered through strong emotionality and therefore is rarely rational or pragmatic, which is exactly what successful appropriation of an in-between place requires above all. Instead, he projects onto it his own feelings and sentiments, mostly negative and weak ones, such as frustration, cowardice, self-pity, envy, hypocrisy, and rage, which is why the places he occupies become for him the embodiment of, or at best coping devices for, his troubles and fears rather than means of revising and reasserting his identity. Even when left alone in the deserted village, he cannot bear the pressure of the emotionally soaked landscape and escapes it through voluntary intoxication, at first using alcohol and then hallucinogenic fungi.

Ironically, the character who is most at ease with the place and its properties is the townsman, Philip Earle. As a man of strong personality and moral credit, he manages to remain amiable and open-minded despite his physical defect, which is also reflected in his spatial perceptiveness. Though a cartographer, the landscape does not represent for him a mere object of mathematical recording but a source of unceasing wonder and enjoyment which he, within given limits, tries to project into the vivid precision of his charts. He is attentive to the changing socio-spatial patterns of the village and, therefore, the only one to potentially understand their impending consequences for its identity. However, as a double-outsider, rejected and scorned by both the villagers and Edmund Jordan, his chances of asserting himself and thus possibly saving at least a bit of the place's "in-betweenness" are too restricted and his futile effort costs him his life. Like most of Crace's works, *Harvest* presents these transitional transformations through the interconnectedness of the characters and the landscape they inhabit. However, the fact that it deals not only with the subjective, experiential dimension of space but also with its analytically objective representation in the form of map making, makes the novel an ingenious example of literary cartography, a narrative that explores the characters' experience of place and their feelings of displacement from a familiar environment, as well as the variable relationship between the lived spatial referent and its abstract cartographic representation.

7. Simon Mawer

Simon Mawer (b. 1948) is the author of fourteen novels, mostly historical fiction, which have been hailed as highly atmospheric, accurately observed, and stylistically precise. His renown, however, did not always correspond with his literary achievements. Prior to the publication of his 2009 novel, *The Glass Room*, Mawer enjoyed the reputation of being "a quiet stylist, a writer's writer" (Crown 2009), but also an author whose works had been generally well-reviewed but had not attracted the interest they deserved. Known mostly as a "mid-list" author (Crown 2009, Cooke 2012), he had never been well-known or best-selling. Having been shortlisted for the 2009 Man Booker Prize, he was even labelled a "black horse" or "the least known" (Crown 2009) of the contenders, who included Hilary Mantel, Sarah Waters, J.M. Coetzee, and A.S. Byatt.

Mawer published his debut novel at the age of 41, having spent over 20 years teaching biology at St. George's British International School in Rome. He had considered writing even earlier on, while studying zoology at Oxford, but he lacked the courage and self-confidence, believing that there were more gifted authors amongst his contemporaries (Crown 2009). But his writing career was affected less by his late arrival on the literary scene, than by a series of failings on the part of his publishers or the literary market. Some of his earlier novels suffered from a wrongly timed release, or were not effectively introduced to the literary market. In her 2009 interview, Sarah Crown therefore notes that "his publishing history reads like a tour of the industry's battlefields, with himself in the role of cannon fodder". Another factor, which Mawer himself considers to have significantly contributed to his slow rise to literary fame and critical and public interest, is his expatriate existence (Lauder 2015). Mawer's former living in Italy[39] and his distaste for attending book festivals and book signings (Lauder 2015) turned him into an outsider within the British literary market, perhaps better known to readers outside Britain.

The apparent lack of literary fame that marked his literary career prior to *The Glass Room* had not prevented him from attracting the attention of various literary prizes. In 1990, his novel *Chimera* (1989) won the newly established McKitterick Prize, awarded to debut novels by authors over 40. The 1997 novel *Mendel's Dwarf*, which Mawer described as a success in the US (Crown 2009), became a finalist for one of the Los Angeles Times Book Prizes for 1999, and a 1998 New York Public Library "Book to Remember." *The Fall* of 2003 won the Boardman Tasker Prize for Mountain Literature and was longlisted for the Man Booker Prize. *The Glass Room* was shortlisted for both the 2009 Booker Prize and the Walter Scott Prize for historical fiction. The 2016 spy novel *Tightrope* won the Walter Scott Prize for Fiction. Mawer's last novel, *Ancestry* (2022), was shortlisted for the same prize. However, the growing literary-critical interest in the author's work has not been reflected in the more academic study of his creation. With the exception of a few scholarly articles, he has not yet been the subject of any monograph, and comprehensive overviews of the contemporary British literary canon fail to mention his contribution.[40]

The lack of more substantial scholarly interest may be related to the author's reluctance to classify his works as historical fiction (Flood 2016). Given the vital role Mawer assigns to the historical and geographical settings of his novels, it is rather perplexing that he openly rejects the label of "historical novelist" (Flood 2016). Mawer typically plants his stories in reality and the degree of attention he pays to the factual representation of historical events, the number of cultural references he includes and the persuasive everyday detail from the life of the periods he nonchalantly includes, do not fail to astound reviewers. Both the reviewers and judges of the Walter Scott Prize for historical fiction considered Mawer's works to be "impeccably researched" (Crown 2009, Sansom 2015, Flood 2016), inhabiting the time and place perfectly

39 According to the biography on Mawer's website, he now splits his time between Italy and Hastings – he accidentally lives close to a place where one of his ancestors was born, which he describes in his latest novel, *Ancestry* (2022).

40 See, for example, Nick Bentley's *Contemporary British Fiction* (2018), Daniel Lea's *Twenty-first-century Fiction: Contemporary British Voices* (2019), or *Contemporary British Fiction* (2007), edited by Richard J. Lane, Rod Mengham, and Philip Tew.

(Flood 2016). In spite of the author's almost cartographic precision as far as historical detail and expression are concerned, he still tends to apply his poetic licence and arranges "the surrounding circumstances to his liking" (Crown 2009). As Rachel Cooke states in her review of *The Girl Who Fell from the Sky* (2012): "[t]he resulting textures are extraordinary, and no page ever reeks of the library: his set pieces are so beautiful you want to read them two or three times over" (Cooke 2012). Mawer seldom situates his narratives in fabricated landscapes and even if he does, the inherent qualities of the fictional landscape quickly give away their sources of inspiration. Mawer's embrace of this strategy is, however, prone to controversy as in the case of *The Glass Room*, which was publicly denounced as a misleading fabrication by the descendants of the Tugendhat family, the former owners of the famous villa that served as an inspiration for Mawer's novel. They claimed that the appealing fictitious story, which was connected so seamlessly with the real place, replaced the real story of the family in the minds of the general public (Hammer-Tugendhat 2012).

Mawer's exact delineations of settings contribute to the accurate evocation of the time and place of his stories, whilst also highlighting their thematic focus. Most importantly, they reflect the mental processes of the protagonists. He tends to situate his novels in places and times of far-reaching social, cultural, and political transformations, which adds to the enthralling nature of his plots. The close connection, if not identification, of the psyches of Mawer's characters and their historical and geographical setting enables Mawer to document their mutual influence and express the complexity of historical developments, while closely inspecting different aspects of individual, national, and cultural identities and their formation. *Tightrope*, a spy novel situated in WW2 France was labelled: "a character study", which "also surveys the state of a nation: Britain too is exhausted, bruised and battered by war" (Pengelly 2015). The protagonists of Mawer's works often act as intermediaries of transition between social, historical, and cultural contexts. As the process of transition naturally involves liminality, it becomes projected into all elements of Mawer's novels, including the liminality of the protagonists, most apparently manifested by their bilingualism, the historical periods, and the spaces and places portrayed in the novels.

Liminality eventually proves to be a productive quality also in view of the classification of Mawer's novels. As stated above, it is challenging to clearly demarcate the genre of Mawer's literary creation. From the thematic point of view, Mawer may be classified amongst authors of historical fiction[41], of spy fiction[42], war fiction[43], or science fiction.[44] If the perspective of the geographical setting is to be taken into consideration, Mediterranean[45] and central European[46] settings play the most prominent role within his works. It is, however, Mawer himself who disputes any straightforward categorisation, rejecting the label of historical novelist altogether (Flood 2016). He accentuates his artistic licence and his refusal to be pinned down by the factual stipulations expected from a historical novelist by an open acknowledgement of manipulation: "I am a novelist. I don't want to tell the truth. I want to manipulate things as I choose. I want to lie" (Crown 2009). He intends to draw from real life, comparing his literary creation to the development of memories which have not happened (Lauder 2015, 2019). The only factor that plays a role in his possible classification as a historical novelist that he is willing to admit is his fascination with the past: "All I do is write novels about what interests me at the time [...] and the recent past is where my particular interest lie" (Flood 2016).

Even reviewers have often been quick to stress the hybrid character of his works – Martin Pengelly characterised *The Girl Who Fell from the Sky* (2012) as "a spy thriller – a literary one for sure" (Pengelly 2015). Reviewing the same novel, Natasha Tripney branded it "a traditional thriller, albeit an intelligent one" (Tripney 2013), with another reviewer stressing that *Tightrope* is "a literary novel in the armature of a thriller, and as such it both follows the routes of a thriller and departs from them" (Pengelly 2015). It often seems that reviewers attempt to counterbalance Mawer's tendency to incorporate "thriller processes" (Mandys 2010) and his classification amongst "seasoned writers of historical spy fiction" (Silman 2019) by attempting to highlight more literary qualities of his novels, which are subsequently branded "humanist" (Brookner 2009), "thoughtful" (Barnacle 2009), and "literary" (Pengelly 2015). Accordingly, Ian Sansom's 2009 review for *The Guardian* described *The Glass Room* as "a novel of ideas, yet strongly propelled by plot and characterised by an

41 Technically, all of his novels may be classified as historical novels as they are situated in a more or less distant past.

42 Spy fiction: *The Girl Who Fell from the Sky* (2012), *Tightrope* (2015), *A Jealous God* (1996).

43 War fiction: *The Fall* (2003), *The Girl Who Fell from the Sky* (2012), *Tightrope* (2015), *The Glass Room* (2009).

44 Novels revolving around science: *Mendel's Dwarf* (1997), *The Gospel of Judas* (2000), *The Girl Who Fell from the Sky* (2012), *Tightrope* (2015).

45 Mediterranean setting: non-fiction memoir *A Place in Italy* (1992), *The Bitter Cross* (1992), *A Jealous God* (1996), *The Gospel of Judas* (2000), *Swimming to Ithaca* (2006).

46 Central Europe setting: *The Glass Room* (2009), *Prague Spring* (2018), *Mendel's Dwarf* (1997).

almost dreamlike simplicity of telling". *The Glass Room* was later defined as "a rare thing: popular historical fiction with integrity" (Sansom 2009) as if to stress its unique duality – its ability to mix typically middle- if not low-brow fiction with more literary nuances. The 1997 review of *Mendel's Dwarf* (1997) also stressed its hybrid nature, marking it "an unusual piece. It's a work of science fiction in the strict sense, but without any of the familiar traits of the genre. It is scientific literature in the literary sense but not the scholarly one" (Kohn 1997).

Simon Mawer addressed this tendency of reviewers to uplift the status of his works and dissociate them from "low-brow literature", such as unfairly undervalued historical fiction, spy fiction, and scientific fiction. In a 2015 interview with Sylvie Lauder for the Czech magazine *Respekt,* he openly rejected the division into low-brow and high-brow literature, as devised by Graham Greene, whom he considers to be his source of literary inspiration and to whom he is often compared (Lauder 2015, Pengelly 2015). Although Mawer explicitly labelled *The Glass Room* and *Mendel's Dwarf* as examples of high-brow literature, his main preoccupation is with the story and the principal theme – they define the form (Lauder 2015). He exemplified this in *The Glass Room*, which sounds (reads) almost like a translation from Czech into English in order to echo its central-European inspiration and setting. In the case of *Mendel's Dwarf*, it adopts the form of a scholarly article, including its vocabulary, structuring and footnotes (Lauder 2015).

With the form being subjugated to the thematic focus, Mawer's works may indeed be considered mainly as novels of ideas, to paraphrase an earlier label. Irrespective of their plot orientation towards historical novels, thrillers, or science fiction, they excel in the evocation of intangible aspects, such as fear (Cooke 2012, Silman 2019), hope (Cooke 2012, Silman 2019), heroism, or bravery (Cooke 2012). They also often tend to revolve around profound philosophical and ethical questions. If a branch of science is portrayed, such as genetics or nuclear physics, it is always from the perspective of its potential and/or actual moral and historical implications, and the same goes for politics and historical events.

Mawer's writing style has earned him comparisons to a number of past and present literary figures. Based on his skilful treatment of spy fiction and his preference for female protagonists, his work has been compared to William Boyd's *Restless* (2006) (Tripney 2013) and Sebastian Faulk's *Charlotte Gray* (1999) (Miller 2012). His fondness for subterfuge and spy fiction has led to him being likened to Ian Fleming

(Pengelly 2015)[47] but perhaps more accurately and frequently to Graham Greene. Mawer has openly acknowledged being inspired by Greene (Lauder 2015), their works often being categorised as literary thrillers with philosophical and ethical implications, which they more often tend to set in foreign countries than in Britain. The degree of realism in Mawer's descriptions of action sequences is close to that found in novels by Eric Ambler (Tripney 2013). Martin Pengelly also mentions William Styron and Philip Roth, whose employment of the erotic as well as young, enthralled narrators can also be found in Mawer's novels (Pengelly 2015). The prominent role of the Mediterranean in his texts as well as his life has led some to liken Mawer to John Fowles and Lawrence Durrell.[48] In an interview, Mawer mentioned the latter and his Mediterranean novels as an influence on him (Sečkař 2010). Lastly, his tendency to thematise science in his fiction earned him a comparison to Michael Frayn (Sansom 2009).

Nevertheless, the author who is most similar to Mawer from the perspective of his writing career and his choice and treatment of prominent literary elements, such as his protagonists, his spatial and temporal settings, and the mutual conditioning and influencing of characters and their spaces and places, is undeniably Jim Crace. Mawer's inclination to situate his fiction in liminal, highly unstable places, such as regions on the brink of profound historical changes or war-stricken, occupied countries, is parallel to Crace's portrayals of communities in transition, i.e. "smaller groups of people, such as settlements, tribes, religious groups, villages and towns, all of whom find themselves on the verge of an historical – social, economic, political, cultural – transformation" (Chalupský 2019, 64). Both authors focus on the revision of identities – both individual, social, and cultural. As they frequently demonstrate in their novels, these processes involve rather abrupt and radical developments and may even take a violent turn.

Crace and Mawer also share a set of beliefs concerning the writing profession and the process of writing. Similarly to Crace, Mawer has always been at pains to define himself as "an intellectual writer" (Crown 2009), claiming that his aim is always to write a story and "nothing else"

47 The protagonist of *The Girl Who Fell from the Sky* and *Tightrope*, Marian Sutro, was called "the female James Bond" by Ian Sansom (2015) in his review for *The Guardian*, a label which Mawer decisively rejected.

48 Mawer expresses his view on Durrell and his literary contribution in *Swimming to Ithaca* by means of a character of a fictitious poet, Geoffrey Crozier: "'The trouble with Larry,' Geoffrey said, 'is that he's really just one of those orientalists that the empire produces. He wants things to fit his own personal vision of the Greeks and the Mediterranean – a piece of folk art, really. All poetry and mythology and dreaming of Byzantium'" (Mawer 2006, 116).

(Sečkař 2010). As he further stated in the same interview, all novels should be motivated by simple storytelling (ibid.) He also rather boldly added that he writes the stories for himself in the first place, not for a particular group of people, and he chooses their subjects based on what interests him. Although he incorporates some innovative aspects into his writing, such as untranslated words and expressions from foreign languages, such as the toponym Mesto in *The Glass Room*, and elements of academic writing in *Mendel's Dwarf*, he has always been "suspicious of experimental writing because it seems to be self-indulgent, and also alienating to the reader" (Sečkař 2010). For Mawer, the governing principle of artistic endeavour should be solely the story (Lauder 2019). He stresses that writers should avoid purposeful moralising as they already reflect contemporary society in their works (Lauder 2019). At the same time, he wants his readers to learn more about some of the lesser-known aspects of history, e.g. Britain's "somewhat under-appreciated role in the making of the atomic and hydrogen bombs" (Pengelly 2015). Most importantly, he instructs his readers about vital aspects of contemporary science and its ethics, such as nuclear physics or genetics, and their role in the historical events of the twentieth century.

If there is one other aspect that Mawer has in common with his contemporaries, and especially with the aforementioned Crace, it is the prominence of nature writing, although not in the traditional sense of the term. Both Mawer and Crace are keen on nature writing, however, each from a different perspective. Where Crace focuses on the unity of humans and the landscape, Mawer, possessing a scientific and teaching background, includes detailed knowledge of individual natural phenomena. Both authors also highlight the connection between storytelling and science, both, nonetheless, from a different perspective. Whereas Crace emphasises the natural need of humans to narrate and connects it with the neo-Darwinian concept of a storytelling gene, Mawer rather stresses the connection between the very essence of modern literature and modern science. He summarised his views on this topic in his 2005 essay "Science in Literature", published in *Nature* magazine. There, he provides the perspective of a novelist who also holds a degree in zoology and spent the majority of his life teaching it. He first stresses that there is no contradiction between fiction and science, despite the traditional expectation to the contrary. Science and artistic creation are not opposite poles, quite the contrary, they share the same core, which comprises imagination and truth. As he puts it: "[f]iction does not stand as the antithesis to fact. Good fiction points to the truth, which is, after all, only where the scientist is trying to go" (Mawer 2005). Mawer detests what he calls the recent false separation of arts and sciences – just as science is "speculative and imaginative" (Sečkař 2010), so novel writing is experimental. Both scientific and artistic ideas live in the minds of their creators. More often than being found in nature, discoveries are made in researchers' heads (Mawer 2005). "The essence is the idea and the enquiry. 'What if?' is the question posed in both literature and science" (Mawer 2005). Thus, the two fields complement each other. As Mawer points out in his 2012 review of Eric Kandel's monograph *The Age of Insight: The Quest to Understand the Unconscious in Art, Mind, and Brain, from Vienna 1900 to the Present* (2012), the complexity of consciousness, which Kandel calls "introspective experience" (Mawer 2012, 444), adds to the impossibility of complete understanding by means of scientific research. He continues: "even when you have explained every neuron, every synapse, every glimmer in the amygdala or flicker in the prefrontal cortex, you still won't have explained what it is actually like to stand in front of a Klimt or Kokoschka and feel the thrill" (Mawer 2012, 445). This is where art and its ability to capture even the most intricate mental processes becomes involved. There is yet another point which connects science and modern art. Here Mawer echoes the main theme of Michael Frayn's *Copenhagen* (1998), pointing out that it is uncertainty that pervades both: "The unreliable particle and the unreliable narrator are two sides of the same weirdly spinning coin" (Mawer 2005). He stresses how modern nuclear physics and other recent theories correspond to art. According to Mawer, the inability of our intellect and imagination to fully embrace modern atomic theory and other intellectual discoveries of the twentieth and twenty-first centuries in their complexity and intangibility reflects how uncertain – "scientifically, morally, ethically and artistically" (ibid.) – we are as human beings.

Mawer's frequent employment of both history and science as chief thematic preoccupations of his novels allows him to explore a number of metaphysical, ontological, and ethical concerns. Mawer's "uncanny ability" (Silman 2019) to capture the intangible, such as love, fear, bravery, loss, hope, and faith, has been highlighted by the majority of reviewers of his works (Samson 2009, Kohda Hazelton 2015, Silman 2019, Cooke 2012). Physics is mingled with metaphysics since he, rather than pointing at their differences, stresses the role of uncertainty as their common core. He sees his fiction as a way to "get to grips with the moral and ethical issues that we face today" (Mawer 2005). The two fields of science his fiction is mainly preoccupied with, which bear the most implications from today's perspective, are nuclear physics (portrayed most notably in *The Girl Who Fell from the Sky*, *Tightrope* (2015), and mentioned also in *Prague Spring* (2018)) and genetics (*Mendel's Dwarf*, *The Glass Room)*. Another field of scientific research that acts as a rich source of inspiration for Mawer's works and also acts as their dominant motif and theme is historical science – including archaeology (*Chimera*), contemporary history (*The Fall* (2003), *Swimming to Ithaca* (2006)), or paleography – the study of ancient biblical scrolls (*The Gospel of Judas* (2000)). But it is not only science that is presented in his works, often it is also a métier, such as architecture (*The Glass Room*), espionage (*A Jealous God* (1996), *The Girl Who Fell from the Sky*, *Tightrope*), or mountaineering (*The Fall*). Although Mawer mostly eschews a teacherly tone, he acknowledges that in some cases his aim is slightly didactic.[49] His approach to both science and various métiers always develops their ethical and historical implications. Thus, both *Mendel's Dwarf* and *The Glass Room* remind the reader of the role of genetics in the development of eugenics and the Holocaust (Brookner 2009). The perspective that Mawer typically adopts, revisiting well-known historical events and scientific facts from unexpected angles, creates surprising connections, attracts the reader, helps the author to avoid a teacherly tone, and stresses the relevancy of the concerns expressed in the work. As a result, Mawer's novels teem with rhetorical questions and sometimes acquire the almost dialogical dimension of early medieval disputations. *The New York Times* review (1998) of *Mendel's Dwarf* points to this aspect of Mawer's creation: "Benedict's inquiries into the chemistry of genius recall theological speculations on the nature of the soul". As a result, the protagonist of *The Gospel of Judas* asks: "Do you need a resurrection?" (Mawer 2000, 76), Benedict Lambert, the main character of *Mendel's Dwarf* ponders on the nature of love: "Isn't love an exchange, a give and take?" (*Mawer* 1997, 184) and Mawer himself addresses his readers in a chapter dedicated to Milada Horáková in his *Prague Spring*: "How do you measure heroism? How do you describe it?" (*Mawer* 2018, 115). Marian Sutro indicates the collective fault in *The Girl Who Fell from the Sky*: "The problem with this war, Clément, is that there are no innocents. You can't stand aside and say it wasn't your fault. It's everyone's fault" (Mawer 2012, 256). An all-encompassing question is asked again in *Mendel's Dwarf* and the answer encapsulates Mawer's own

49 *Mendel's Dwarf* was described as being reminiscent of his lectures by his students (Lauder 2019). With *Prague Spring* his aim was "slightly didactic", he endeavoured to "inform people in the English-speaking world more about what happened in Czechoslovakia and what the implications of that were" (Vaughan 2018).

beliefs in the decisive role of uncertainty in contemporary science, art, and life: "*Why?* Of course the question is false. Scientifically, I mean. Philosophically as well, in all probability. We are what we are; there isn't anything else. But still you find yourself asking, don't you? WHY?" (Mawer 1997, 265). Mawer's works tend be novels of ideas, powered by their captivating plots and striking simplicity of expression.

One of the hallmarks of Mawer's writing, which reflects the previously mentioned philosophical aspects, is his focus on identity – personal, national, and cultural. *Tightrope* is therefore described as "a character study" as, apart from the life of the protagonist, Marian Sutro, who is recovering from torture and imprisonment, it surveys the state of a nation: "Britain too is exhausted, bruised and battered by war" (Pengelly 2015). There is another way through which Mawer demonstrates his keen interest in identity and its major components and that is the role of language. As he situates his plots in liminal spaces and often at the seam of two historical periods, he features bi – or even multilingual societies, and both similarities, differences, and spaces between languages serve as a rich source of inspiration. Sarah Crown considers "an exploitation of the slippages and spaces between languages" (Crown 2009) as one of the staples of his writing. A quote from *The Glass Room* illustrates Mawer's use of false cognates to express the impossibility of one language fully reflecting another: "Tomáš always referred to the gymnasium as the Glass Room. There is a language problem here. The word he used for room, *pokoj*, can also mean peace, tranquillity, quiet. So when he said 'the glass room' he was also saying 'the glass tranquillity'. Thus does one language fail to make itself felt in another. He loved the Glass Tranquillity" (Mawer 2009, 333).

His interest in identity is also reflected in his focus on the recent past (Crown 2009) as its understanding also conditions our comprehension of the present: "However, I think our collective past should be important to everyone: if we don't comprehend where we've come from, then we won't have any idea where we are going" (Flood 2016). Mawer's tendency to incorporate alternating timelines, thus strengthening the connection between the past and the present, add to the exceptionality of his writing, which can be seen as transcending the genre of historical fiction "adding something that a nonfiction treatment could not" (Miller 2009).

Mawer's latest novel, *Ancestry* (2022), revisits the phenomenon of the past and its role in human lives. The novel bears the famous last line from Francis Scott Fitzgerald's *The Great Gatsby*: "So we beat on, boats against the current, borne back ceaselessly into the past" and opens with a rhetorical question: "What is the past?" (Mawer 2022, 1). Mawer is quick to answer the question from a scientific point of view, stressing the presence of the past within us in the form of "that acronymic DNA that we have been bequeathed" (Mawer 2022, 1). He is also very much aware of its illusory nature, which is an idea expressed by means of one of the characters in *The Glass Room*: "Why should I be interested in finding out about the past? The past is an illusion" (Mawer 2009, 335). This belief also contributes to his manipulative tendencies as far as the depiction of the past is concerned (Crown 2009, Flood 2016) and the lack of, or disdain for, absolute historical accuracy. In words of one of the characters from *Swimming to Ithaca*, there is not a big difference between writing of a story or history: "'Never forget,' Thomas says, 'that the word "history" is cognate with the word "story". What I mean to say by this is that history is, essentially, a narrative. Just like a novelist, the historian is creating a narrative intended to explain something'" (Mawer 2006, 37).

The preface of *Ancestry* is concluded with a comparison of lifeless artefacts with living, feeling existence: "Where is the flesh and the blood? Who were the people? What did they feel? Where have they gone?" (Mawer 2022, 1). Not only does this succession of rhetorical questions encapsulate the motivation behind his writing, but, together with the rest of the novel, it also reveals the personal nature of *Ancestry*, his most openly autobiographical novel so far. Mawer's stance on the inclusion of autobiographical details is rather disparate. On the one hand, he endeavours "to look at something else, some other stories outside of me, and try to get it in" (Sečkař 2010) and claims to be very "suspicious about autobiographical novels" (Sečkař 2010), on the other hand, he acknowledges that the majority of his works bear marks of his personal experience.

His scientific and teaching background is apparent in most of his works; both *Swimming to Ithaca* and *Ancestry* feature an apparent autobiographical aspect; *Mendel's Dwarf* and *The Glass Room* were inspired by Mawer's visits to Brno in search of more information on Johann Gregor Mendel, a nineteenth-century botanist and the founder of genetics (Lauder 2015, 2019); the leitmotif of *Prague Spring* – hitchhiking through Europe in the summer of 1968 – is based on Mawer's own experience (Vaughan 2018); *Chimera*, *The Girl Who Fell from the Sky,* and *Tightrope* portray the SOE and its agents who both of Mawer's parents worked with during WW2 (Pengelly 2015, Lauder 2015, 2019); the Mediterranean setting of *Chimera*, *The Bitter Cross* (1992), and *Swimming to Ithaca* (2006) reflect the novelist's life-long bond with the Mediterranean; *The*

Fall (2003) was inspired by Mawer's past and his passion for climbing (Crown 2009).

The Fall demonstrates that "climbing's more than a sport, it's a way of life" (Crown 2009) and its climactic scene is based on Mawer's own fall and subsequent entrapment on a shallow ice ledge on the ice wall of Ben Nevis (Mawer 2010), which he described in an article entitled "Once Upon a Life" for *The Guardian*. Mawer refers to this moment as a turning point which led him to abandon a "curious split life" (Crown 2009), strung between two poles: "One pole was the hedonistic world of the Mediterranean, always a draw to the budding writer and particularly to one who, with an adolescent's taste for purple prose, had been swept away by Lawrence Durrell's *Alexandria Quartet*. The other pole was the mountains" (Mawer, "Once Upon a Life", 2010). Mawer's passion developed when he took a teaching position on Guernsey and he soon started going on climbing expeditions in Scotland. At the same time, his father was stationed in Malta with Mawer experiencing the "end-of-empire opulence [...] living in super-luxury, then coming back to Scotland and sleeping in bothies" (Crown 2009). This "dual existence" (Mawer, "Once Upon a Life" 2010) embodied another aspect intrinsic to Mawer's life – he associated the Mediterranean with writing and Scotland with climbing. The explosive resolution took the form of a near fatal climbing accident and thus the Mediterranean won. And writing along with it.

Some of the aspects of the experience became the cornerstones of Mawer's poetics: the end of the empire days in Malta, together with the oscillation between the extremes of extravagance and austerity, both in terms of the practicalities of Mawer's existence and the landscapes of Scotland and the Mediterranean. The first prominent example is his frequent employment of rather extreme dualities, such as "rationality and irrationality" (Mawer in Sečkař 2010) or "order and chaos, impulse balanced by propriety" (Crown 2009), "shuttlings between light and dark surface" (ibid.). The second aspect reflecting his unique experience is manifested in his penchant for liminal characters, settings, and situations, or "shifts between states [...]" as Sarah Crown called them in her 2009 profile for *The Guardian*.

The author's relationship with the Mediterranean has been a long and complex one – not only did he spend a part of his childhood there since his father's RAF service took the family to Cyprus and Malta, but he also spent the majority of his adult life living in Italy, teaching biology at a British international school in Rome. The Mediterranean Mawer depicts in his novels is a place of rapid and often conflicted historical and cultural developments, e.g. the liberation movement in WW2 Italy in *Chimera*, the Mediterranean of the sixteenth century with the Knights of Saint John confronting Islam and Protestantism in *The Bitter Cross* (1992), the last days of the troubled British Mandate in Palestine in *A Jealous God* (1996), or Cyprus in the days of EOKA bomb attacks in *Swimming to Ithaca* (2006).

Mawer's inclination to incorporate personal experience in his writing: "anything in a novelist's life is grist to the mill of his or her craft" (Mawer, "Once Upon a Life", 2010) is perhaps most apparent in his choice of foreign settings. Marcel Berlins calls him a "superb chronicler of past events in foreign countries" in his 2018 review of *Prague Spring* for *The Times*. It was his nomadic childhood ("my mother worked out that we've moved something like 20 times in 22 years" (Crown 2009)), which greatly influenced his own uprootedness: "I'm still not certain where I come from" (Crown 2009) and his "need to be away, the fascination with difference" (Crown 2009). He moved to Italy in order to escape the depression he associates with Britain. As he explained in an interview with Marek Sečkař, he enjoyed returning to Britain since he was able to perceive it from a foreigner's perspective, which some associated with his writing: "I think people say that my writing is not typically British, that there's something European about it" (Mawer in Sečkař 2010). Being an outsider and writing from a foreigner's perspective is something inherent in Mawer's creation no matter which region he describes or lives in – be it the Mediterranean or Britain: "I live in Italy, and I'm an outsider in Italy despite having lived there for 40 years. I go back to England now quite regularly and actually have a house there, and I'm also an outsider there" (Vaughan 2018). Mawer considers novelists "natural outsiders" (Vaughan 2018). The foreign viewpoint allows him to defamiliarise even well-known literary terrains. It is a view shared by Celine Low, who compares the novel *The Glass Room* to "a museum that connects the Czechs not only with their history but also with the world, through the lens of the author who curates this museum as a foreigner" in her master's thesis "The Topos of Glass at the Intersection of Architecture and Literature" (2021). This ability provides him with a significant advantage – as Sylvie Lauder claims in her 2015 interview "only a foreigner will see things we are unaware of or unable to perceive so clearly".

Besides the Mediterranean, the region of central Europe acts also as a rich source of inspiration for Mawer. Mawer's familiarity with the Czech Republic and the space of central Europe is considerable. Having known it for over 25 years (Mawer in Vaughan 2018), Mawer claims to admire the turbulent history of the region, even stating that his "heart is in the Czech Republic" (Lauder 2015), yet would not wish to experience it himself. The perspective that he regards as a source of frustration from the point of view of being an outsider is linguistic (Vaughan 2018). Mawer often demonstrates the inability of one language system to mediate the other without any shift in meaning by employing untranslated and untranslatable words from different languages: "'Leave Tatínka in peace,' Liba says, ushering the children to their breakfast" (Mawer 2009, 89). "On the upper floor there were rooms, *zimmer*, boxes with walls and doors; but down here there was room, *raum*, space" (Mawer 2009, 71).

Despite his apparent distaste for contemporary political subjects, such as Brexit (Kadlecová 2018), Mawer places his works in the midst of epoch-making events, most frequently cultural, political, and social conflicts. His interest in sudden spurts of liberal thinking and their abrupt suppression is apparent especially in the novels set in central Europe: *The Glass Room* and *Prague Spring*. Both novels might be read as geopolitical fantasies, "bringing its Czech audiences the promise that the desired Western identity is within reach" (Eberle 2018, 172). Although he rarely mentions his political affiliation in his interviews, Mawer commented on it in his interview with Kateřina Kadelcová for *Reflex* magazine in 2018, upon the publication of *Prague Spring*. Mawer described the Prague Spring as a tragic event which prevented the world from learning whether it was possible to reform communism. He even contradicted Václav Havel, the former president of the Czech Republic, an icon of dissent, and a political prisoner of the communist regime, claiming that in his opinion, communism was reformable (Kadlecová 2018). Compared to his earlier stance, he considers himself to be "inclined towards the politics of the left more than ever before" (Kadlecová 2018) having experienced the financial crisis of the 2010s, which made him acutely aware of the deficiencies of the free market and capitalism.

Mawer's preference for highly intricate historical periods, explosive settings, and complicated ethical and moral themes is reflected in his choice of similarly complex protagonists. Typically bilingual and acting as outsiders, they embody the liminality of the situation in their dual (linguistic) citizenship. In spite of the intricacy of Mawer's texts, they are most often characterised by "an almost dreamlike simplicity of telling" (Sansom 2009), "[t]he clarity with which it is written is almost unfamiliar and certainly to be admired" (Brookner 2009). As Anita Brookner further pointed out in her review of *The Glass Room*, "[i]t is its unfamiliar purity which is its outstanding feature" (Brookner 2009) whilst other reviews praised its "icy and disturbing elegance" (*The Scotsman* 2018 review of *Prague Spring*). One of the reasons why Mawer merges thematic complexity and relative formal simplicity may be attributed to his scientific background. In her 1998 *The New York Times* review, Francine Prose commented on *Mendel's Dwarf*, saying that: "the pleasure of his novel comes from the chance to watch him consider the mystery of the world, to report on the clarity with which nature speaks to us, at least on the cellular level" (Prose 1998). Seeing otherwise complicated matters through the lens of science allows for almost disturbingly straightforward statements such as: "[t] he so-called genetic code evolved simply to work. It is not a code: it is a language, and a disturbingly simple one" (Mawer 1997, 120). Another attribute which is often highlighted in connection with Mawer's tendency towards textual clarity is the frequently brisk pace of his works (Tripney 2013). There is also a strong sense of rhythm in his writing, stretching from the level of sentences to the overall structuring of the individual novels. The question is how the novelist manages to centre his works in the midst of highly complex historical and geographical settings, populate his novels with liminal characters, and evoke a keen sense of place and time while maintaining a fast-paced, clearly structured and often circular plotline. The answer is to be found in a set of qualities whose combination contributes to the uniqueness of Mawer's writing.

Firstly, Mawer's scientific and teaching background is reflected in the tone and the style of his writing. In his 2015 interview with Sylvie Lauder, Mawer explained the motivation behind his critically acclaimed novel, *Mendel's Dwarf*, and he acknowledged that while he did not want to sound teacherly or assume a mentor-like position, he still wanted to approach the subject of biology, and more importantly, genetics and its ethical and historical implications. On reading it, some of his students claimed that *Mendel's Dwarf* was like listening to his lectures. In another interview focused on *Prague Spring*, he admitted that his intention was "slightly didactic" and that he wanted to enlighten the English-speaking world about the events of 1968 in Czechoslovakia and point out their wide-reaching implications (Vaughan 2018).[50] It is also the very act of choosing either decisive historical events or scientific research as pivotal subject matter of his fiction that leads to the reviewers' tendency to emphasise Mawer's "mentor-like" position (Mandys 2010) and sometimes

50 Some reviewers considered *Prague Spring* to be the most distinctive reflection of the historical events commemorating its 50th anniversary (Konrád 2021).

criticise it – as Veronika Krajíčková did in her 2019 *iLiteratura.cz* review in which she accused Mawer of "authoritative exposition" in *Prague Spring*. Jonathan Myerson also wrote in his review of Mawer's latest literary venture, the 2022 *Ancestry*: "But the siege of Sevastopol, however evocatively fictionalised, can't help but feel like a history lesson when the story we really want to follow is Ann's" (Myerson 2022).

Another significant aspect that contributes to the clarity of Mawer's writing, but which may also be viewed as emphasising its didactic tendencies, is the way in which the plot is structured. There are two strong tendencies observable in the structuring of his works: the first is his preference for almost circular plots, the second is his partiality for parallel plot lines. The former appears already in Mawer's first novel, *Chimera* (1989). As the novel explores archaeology and both the recent and distant past, in this case the Etruscan settlement of Italy as the subject matter of the novel, it eventually contributes to its mythical quality. This tendency to bring the plot full circle appears in the majority of Mawer's works, but in some cases it has been deemed too pedantic. Some reviewers feel that it verges on the sensational or the melodramatic, e.g. Ian Sansom mentions this tendency in his review of *The Glass Room*: "As it draws towards its inevitable conclusions, the novel becomes perhaps too comfortable a read" (Sansom 2009).

The use of parallel timelines, which adds to the cyclicality of the plots, has become a hallmark of Mawer's writing. They usually connect the past and the present, reinforcing their junction and establishing a dialogue between different eras. This tendency expresses the author's preoccupation with history and its impact on the present: "I think our collective past should be important to everyone: if we don't comprehend where we've come from, then we won't have any idea where we are going" (Flood 2016). Besides parallel plotlines, the connection between the past and the present is often expressed by means of a unifying feature, and in Mawer's fiction it often takes the form of an object or a character, e.g. the Landauer villa in *The Glass Room*, the Italian village of Vetrano in *Chimera*, a set of family photos in *Swimming to Ithaca*, or a person, most often a child, such as Helen Harding in *A Jealous God* or Benedict Lambert in *Mendel's Dwarf*. The existence of multiple timelines is reflected through the narrators. Mawer uses two categories of narrator, often alternating them within one novel – there are omnipresent, authorial third-person narrators who add to the authoritative tone of the works, and then there are partial and almost unreliable narrators. Some of the narrators also act as the protagonists of the novels, such as Sam in *Tight-*

rope, Benedict Lambert in *Mendel's Dwarf*, or *Chimera*'s Anthony Lessing and *The Gospel of Judas*'s Leo Newman.

Mawer does not limit the use of parallelism to the structuring of the plot; he also uses it on the level of literary expression itself. He likes to use anaphora in his prose to enrich it with elements of poetic diction and to strengthen the impression of analogy, as in the description of an explosion in the 1996 novel *A Jealous God*:

> Five minutes later, at 12.37, seven hundred and seventy pounds of TNT, packed into milk churns and placed in the Regence Café directly beneath the Government Secretariat, detonated. Focused by the confines of the basement the blast was directed upwards through the six stories of concrete, stone and steel. It blew through floors and collapsed walls as though they were made of cardboard. It blew a column of smoke and yellow limestone dust high into the blue Jerusalem sky, high above the Hinnom Valley and the walls of the Old City, high above the Dome of the Rock and the Western Wall of the Temple Mount, high above the Church of the Holy Sepulchre and the Al-Aqsa mosque and the Hurvah synagogue. It blew people and furniture and filing cabinets to pieces with a fine indifference. (Mawer 1996, 13)

Not only does Mawer include poems in his novels (*Chimera*), most often by famous writers such as T. S. Eliot, but he also writes poetry himself – his website features examples of "Czech poems" and poems falsely attributed to the fictitious poet Geofrey Crozier, who appears in *Swimming to Ithaca*.

Mawer's choice and treatment of characters complements the major preoccupations of his literary creation. They tend to be highly complex and engaging (Askew 2000), and, as the epitomes of liminality, they mirror the unsettling qualities of their historical and geographical surroundings. They often assume the role of outsiders which enables them to provide a more engaging perspective. Some reviewers have highlighted Mawer's ability to create outstanding and convincing female characters, most often referring to Marian Sutro, the main character in *The Girl Who Fell from the Sky* and *Tightrope* (Pengelly 2015). However, Hana Hanáková from *The Glass Room*, or Helen Harding from *A Jealous God* also deserve to be mentioned in this regard.

Mawer does not eschew sexuality and often presents it as one of the chief sources of his characters' motivation. Some reviewers, however, highlighted this aspect almost with surprise. In his review of *The Glass Room* for *The Financial Times*, Richard T. Kelly noted that it is "indeed

[...] preoccupied by flesh and sexuality" (Kelly 2009), whilst Kateřina Svátková stressed it in her 2018 *iRozhlas* interview: "You put a great emphasis on physicality and sexuality – these are themes which almost always play an important role in your books". Rachel Cooke criticised Mawer's "interest (it verges on a fixation with Marian's genitals)" in her review of *The Girl Who Fell from the Sky* in 2012. Mawer commented on these remarks, suggesting that sexuality is a basic human need, which conditions our behaviour, influences human relationships, and generates a great deal of energy. According to him, to omit it from literature would be "hypocritical" (Svátková 2018).

If there is a component that seems to dominate all other aspects of Mawer's writing, it is his choice of geographical and historical settings. He typically situates his plots on the verge or in the midst of existentially threatening historical events; most frequently he opts for the key events of the twentieth century, such as WW2, the Cold War, and the fall of the British Empire. There are also works situated earlier – in the nineteenth and even the seventeenth century, although those set in the twentieth century clearly predominate. In Mawer's novels, the present and the past are interconnected, the parallel plotlines encouraging a dialogical reading. Mawer depicts a world of clashing worldviews and moral and ethical principles. The geographical settings of his novels mirror his preoccupation with multicultural areas at the onset of a conflict, such as the Mediterranean or central Europe, but also his autobiographical projection. His unique qualities, such as his precision of description, skilful mixing of fact and fiction, and his ability to capture the essence of complicated concepts, are paired with and contribute to a profound sense of place. It can be said that the majority of Mawer's novels derive their meaning from the synergy between their individual aspects, but, most importantly, the organic relationships between the protagonists and their settings. What needs to be stressed is that what initially appears to act as a setting often turns into the central conceit of the novel. Mawer typically establishes a powerful trope in the centre of his novels, but those tropes turn out to be mostly spatial, testifying to the substantial topocentric qualities of his writing. The most self-evident example of this tendency is to be found in *The Glass Room* where the eponymous room acts as the "haunting conceit at its centre" (Miller 2012). Many of his novels operate on the same principle. Mawer's first work, *Chimera*, revolves around an archaeological dig in the ancient Etruscan town of Vetrano. In *Tightrope*, similarly to *The Girl Who Fell from the Sky,* an eponymous conceit embodies the central aspects of the novel. Mawer also wrote novels which are less spatially inclined, e.g. *Mendel's Dwarf* or *The Gospel of Judas*, nevertheless, those in which the spatial is central prevail.

The final element of Mawer's work to be mentioned is his approach to character, place, and space. Substantial topocentric qualities of his poetics are exemplified by the actual fusion of characters and the places and spaces they inhabit. Whereas other similarly oriented authors, most notably Jim Crace, illustrate how the places and spaces reflect or determine the characters' mental states, evoke atmosphere, and develop the plotline, Mawer focuses rather on the traumatic aspects of this connection. The characters as well as the places are liminal and yet the process of transformation affects them differently. Whereas the places and spaces are often left untouched and some of them are even "indifferent" (Mawer 2009, 100), protagonists are often crushed under the weight of dramatic and mostly tragic circumstances. On the other hand, as he repeatedly proves, the mere existence of spaces and places is conditioned by human presence: "A house without people has no dimensions. It just is. An enclosed space, a box" (Mawer 2009, 308). Mawer's topocentric poetics and his thoroughly humanist understanding of place and space occupy the central position in his novels. This tendency is evident in the synergistic connection between character, setting – both spatial and temporal – and historical, social, and cultural contexts.

8. *Chimera*: Pioneering Simon Mawer's (Spatial) Poetics

Simon Mawer published his debut novel, *Chimera*, in 1989, having spent over 20 years teaching biology at St. George's British International School in Rome. As Mawer published his novel at the age of 41, he became a contender and, owing to the considerable qualities of the novel, also the first recipient of the newly established McKitterick Prize, which is typically awarded for either a published or unpublished first novel by a novelist over 40. While *Chimera* marked Mawer's first foray into the world of published authors, it introduces a fully-fledged author capable of producing dense, mature storytelling, apposite descriptions, and rich and nuanced portrayals of both the distant and less distant past and the present. The novel, which is sadly out of print today and whose copies may be painstakingly tracked down on *Abebooks* (Pengelly 2015), pioneers Mawer's thematic focus as well as his chief structural and formal preferences. *Chimera* marks Mawer's first immersion in the subject matter of war, resistance movements, and espionage as well as his first work set in the Mediterranean, which might be considered, apart from the region of central Europe, as his typical choice of setting. *Chimera*'s keen sense of time and place results from the organic connection between the protagonists and their setting. The novel also skilfully incorporates a field of science, in this case archaeology, in its thematic focus.

Mawer asserted the role of *Chimera* as a pioneering work in his 2015 interview by *The Guardian*'s Martin Pengelly. Discussing the publication of *Tightrope* (2015), the follow-up to the successful spy novel *The Girl Who Fell from the Sky* (2012), he acknowledged several thematic parallels between his works, parachuting into the enemy's territory being one of them: "The first novel I published, *Chimera*, [...] is set in Italy but it's got a man who is dropped in Italy in the war and then comes back after the war to explore Etruscan archaeology. This has always been there, this idea" (Pengelly 2015). The same interview, similarly to a 2009 interview with Sarah Crown, postulates Mawer's inclination to incorporate "personal experience" in his writing.[51] Mawer himself corroborated that "anything in a novelist's life is grist to the mill of his or her craft" (Mawer "Once Upon a Life", 2010). Accordingly, it was his life in Italy, and more specifically the region of Tuscany, which gave him the incentive to revisit writing again after his initial attempts stalled: "I started on a story inspired by places around here. That became *Chimera* – my first book" (Crown 2009).

The history of the author's relationship with the Mediterranean has been a long and complex one – not only did he spend a considerable amount of time in the Mediterranean region as a child, mainly due to his father's RAF service requiring him to be stationed at various air bases, but he also spent the majority of his professional career in Rome. He described his own experience of arriving in Cyprus as a child in *Swimming to Ithaca* (Crown 2009), one of his most autobiographical novels: "Shock. That was the word. The shock of sensation: of noise, of smells, of sights, the uneasy sensation of tripping across gangway, clasping Paula's hand. The shock of sunlight on hot stone. Dust, fine and yellow" (Mawer 2006, 72). The fascination with the Mediterranean is palpable in Mawer's writing, which is imbued with a sense of place, including the region's history, local colour, and distinctive poetics. He emphasises the region's complex and often conflicted historical and cultural development by situating the plots of his Mediterranean novels in distinctly tumultuous, tense periods resulting from the clash of different cultures at a given historical moment.

Surprisingly, given the prevalently historical nature of his novels, Mawer does not regard himself as a historical novelist. What characterises Mawer's fiction is his frequent drawing on real life, including his personal experiences and preferences, and adapting some of its features to his liking. One of his main guiding ideas is that fiction is liberating for the writer (Pengelly 2015) and that as a novelist, he can manipulate things as he chooses, or even lie (Flood 2016). Although his work is rarely mentioned in recently published academic overviews of contemporary British literature, he may be classified amongst authors who, like him,

51 As Mawer revealed to Pengelly, his keen interest in the SOE and its agents, which he developed both in *The Girl Who Fell from the Sky* (2012) and its sequel, *Tightrope* (2015), has been influenced by his mother's experience of working with the famous SOE Anne-Marie Walters, also known as Colette.

focus on historical themes, narrativising the past and analysing and strenghtening the parallels between the past and the present.

In his 2018 monograph *Contemporary British Fiction*, Nick Bentley attributes these qualities to contemporary historical fiction. Mawer's rejection of complete verisimilitude in his works, as well the ability of his text to comfortably inhabit the past, point in the direction of Linda Hutcheon's concept of "historiographic metafiction": a literary method which challenges or even rebuts the usual, universal methods of distinguishing between historical facts and fiction (Bentley 2018, 95). Hutcheon focused mainly on the self-conscious and self-reflexive properties of the writings she analysed. Jerome De Groot, the author of two monographs on the subject of contemporary historical fiction: *The Historical Novel* (2009) and *Remaking History: The Past in Contemporary Historical Fiction* (2015) focuses on similar qualities of historical fiction and in particular, he examines the nature of the narrativisation of the past, as "[h]istory is other, and the present familiar. The historian's job is often to explain the transition between these states. The historical novelist similarly explores the dissonance and displacement between then and now, making the past recognisable but simultaneously authentically unfamiliar" (De Groot 2010, 3). At the same time, he asserts that fiction, and novels in particular, are no longer perceived as merely fictitious and therefore dubious (De Groot 2016, 6). Quite the contrary, throughout his monographs he repeatedly demonstrates that narrativisation conditions the very understanding of the notion of pastness and thus different fictitious representations of the past act as highly useful tools for its investigation. Mawer's works are part of this effort to present the past in a way that places emphasis on its collective nature and its impact on the present.

Whilst *Chimera* is Mawer's writing debut, it is a mature work that incorporates almost all the hallmarks of his work, including its poetic and thematic focus as well as key formal aspects and structural preferences. The novel pioneers the novelist's tendency to feature impeccably researched period detail in order to build extraordinary set pieces. Both of these aspects, combined with Mawer's precision of expression, contribute to his fiction's ability to perfectly inhabit its space and time. In *Chimera*, Mawer introduces what has since become the structural staple of his fiction: multiple timelines. Set in Italy, in the Tuscany region, in the fictional town of Vetrano, the story is composed of two alternating timelines, one set in the period from the autumn of 1943 to the spring of 1944, and the other set thirty years later in the same place. Both periods, although seemingly more distinctively the one set during WW2, are marked by a great deal of tension, imminent danger, and instability. The wartime plotline revolves around the endeavours of the Italian Resistance, led by an English SOE agent, David Hewison. The more recent parts of the plot revisit the outcomes of tragic war events and their continuous impact on the survivors as they resurface in the present. *Chimera* revisits other layers of the past since the town of Vetrano is also the location of an enormous archaeological excavation of the Etruscan town of Lucri, which was most likely attacked and destroyed by the Romans in the fifth century BCE. Mawer gradually develops correspondences between the present and both the more and the less distant past until they converge in a tragic climax at the end of the novel.

8.1 Liminality in *Chimera*

Apart from the typical historical and geographical setting, *Chimera* introduces another prototypical aspect of Mawer's poetics: liminality. The term itself was originally coined by Arnold van Gennep in his anthropological study of the rites of passage of various cultures as a description of rituals which, when undergone, position the individual in a space between two clear polarities (Turner 1970, 93). From the contemporary perspective, liminality correlates mainly with postcolonial discourse and its vision of "in-between, transcultural" space (Ashcroft 2007, 117). As far as Mawer's novels are concerned, the concept of liminality operates on multiple levels as the novelist often chooses to develop his characters synchronically with their historical and geographical settings. Mawer's novels are built upon the interconnectedness of all their themes and motifs, and one of the key shapes that this level of interconnectedness takes is the parallel developed between the protagonists and the ways in which their qualities echo the volatile, liminal nature of the places, cultures, and periods in which the stories are set. *Chimera* even makes a point of creating a connection between its two protagonists, so that David Hewison and Anthony Lessing can be seen as almost direct reflections of each another.

Anthony Lessing is a beady-eyed visitor to his uncle's Italian villa. David Hewison, Anthony's uncle, plays the part of "[a] prodigal; a traitor to the family; a spy floating down through the Italian sky beneath a parachute; a discoverer of lost civilizations; a hero" (Mawer 1989, 11). It is revealed that he was a member of the SOE who parachuted into Italy and organised the resistance in Vetrano and the surrounding area.

At the end of the war, he comes back to the place and uncovers the lost Etruscan city of Lucri. While doing so, not only does he abandon the "indissoluble hybrid" (Mawer 1989, 28) of the Hewison family and firm, but also invests a considerable portion of their riches into financing his extensive archaeological project. Anthony Lessing, the novel's narrator, replicates his uncle's qualities in many ways, one of which is being an actual spy. David served as an SOE agent, but Anthony is spying on him, calling himself a "voyeur of Hewison's past" (Mawer 1989, 228), not, as David wrongly assumes, for the sake of the Hewison clan, but rather for his own purposes, both attracted to and later repulsed by his uncle's actions. David is perceived, first by his nephew and later in the plot by several other characters, as a "mythic figure, half noble, half cunning, wholly inimical to those relations who had peopled my childhood" (Mawer 1989, 27). It is maybe his rebellion against his business-oriented family which fascinates Anthony and that he would like to replicate in his own life. But it is not only in Anthony's view that David resembles a classical hero, with "a classical acting mask, an archetype" (Mawer 1989, 24). In wartime, he was seen as a "godlike" figure, "heroic in the classical sense. A Perseus. A man who swept down from the skies at the very moment of our greatest need, when everything around was chaos and the ordinary decencies of society had been thrown aside, when we had almost descended into anarchy" (Mawer 1989, 160).

Alongside the carefully placed classical references, Mawer develops another quintessential quality of his characters: linguistic hybridity. Mawer's writing often explores the slippage between languages, highlighting the gaps and spaces between individual words and their counterparts in different languages.[52] In *Chimera*, compared to other novels, this tendency is rather muted. By studying the etymology of individual words in order to construct a dense system of analogies within the novel, it is shown that the majority of Latin words and related phenomena were derived from the Etruscan. As a result, *Chimera* continually reinforces the vision of Roman civilisation as hopelessly unoriginal, derivative, and mostly cannibalistic towards other cultures. In the WW2 part of the plot, especially its beginning, David Hewison's hybridity mostly causes unease since he is an English parachutist speaking native Italian due to his Italian heritage. Others are mostly "wary of him. He spoke Italian like a signore, and yet he was English. Occasionally nowadays he would

52 "'Ciao'. Which comes from the Venetian dialect and means Schiavo, slave. Your slave" (Mawer 1989, 241).

lapse into a very convincing *romanesco* dialect, yet he was a *signore*" (Mawer 1989, 79). The enigmatic, contradictory nature of his existence is even amplified by his political impartiality in "a world where everyone had some side to take" (Mawer 1989, 79) and he immediately becomes an object of suspicion.

Mawer channels both the hybrid and mythical aspects of the structural aspects of the novel, namely of the protagonist, of the plot as well as of the setting, into the statue of a chimera[53], an Etruscan bronze discovered by David Hewison, which acts as both a motif and a symbol of the man himself. Once Anthony arrives at Villa Rasenna, David Hewison's Italian residence, out of the many archaeological findings scattered around as if they were "ordinary objects of domestic life" (Mawer 1989, 8), the object that attracts him the most is the statue of a chimera, "the size of a small cat, twisted and contorted, sprung tight with rage" (Mawer 1989, 9). On this occasion it is Lara, Hewsion's much younger wife, who pats the head of the bronze, smiling "ruefully at me as though seeking reassurance" (Mawer 1989, 9). David Hewison treats the statue in a similarly pet-like way, "caress[ing] its lion head as though nuzzling a puppy" (Mawer 1989, 52). Far from a comforting sight at the beginning, the statue becomes more and more animated and sinister as the plot proceeds towards its tragic climax (Mawer 1989, 211, 282). The analogy between the statue and the protagonist, both haunted by their curious hybrid existence, is carefully built upon, only to be fully exploited in the denouement. It is revealed that David Hewison not only participated in the kidnapping of Lara's father, but that he personally killed him in order to gain the trust of the resistance movement leaders who were wary of his hybrid loyalty (Mawer 1989, 225). Furthermore, Lara's supposed father, Alessio, develops the parallel himself, criticising David's lack of involvement: "Brought up here, I suppose. But not wholly Italian. There's no involvement, no passion in you. You're a hybrid. [...] A hybrid Italian. A chimera" (Mawer 1989, 223). Ironically, the very quality that made David a perfect fit for an SOE agent is repeatedly questioned and challenged, while his efforts at proving his steadfast commitment ultimately result in tragedy.

Mawer's tendency to populate his works with liminal, hybrid characters and to echo their nature thematically by setting the plotlines in explosive periods, spaces, and places marked by tension and transformation, seeps into another thematic aspect of his novels: their focus

53 The chimera was a mythical monster that was a mixture of various beasts; it had two heads – a goat's and a lion's – and a serpent's tail.

on literal and metaphorical transitions. In her 2009 interview, Sarah Crown posits that "shift between states is something Mawer returns to repeatedly in his work" (Crown 2009) and that "these two threads – order versus chaos, impulse balanced by propriety – pursue each other through his fiction as through his life, intertwining and grappling down the pathways of his novels" (Crown 2009). Mawer himself credits the role of his upbringing – split between the Scottish Highlands and the luscious Mediterranean – as an inspiration for his writing. In *Chimera*, David's and Anthony's hybrid existence thematises their uprootedness and their inability to commit, and as the novel develops, the significance of these qualities moves from the personal sphere to the national and even the universal. David's as well as Anthony's conflict of loyalties, torn between what is personally desirable and what is universally moral, is reflected in a number of metaphorical transitions, which mostly take spatial form. Mawer employs the Mediterranean region, and Italy in particular, to exemplify the situation of the two men, David and Anthony, oscillating between two extremes, caught between two opposing poles: "'What is it about this country?' [...] It seems a place where anything can happen – the very worst and the very best, too often at the same time. It throws a kind of magnetic field around it, doesn't it? A magnetic field with innocence at one pole and corruption at the other, and the wretched people strung out in between like little vibrating compass needless." (Mawer 1989, 202)

An extensive use of liminality as a key quality of the characters and the settings, together with the emphasis Mawer puts on the interconnectedness of the individual thematic and structural aspects of his works, results in frequent use of different kinds of parallelism. This can already be seen at the structural level of his text, where he often employs repetition of a similar sentence structure with minor variations, usually for the sake of gradation. This use of analogous structures, together with the repetition of a particular sentence element, adds to a distinctive rhythm and makes Mawer's prose transcend its nature and venture into the realm of poetry and its use of anaphora: "No doubt that there was a family who made the votive objects for the shrine. No doubt they were rich as well" (Mawer 1989, 67); or: "And he felt tired, physically tired of struggling through this damned wilderness, but also tired of having to be understanding towards a man whom he had disliked ever since Clara had first spoken of him; tired too of having to admit to himself that Alessio was not the insensitive fool that he had always imagined" (Mawer 1989, 224). To further strengthen the poetic element, Mawer also juxtaposes contrasting elements in parallel structures, resulting in a haiku-like tension: "An evening of strong contrasts: the storm outside, the shabby stillness within" (Mawer 1989, 276). As far as figures of speech are concerned, the most prominent is probably a simile whose explicit comparison of two elements could be seen as another example of the author's extensive use of parallelism: "A primaeval stillness seemed to fill the opening, like water filling deep pool" (Mawer 1989, 92), "the backstairs wisdom is that he treats his employees like his prized Guernseys: feeds them well, milks them hard, and sells those with a low yield" (Mawer 1989, 104).

8.2 Parallelism in *Chimera*

From the point of view of the arrangement of the novel, the alternation of chapters set in the present and set in the past underlines both the interconnectedness of the two timelines and an intricate system of analogies between the two plotlines, the characters, and the settings. Anthony mirrors his uncle David in a number of ways. Initially, Anthony sees David as a tempting model for severing ties with the overbearing Hewison family business. Later, he shares his uncle's passion for his wife, Lara, as well as his desperate "search for a past" (Mawer 1989, 108). While David finances and participates in the archaeological uncovering of the ancient town of Lucri, Anthony, in turn, examines his uncle's past and mostly his involvement in the resistance's war effort, which resulted in the killing of fifteen villagers as well as the father of David's current wife, Vincenzo Alessio, one of the leaders of Mussolini's new republic. Despite Anotny's perception of himself as a saviour, he is shown to have the same domineering nature of both his uncle and his family.[54] Anthony's intrusion into the lives, history, and marriage of Lara and David matches the intensity of David's earlier involvement with Lara's family, and, as Mawer skilfully evokes, his excavation of Lucri, which marks his contemporary domination of the town of Vetrano and its past. The parallel between the archaeological dig and the process of excavating the past is developed most prominently in the novel. It would be reductive, however, to limit the interpretation of the dig to its symbolic interpretation as a way of communing with the past, since the excavation site at the centre of the

54 Lara even points out the similar dominant nature of the two men, David and Anthony: "It was something about the way you were standing, looking around. Not a facial resemblance at all, more an attitude, a sense of ownership. I sat in the drawing room watching you and thinking, how like David" (Mawer 1989, 148).

novel represents one of the leitmotifs as well as the central spatial conceit of the novel.

As far as historical parallels are concerned, the novel draws parallels between Roman civilisation devouring Etruscan culture, the German occupation of Italy, and the actions of Anthony and David. Inspired by the excavation site, but also the surroundings of Vetrano, a host of analogies are drawn between Etruscan and Roman and, by extension, between Italian and German. Through the process of comparing and contrasting these cultural and historical influences, *Chimera* introduces several pivotal aspects of the dichotomy between the Etruscan and the Roman. Although the archaeological research suggests that the town of Lucri was last inhabited in the fourth century BCE, before the Romans burnt it down, the novel repeatedly underlines the mystical nature of the place. The Etruscan mindset differs dramatically from the Roman one; it is described as being less rational, full of mysticism and "archaic fatalism" (Mawer 1989, 108), governed by a "mysterious sense of pattern and design" (Mawer 1989, 108). The Etruscan ethos "to submit and endure" (Mawer 1989, 108) seems to permeate the place, tinting the local colour so that: "Here was none of that Renaissance optimism which, for all that the twentieth century has done, one can still feel in the Florentine countryside. Here, in the place where David Hewison has made his home, there was something altogether darker and less reasonable" (Mawer 1989, 14). What is more, the nature of the place, described as "an ancient wilderness" (Mawer 1989, 60) with little to no connection "with the world of man" (ibid.), adds to its mystical image. Anthony is rather stunned by this "strange world, a world suffused with magic and a submission to the forces of nature that was almost oriental in its character, almost Hindu" (Mawer 1989, 109), David, on the other hand, is attracted and becomes deeply committed to its rather dark, disturbing nature.

8.3 Idiosyncratic Conception of Time in *Chimera*

The notion of archaic Etruscan fatalism is amplified by the introduction of the cyclical, mythical concept that acts as a source for the organisation of the plot. *Chimera*'s verbal fabric resonates with meticulously interconnected elements. This effect is even amplified by the repeated references to T. S. Eliot's *Four Quartets*: "In my beginning is my end" (Eliot 2004, 177). One of the most obvious manifestations within the plot is the sphere of relationships. Anthony and Lara's illicit love affair duplicates that of David and Lara as well as that of David and Clara. Once it is revealed that David knowingly married his own daughter, Lara, and murdered her father, he commits suicide. Although Lara herself pointed out the great similarity between David, her husband and father, and his nephew, Anthony, in true classic tragedy fashion, she resumes her relationship with Anthony, David's reflection: "not with love but rather as though she was fulfilling part of a ritual" (Mawer 1989, 298).

Kevin Greene, the author of the concise volume *Archaeology: An Introduction* (2010), sees humanity's contemplation of its origins as "a very early aspect of human consciousness" (Greene 2010, 9). He delineates two basic conceptions of time associated with different cultures, civilisations, and periods – a line and a circle. Whereas some perceive time as "going around in an endlessly repeating circle of life, death and rebirth" (Greene 2010, 6), others adhere rather to a linear conception of time. It is the latter group that has inspired historical thinking and the emergence of the historical sciences in general. From the narrative point of view, this dichotomy of time conceptions takes on different dimensions. The circular one, tied to the image of the circle, is connected with mythical time (Freeman 1998, 27) whereas the one "tied to the image of the line" is associated with historical time (Freeman 1998, 27). Mark Freeman dedicated his 1998 study "Mythical Time, Historical Time, and the Narrative Fabric of the Self" to a thorough scrutiny of the interrelationship of "time, experience, and self via the idea of narrative" (Freeman 1998, 27). His aim, apart from a significant reconsideration of the roles of the previously mentioned variables, is to recognise the complex and deep-rooted set of connections between myth and history and life and literature (Freeman 1998, 27). In his article, Freeman presents the following paradox: On the one hand, there is a clearly discernible tendency to reject a positivist approach to the presentation of human lives and instead present them in a more lively and human way, framing their stories by means of some generally recognisable narrative. On the other hand, there is a tendency to denigrate the nature of a narrative as something artificial, imposing, and almost coercive, something distant and isolated from the otherwise formless and meaningless fabric of life (Freeman 1998, 28).

In seeking a solution to the dilemma that initiated his study, Freeman refers to Frank Kermode's insightful 1967 monograph, *The Sense of an Ending*. Kermode highlights the linear nature of time, which causes each moment to be singular, unrepeatable, and preceded and followed by another, as one of the factors contributing to the human desire to feel that one's existence is "related to a beginning and an end" (Kermode 1967,

4). Another aspect of the effort to confront (or console) the relatively formless nature of human life is to contain it within a narrative ("fictive concords with origins and ends" (Kermode 1967, 7)). A narrative is supposed to step "into the picture to give form to the flux, to make it all seem like there is a point, a purpose, a meaning" (Freeman 1998, 29)[55]. There are a number of questions that arise from the tension between the two directions the perception of narrative might take. If narratives are essentially untrue, why and under what circumstances should they be seen as valuable? Where should one draw the line between a useful narrative and more or less far-fetched fiction? As Freeman points out, a significant number of modern and postmodern works resolve this issue by adopting a rather documentary attitude to human experience, citing Sartre's *Nausea* as an example. Kermode reminds his reader of the need to distinguish between the factual and fictive nature of narrative: "once we forget the fictive nature of fictions, we regress to myth" (Freeman 1998, 29). In this context, should the nature of myth be regarded solely as archaic and regressive? In order to analyse myths and their connection to the process of narrativisation as a way of providing a coherent shape to human life, Freeman turns to an influential work on the ritual repetition of mythical events turned into paradigmatic models (viii), Mircea Eliade's *The Myth of the Eternal Return: Or, Cosmos and History* (1954).

According to Eliade, the habitual division of conceptions of time into a linear or historical one and a circular or mythical one, as observed in the writings of Kevin Greene or even Mark Freeman, is only an apparent one. What this dichotomy fails to register is the way in which traditional societies, often considered incapable of connecting the conception of time with the image of the line, in fact deliberately revolted against concrete time (Eliade 1954, xi) and rejected it because of its lack of meaning, which reflected its haphazard, ephemeral nature. Eliade's monograph is mostly concerned with archaic ontology and the way in which it seeped into the behaviour of humans in premodern periods. While observing the typical behaviour of premodern humans, Eliade came across rigorous observation of ritual patterns based on paradigmatic models, which was a way of revolting against the lack of meaning of linear, historical time. Not only did Eliade observe a great deal of "nostalgia for a periodical return to the mythical time of the beginnings of things, to the Great Time" (Eliade 1954, xi), but he also

55 Humans' inclination towards coherence and order is often satiated by religion (Freeman refers to a "proto-religious" belief (1998, 30)).

realised that the observation of ritual patterns allowed "the Cosmos and society to be periodically regenerated" (Eliade 1954, viii). The monograph reveals an original ontological conception based on the notion of perpetual repetition – any action "acquires meaning, reality, solely to the extent to which it repeats a primordial act" (Eliade 1954, 5), and thus concrete time develops a connection with the mythical dimension. There are two moments – the one when the action was first performed by a forbear or a celestial being, and the one that reflects the original in the present time (Eliade 1954, 21). Thus, every act becomes a version of the original act and repeats the archetype. Surprisingly, the real dimension is acquired only through repetition, "everything which lacks an exemplary model is meaningless, it lacks reality" (Eliade 1954, 34). Historical time is suspended as it becomes irrelevant and each repeated act or gesture connects an individual not only to mythical time but also to reality. Therefore, according to Eliade "Any meaningful act performed by archaic man, any real act, i.e. any repetition of an archetypal gesture, suspends duration, abolishes profane time, and participates in mythical time" (Eliade 1954, 36).

Chimera exemplifies this quality by introducing parallel timelines that strengthen the fatalistic, cyclical conception of time and action. Events of WW2 are shown to have immediate effect on the present, both on a personal as well as national level. Furthermore, the dramatic and often tragic situations associated with the German occupation of the country are presented as reflections of the tumultuous history of the region, and in particular the violence of the Etruscan civilisation being engulfed by the Roman invaders. Human relationships follow a cyclical pattern – they duplicate across generations. The novel and its plot demonstrate how the present and the past are inextricably linked – only towards the end does the narrative come full circle: "Seeds sown long ago germinate and blossom and die, but they have made other seeds whose time will come sooner or later; and so it goes on. Full circle" (Mawer 1989, 298). This quality is repeated in the rest of Mawer's work and can be regarded as his homage to archaic ontology.

8.4 Thematisation of Archaeology

If there is yet another pivotal aspect of Mawer's works presented in *Chimera*, it is his tendency to incorporate and thematise a field of knowledge or science. Once again, Mawer's inclination may be explained on the background of his personal experience – he read biology at Oxford University (Crown 2009) and later became a teacher, first on the island of Guernsey and later in Rome. His presentation of this knowledge seeps organically into the texture of the novel, echoing and reflecting its thematic preoccupation, but also providing an enlightening side effect. The didactic aspect of Mawer's texts does not only stem from his former pedagogical profession, but is also rooted in his overall vision of fiction and literary creation, which he indicated in his 2005 essay "Science in Fiction". In his view, fiction and science do not stand in opposition since they are energised by the same questions, they share similar methods, and the results they strive to attain mostly share the same quality: truthfulness. There are numerous fields of knowledge Mawer incorporates into his novels, from both science and the humanities. The level of thematisation of these fields of knowledge is such that they become an integral part of the plot on both the literal and the metaphorical level, but they also mark the process of reading and interpreting the plot. Mawer not only brings fresh insights and interesting observations to the fields of knowledge he presents in the novels, but he also aptly summarises and re-evaluates some of their foundational aspects. In the following quote he contemplates the nature of historical inquiry and profoundly re-evaluates the outcomes of archaeological research into Troy:

> But do we ever understand, I wonder? However much we pick it over do we ever understand? Look at the great themes: tragedy, fate, all that kind of nonsense. Take the greatest of them if you like: the Trojan War. What do we the archaeologists find? A habitation level – Troy VIIa – which was nothing but an impoverished fortress covering five acres; no evidence there was such a thing as a war with the Greeks: rather, much evidence that there could not have been, at least not in Homer's terms. No, the drama which you read is Homer's alone, not Agamemnon's or Priam's. [...] The reality, always, is rather mundane; bathos rather than pathos, I'm afraid. (Mawer 1989, 138–139)

In *Chimera*, Mawer's keen interest in history and place meets his interest in science in the form of archaeology. The role of the central symbol and leitmotif is therefore taken by the archaeological dig of the ancient Etruscan town of Lucri, situated in the vicinity of the fictitious Tuscan town of Vetrano. From the very outset, Mawer's atmospheric depictions echo and repeatedly amplify the coexistence of different cultures, civilisations, the present, and the past. Vetrano's buildings are thus "a kind of architectural palimpsest" (Mawer 1989, 5).[56] and the inside of Villa Rasenna[57], the residence of David Hewison and his strikingly beautiful and much younger wife, Lara, is decorated by artifacts from the excavation with "vases and urns and bronzes scattered about as though they were nothing more than the ordinary objects of domestic life" (Mawer 1989, 8). As the plot evolves, archaeology is presented less as a motif and more as a theme. Eventually, the whole narration of Mawer's *Chimera* assumes the role of an excavation.

The excavation in question is described as "thrilling in its concept, anachronistic in its scale" (Mawer 1989, 44), harking "back to the almost legendary excavations of the past, to Schliemann's Troy and Mycenae, to Evans' Knossos, to Woolley's Ur of the Chaldees" (Ibid.). In his typical fashion, Mawer presents characters whose palimpsestic identities and backgrounds he painstakingly reveals as he strips away the successive layers of their stories. The narration thus follows a natural human tendency to be interested in origins, which Clive Gamble, the author of the comprehensive *Archaeology: The Basics* (2015) ascribes to the "archaeological imagination of the humans" (Gamble 2015, 1). He describes archaeology as one of the fundamental ways in which humans organise reality, acting as "one of the ways in which we remember" (Gamble 2015, 2). According to Gamble, not only do we routinely employ standard archaeological techniques, such as excavating, measuring, and describing, but we also use these procedures in both their literal and metaphorical sense as "metaphors to investigate our inner selves. Every time we 'dig into the

56 Mawer does not reserve this layering tendency for Vetrano and its surroundings. Rome has similar qualities reflecting time and culture: "Rome is a preposterous city, a colossal fluke, a scrap heap of every past and every idea which Europe has ever suffered. Here you can have anything you please, any epoch, any philosophy, any political system. Any illusion too" (Mawer 1989, 239).

57 Villa Rasenna is described in a similar way to a number of places housing Mawer's narration, most notably the eponymous Glass Room – as an impartial relic, indifferent to the drama revolving around it and within its walls. Its ability to resist the constraints of history, time, and human activity approximate it to Foucault's conception of heterotopia – a place similarly representing, contesting, and inverting other places. "At the top of the avenue the Villa Rasenna stood behind its screen of umbrella pines in marvellous counterpoise to my own disquiet. It calmed me. The house seemed unmoving and unmoved. It had the quiet sensation of the centuries about it, a sense of agelessness acquired through age, a rocklike passivity which had given it resilience against every human current flowing past. It was an observer, not a protagonist. [...] Then I had seen the house as a kind of metaphor, a contrast to Poggio Sanssieve. But now I saw it almost as a deity, a cult object standing above the tide of human affairs and looking down on me as though at a piece of flotsam swirling around its base." (Mawer 1989, 258)

subconscious' or 'peel back the layers of personality' we are imitating archaeologists" (Gamble 2015, 2). Gamble emphasises the mutual influence of the mental and physical processes since archaeology is defined as "the study of the past through materials and material remains. It is about three things: objects, landscapes and what we make of them" (Gamble 2015, 2). Echoing the implications of Mawer's narrative technique, as well as one of *Chimera*'s central subject matters, Gable characterises archaeology "as a social activity involved in the creation of a memory that may be local, national or even global in scale and complexity" (Gamble 2015, 2). Mawer's conception of archaeology echoes this vision as the dig exceeds its role as an instrument of disinterested dissection of the past and, as is repeatedly demonstrated, "becomes an act of empathy and communion" (Mawer 1989, 44). For David, the dig is a decisively living entity and he sees the archaeological findings not as "a dead past, it is more a living thing, a resurrection" (Mawer 1989, 243).

One might define David's main source of motivation as atoning for his sins and foolishly trying to revive the long dead. But his connection to the past seems to be more profound. During his time as an SOE agent, while supervising a night drop, he "could hear the mules snorting and stamping on the ramp. There was the cursing of the drivers, the crack of whips, the swaying of the loads: bales of cloth perhaps, sacks of grain, baskets of metal-bearing ore from the Tolfa hills. And the helmeted guards standing impassively at either end of the narrow gangway" (Mawer 1989, 58). Although this type of daydreaming can be categorised as a form of escapism, a coping mechanism, or pure fantasising, Nadia Durrani and Brian M. Fagan, the authors of another recent introduction to archaeology, connect the very origins of archaeology with fantasy realms and treasure hunting. Archaeology is "the stuff dreams are made of – buried treasure, gold-laden pharaohs, and the romance of long-lost civilizations" (Fagan and Durrani 2016, 3), which is reminiscent of Freud's approach to the discipline, which will be developed later. The authors highlight the fact that ancient cultures had speculated about their ancestors, with the Greeks and Romans being particularly captivated by their barbarian ancestors "who drank from cups made from human skulls" (Fagan and Durrani 2016, 6). They place the beginnings of archaeology in the European Renaissance, which brought a wave of interest in classical civilisations. The roots of the scientific discipline are far from scientific, since they are surprisingly to be found in "treasure hunting" (Fagan and Durrani 2016, 6).

Accordingly, many of the founding figures of the nineteenth century were either adventurers or professional travellers (Fagan and Durrani 2016, 15). Some of them, most notably Heinrich Schliemann, a German businessman, were preoccupied with the past and its literary rendition to the point of obsession.[58] Schliemann's methods were considered to be unscientific even in his day, but his zeal captivated the imagination of a number of his contemporaries. Writers were drawn not only by the great amount of mystique that was generated, but also by the idea of the possible co-existence of several historical layers, buried one on top of the other beneath the surface of the contemporary cityscape. Richard Lehan, one of the founders of modern literary urban studies and the author of the influential *City in Literature* (1998), attributes this fascination with archaeology to the growth of interest in urban archaeology and landscapes, predominantly urban ones, which found its artistic expression in modernist literature (Lehan 1998, 79).

Eventually, this conception of a predominantly vertical spatial structuring became a prolific trope. Fascinated by Schliemann's excavation of Troy, Freud developed an analogy between the human mind and the Eternal City of Rome in his *Civilization and its Discontents* (1930) in order to express the peculiar quality of the workings of the mind, from which nothing can vanish: "[s]ince we overcame the error of supposing that the forgetting we are familiar with signified a destruction of the memory-trace – that is, its annihilation – we have been inclined to the opposite view, that in mental life nothing which has once been formed can perish – that everything is somehow preserved and that in suitable circumstances (when, for instance, regression goes back far enough) it can once more be brought to life" (69). Just as memories mark the human consciousness, the past has left marks that both resurface and remain buried beneath the contemporary city (Freud 1978, 70):

> The assumption that everything past is preserved holds good even in mental life only on condition that the organ of the mind has remained intact and

58 Schliemann decided to provide material evidence for the existence of Homer's *Iliad* and *Odyssey*. His actions and thinking lacked precision and scientific documentation, but they abounded in both enthusiasm and sensationalism. He claimed to have located Homeric Troy in Turkey in 1871 and, employing engineers who participated in the building of the Suez Canal, he discovered "seven ancient cities superimposed one on top of the other" (Fagan and Durrani 2016, 15) and treasure which, in contradiction to his claims identifying it as the king Priam's wealth, consisted of isolated gold artifacts gathered over a period of many months. He then stormed, surrounded by the same aura of adventure and determination, into Mycenae in Greece in 1876. Although Schliemann was persuaded that he gazed at the face of another Homeric king, Agamemnon, archaeologists date these finds to at least three or four centuries before the Trojan War.

> that its tissues have not been damaged by trauma or inflammation. But destructive influences which can be compared to causes of illnesses like these are never lacking in the history of a city. [...] Demolitions and replacements of buildings occur in the course of the most peaceful development of a city. A city is thus a priori unsuited for a comparison of this sort with a mental organism. (Freud 1978, 71)

In *Chimera*, the plot itself becomes the site of an excavation, with scattered pieces of information and hints resembling "fragments found in the floor of an excavation trench. Some proved to be nothing more than flakes of oxidized bronze, green with Verdigris and without form of substance. Others were treasure" (Mawer 1989, 34). The ancient town is repeatedly anthropomorphised to demonstrate both the viability of the past as well as to accentuate the parallel between Lucri's "fossil skeleton" (Mawer 1989, 43) and the process of dissecting David Hewison's life and past. The process of excavation proves to be radical, if not brutal, at some points: "Over the decades, like anatomists flaying a corpse, the archaeologists had meticulously stripped the promontory of its skin of soil to lay bare the bones and sinews of the ancient city, the shadowy structure of its houses and streets" (Mawer 1989, 42). As one of the characters points out: "[t]he problem with archaeology, the thing that has always worried me, is that whatever you try to understand you end up destroying" (Mawer 1989, 146). Therefore, as the story itself unravels, the narrator, Anthony, and the readers excavate David's past sins, with results that are as disturbing as they are tragic.

8.5 Thematisation of Catholicism

The peculiar historical and spatial connectivity of *Chimera* is underlaid by a number of direct and indirect references to morality, spirituality, and belief. The novel's preoccupation with ethical questions follows the blueprint of classical tragedy in which characters are made to face a host of moral questions, ranging from killing to adultery and even incest. The narration also repeatedly highlights the fact that both the protagonists, i.e. Anthony Lessing and David Hewison, belong, albeit reluctantly and almost unwillingly, to a long family tradition of Catholicism. The religion is compared to a hereditary disease haunting the family line and manifesting itself in strange ways (Mawer 1989, 31). David, almost as if to foreshadow his considerable feelings of guilt, is "bereft of faith perhaps", but "still looking for a confessor" (Mawer 1989, 31). He also admits that he substituted his faith with his relationship to Lara, which he likens to "a spiritual experience" (Mawer 1989, 31). Anthony, on the other hand, commits to his "residual" Catholicism, with "something of the form and the moral framework but little of the spiritual belief" (Mawer 1989, 31). David's inherent Catholic morality also acts as an incentive to finance the archaeological dig in Vetrano. By recovering the lost Etruscan town of Lucri, David intends to expiate the sins connected with his involvement in the war there. Whether it is his part in the killing of forty local men as an act of retribution for the failed operation he led, his killing of the husband of his lover, Clara, or his marriage to his own daughter remains obscure, but what is clear is that he sees his mission as "an offering to the people of Vetrano" (Mawer 1989, 90), who "were nothing, a people without significance, without a history" until the finding of Lucri (Mawer 1989, 90). In spite of David's dubious proclamations about providing the people of Vetrano with a past, it seems to be mainly his personal mission to wash away his sins in a biblical sense, regardless of the irrationality of such an endeavour.

In his oft-cited lecture "The Englishness of English Literature" (1996), Peter Ackroyd, who has devoted a great deal of his writing to the influence of *genius loci* on English national identity, claims that, contrary to contemporary belief, there is such a thing as the English spirit or genius (Ackroyd 1995, 12). Despite the contemporary distaste for cultural aspects tinged with nationalistic, imperialist, and colonialist undertones, Ackroyd proclaims the existence and even the virtues of Englishness. As one of the vital aspects of the English tradition, he emphasises the residues of Catholic thinking, which he envisions as an irrational and dynamic and visionary part of English consciousness (Ackroyd 1995, 18–19), often confronted and diminished if not entirely annihilated by English criticism representing a "form of secular Protestantism" (Ackroyd 1995, 17). In Ackroyd's view, "Catholicism tends to emphasise the significance of authority and historical tradition, whereas Protestantism emphasises the moral value of individual experience" (Ackroyd 1995, 17). Applied to the two protagonists of *Chimera*, David and Anthony, one can almost see them standing in an opposition, representing the diminishing grip of the Catholic strand within the family. The residual Catholicism of both characters, as seen from the perspective introduced tentatively by Ackroyd, partly elucidates the motivation behind their rather disturbing actions. David, as a member of the older generation and therefore possibly the one with a tighter connection to his belief, envisions his role as a protector of the people of the village and their past, as a man ridden with guilt spending "a lifetime and a fortune trying to absolve himself" (Mawer 1989, 91), whereas Anthony is more concerned with finding his own place in the world, using his uncle as a source of inspiration and ultimately disposing of him and replacing him in a mythical fashion.

The prominence of the excavation site as the central (spatial) conceit of the novel is proved by its ability to draw parallels between the characters and their behaviour, but it also highlights analogies between the characters and the cultural and historical context, namely the clash between the Etruscan and the Roman cultures. The Roman culture, a parallel to the German occupation of Italy, invaded and subjugated the Etruscans, much like the imperious nature of David and Anthony and their domination of people and physical spaces. Mawer gives such prominence to the spatial poetics that it often seems as if though the characters are mere extensions of the places and spaces rather than the other way round. *Chimera* opens up a whole range of historical, existential, psychological, and even ontological questions on the background of a careful dissection of the treatment of a place.

Both David and later Anthony are aware of the intricate web of both tangible and intangible spatial relations that underlie the landscape of Vetrano and repeatedly refer them back to its mythical, pagan past. *Chimera*'s emphasis on the intersection of its temporal and spatial aspects calls for the application of various interdisciplinary approaches that have recently dominated the field of literary studies (Peraldo 2016, 1). One of these approaches, psychogeography, is characterised as a literary study of the "relationship between the urban environment and the behaviour of its inhabitants" (Coverley 2018, 18) by one of its key proponents, Merlin Coverley. Although *Chimera* may not be characterised as a fully-fledged urban novel, it is possible to analyse it from the point of view of psychogeography because some of its aspects adhere to the pivotal aspects of psychogeographic inquiry, such as the explicit connection between the past and the present, the evocative landscape, and the physical and metaphorical archaeological investigation of the past. While both Ackroyd and Coverley refer mainly to a mental and abstract landscape underlying the physical one, *Chimera* revolves mainly around the archaeological uncovering of the physical site from the past, a lost Etruscan town. The re-discovered town of Lucri acts both as an expression of spatial and historical unity and as a symbol of the careful exposure of layers and layers of lost, forgotten, or deliberately concealed parts of the past with "the archaeologists painstakingly peeling away successive deposits and exposing a new truth at each level" (Mawer 1989, 91).

8.6 Place and Space in *Chimera*

Mawer's inclusion of archaeology as both the subject matter and a narrative technique echoes the preoccupation of several interconnected approaches to literary space. Firstly, psychogeography, whose field of research is, however, almost exclusively connected to urban settings and, more importantly, to London. Although this approach suffered a form of backlash, mostly because of its previous overuse within the context of any literary depiction of London (Coverley 2018, 31), it is experiencing a revival, however, its predominantly London focus is contrary to the needs of its application to *Chimera* (Coverley 2018, 142–3). Psychogeography and its limitations motivated the creation of two new recent approaches: *deep topography*, developed by Nick Papadimitriou (Self), and *deep locational criticism*, delineated by Jason Finch in his *Deep Locational Criticism: Imaginative Place in Literary Research and Teaching* (2016). Both of these approaches analyse the effects of the environment, both natural and man-made, on the human psyche (Finch 2016, 199). The central position of place as the centre of the study echoes the approach of geo-centred geocriticism of Bertrand Westphal. Even more importantly, both deep topography and deep locational criticism involve archaeological research as one of the key aspects of their respective fields of research. At the same time, both of these approaches study real places and their artistic reflections. They both share some aspects with the axis of study of *Chimera*, which is set in a real region, albeit in a fictional town. Therefore, their application to the text may concern only selected aspects and serve mostly as additional sources of analysis.

One of the ways in which *Chimera* addresses the notion of places and their mutual conditioning with human activities, lives, and minds is the depiction of the different attitudes of the Etruscans and the Romans to the landscape. The stark contrast between the Etruscan approach, which results in organic union, and the harsh interventions of the Romans, is mirrored by the effects of the German occupation and by contemporary, industrialised approaches to the landscape. This line of interpretation reflects ecocritical concerns, which, like geocritical approaches, highlight the intersections of human consciousness and existence with its environment. No longer limited to the study of the natural world, ecocritical thinking calls for an inclusive approach that also involves "less obviously 'natural' landscapes" (Armbruster and Wallace 2001, 4). From the point of view of Mawer's novel, some of the most striking thematisations of humankind's approach to the environment are the references to the fundamental differences between the Romans and the Etruscans in their attitude to the environment. The Etruscans are repeatedly described as being able to achieve harmonious union with the natural world: "It was impossible to say whether the narrow gap which broached this defence had been cut or whether it was natural, so intimately did these distant people know their landscape, so perfectly could they mould it. Here there was no intrusion on the land: nature and man's work seemed an organic whole" (Mawer 1989, 59). In contrast to these gentle, balanced alterations of the landscape, the Roman interventions are shown to be conspicuous and markedly domineering. From the point of view of an ecocritical reading of these two contrasting approaches to the landscape and the natural world, an equally critical approach is assumed towards modern Italian infrastructure: "Conquest my dear fellow, pure colonial conquest. The white Americans did it with their railways, the Romans did it with their roads; just as the present Italian governments are conquering the South with the *autostrada*" (Mawer 1989, 256).

The disparities between the Etruscan and Roman cultures are also explored from the perspective of dominance and submission. The marked contrast developed between the Etruscan and the Roman element thematises the aspects of dominance and submission, destruction and creation, guilt and forgiveness. Expressed mainly through different parallels, these aspects illustrate a number of connections between human consciousness and its environment, which is the basis of "interdisciplinary, multicultural, and international" (Glotfelty 1996, xxv) ecocritical study as stipulated by Cheryll Glotfelty in *The Ecocriticism Reader: Landmarks in Literary Ecology* (1996). Pioneering the approach proposed by Armbruster and Wallace, Glotfelty voices the common preoccupation of the contemporary humanities as well as other scientific fields – their effort to overcome a fragmented vision of the world and replace it with an inclusive and highly complex interdisciplinary perspective. Although Glotfelty's message is primarily directed at humanities scholars, whom she urges to educate themselves in science so that they are able to meet the requirements of the interdisciplinary nature of the ecocritical approach, similar efforts are to be found in more exact fields of science, such as geography. The continuous merging of individual scientific fields, but also of science and art, suggests a continued effort to overcome a traditional, rather rigid division based on the dualistic tendencies referred to by Armbruster and Wallace. Tim Creswell, the author of *Place: An Introduction* (2004), an overview of a central and yet shockingly complicated fundamental concept of both geography and the humanities and social sciences, points out a similar strategy in writing about places while trying to engage with them in their complexity (Creswell 2004, 19, 23). Creswell understands "place" as a way of human existence, or being in the world (Creswell 2004, 18), and determines humanistic geographers, neo-humanists, and phenomenological philosophers as the proponents of this stance (Creswell 2004, 56).

Chimera illustrates this approach to place as the way in which the protagonists interact with their surroundings reflects their approach to existence in general. The characters' motivation, behaviour, desires, needs, and qualities are expressed through their complex relationship to places and the way in which they interact with their surroundings. David Hewison's possessive, controlling nature is therefore revealed mainly by means of his treatment of the excavation site. He is seen striding through the place "like a senior officer visiting regimental lines, with head thrust forward and hands clasped behind his back" (Mawer 1989, 41). The narration repeatedly personifies the excavated town, "the fossil skeleton of Lucri" (Mawer 1989, 43), referring to its "bones and cavities" (Mawer 1989, 60), and thus highlights both its animate, human-like nature and David's tendency to manipulate it, which extends to human characters as well. Largely because their relationship began when Lara was very young, Anthony views Lara not only as David's "possession", but even as his "creation" (Mawer 1989, 179). What motivates his treatment of the excavation site, besides something "more than a fascination: a light of pure possession" (Mawer 1989, 42), is yet another aspect of its multifaceted symbolism, its acting as an embodiment of the past.

Hewison insists on enlivening the place, claiming that "[i]magination is the key" (Mawer 1989, 45). Not only does he wish to put himself into "some kind of context, any context" (Mawer 1989, 46), thus severing ties with his family, but he also wants to take "back his own past as well" (Mawer 1989, 46). To control an excavation site, then, is to possess its past, and even one's own past, and perhaps to erase past wrongdoings, such as killing the father of one's wife or committing incest. Why Hewison sympathises with the Etruscans and why the Etruscan village mediates Hewison's past is explained mainly by means of their shared liminal character: "He [...] loved the pieces, and loved the strange people who had made them, perhaps because he saw in them a people who, like him, had not quite fitted into the world which they had inhabited" (Mawer 1989, 52). Moreover, Hewison searches "for a past" (Mawer 1989, 108) and decides to dignify these unknown, unseen, underrepresented people with the same. At the same time, he wants to determine a new identity, a new life that would be his alone, separate from his family (Mawer 1989, 77). Given the parallels between the characters of David and Anthony, both the former's actual archaeological research and the latter's metaphorical probe into his uncle's past may be seen as efforts to possess (and manipulate) the past as well as to contextualise or recontextualise oneself.

Chimera is Mawer's literary debut, but it already displays all the vital aspects of his literary contribution: describing the essence of the intangible through his apt use of complex spatial motifs and metaphors. His writing often revolves around and contributes to an exceptional unity of space, place, time, overall aesthetics, and the characters' mental processes. The resulting intersection of the symbolic, the mental, the physical, the aesthetic, and the experiential may be regarded as emblematic of Mawer's poetics.

The qualities of *Chimera*'s protagonists, perhaps most obviously their bilingualism – they switch between English and Italian – demonstrate Mawer's tendency to mark his characters, as well as the communities to which they belong, with liminality. Mawer's plotlines revolve mostly around historical transitions, involving territories, cultures, religions, communities and, obviously, individuals. The prevailing liminal quality is therefore the result of a complex interplay of parallels and reflections, resulting in a detailed study of character as well as a convincing portrayal of the place and space of the period and its cultural and historical development.

This chapter seeks to establish *Chimera* as a pioneering work of Simon Mawer's poetics and, in particular, his treatment of place and its pivotal position in the context of his writing. The way in which he approaches different places in his fiction is synchronised and synergised with all other aspects of his creation. This complex treatment of the category of place requires an equally wide-ranging, inclusive and interdisciplinary set of analytical tools, exemplifying Eric Prieto's call for an inclusive approach to the geocentric study of literature (Prieto 2011, 25). The way in which the text of the novel engages with the mutual intersections, conditioning and constructing of culture and nature reflects an ecocritical perspective while closely following Prieto's call to challenge the positioning of humanity "outside or above the natural order" (Mawer 1989, 25).

Mawer typically employs a prominent spatial motif – in this case it is the archaeological excavation of the ancient Etruscan town of Lucri. Mawer's choice of the scientific field of archaeology, with its natural connection to the past, exemplifies Mawer's penchant for using different kinds of parallelism in his fiction in order to project the major themes of the novel, such as the relationship between past and present, human and place, or moral dilemmas. On closer inspection, the conception of archaeology in *Chimera* quickly outgrows the role of leitmotif and assumes the role of both symbol and narrative approach. In terms of literary criticism, the discipline that responds the most readily to this conception is *psychogeography* and, from a more contemporary perspective, *deep topography*. At the same time, it resonates well with the common denominator of both ecocriticism and geocriticism, which is their shared call for inclusivity and interdisciplinarity. The novel provides a unique perspective on place, which it simultaneously presents from a number of different angles. The prevailing perspective may be classified as a phenomenological one, in that the place in question outgrows the limits of a singular, clearly demarcated entity and becomes a universal expression of spatial experience.

The cyclical structuring of the plot, emphasised by a number of references to literary works concerned with the cyclical nature of time, together with the intricate interplay of analogies and parallels, enhances and contributes to the mythical dimension of the narrative, which can be interpreted as either a source of narrative framework or as a return to pre-classical, archaic ontology. The unique treatment of spatial aspects of the novel, together with the dense complex of parallels and analogies that form the thematic component of the plot, contribute to *Chimera*'s multi-layered identity, which is reminiscent of the significance of its title. Mawer's first work is part war novel, part romance, and part historical novel, posing a series of gnoseological, ontological, and ethical questions. *Chimera* thus heralds the future course of Mawer's creation, which may be perceived as a phenomenological probe into the perception of place, space, and time.

9. Thematising Science and the Region of Central Europe in Simon Mawer's *Mendel's Dwarf*

This chapter presents *Mendel's Dwarf* (1997), the first of Mawer's novels to be set in central Europe. Although the novel cannot be said to develop the spatial element to the same extent as the rest of the works analysed in this monograph, it nevertheless deserves attention because it embodies other vital aspects of Mawer's creation. First and foremost, it introduces perhaps one of the most intriguing and complex protagonists Mawer ever conceived. Benedict Lambert is a highly idiosyncratic character in general and even more so in the context of Mawer's work. He, unlike a plethora of other characters, is not characterised by means of and in connection with the places and spaces around him.[59] His part in the plot is complemented by science as a theme and a motif; it even seeps into the textual aspects of the novel, which at times reads like a scholarly paper rather than a novel. As he is wont to do, Mawer introduces another, parallel plotline centred around the life of Gregor Mendel, a brilliant scientist, a real historical figure, and a distant relative of the fictitious Benedict. This part of the story is already endowed with typical elements of Mawer's poetics, including its prominent spatial aspect. He accurately and atmospherically describes Brno, the second biggest city of what is now the Czech Republic, and its highly multicultural life in the days of the Austro-Hungarian Empire during the lifetime of Gregor Mendel. *Mendel's Dwarf* thematises science in general, genetic research and its theoretical, practical, and ethical implications, but also the space

59 If, however, Mawer employs a spatial element for the sake of characterisation, it is strikingly apt: "Miss Piercey, lying on my bed again, lying in the light of day seeping through the curtains into my underground lair, lying with her smile, telling the truth with her closed and averted eyes" (Mawer 1997, 225–226).

of central Europe, which has since become one of the main focuses of Mawer's work.

Having been familiar with it for over 25 years (Vaughan 2018), Mawer claims to admire the turbulent history of the region, stating that his "heart is in the Czech Republic" (Lauder 2015). Until the publication of *The Glass Room* (2009), *Mendel's Dwarf* (1997) had been considered to be his most critically acclaimed novel, having been a finalist for the Los Angeles Times Book Prize for 1999, longlisted for the Booker Prize, and selected (alongside Jim Crace's *Quarantine*)[60] for The New York Public Library's 43rd annual Books to Remember from 1998. The inspiration for the novel was Mawer's first trip to the Czech Republic, when, arriving by train from Vienna, Brno was the first place he saw. As Mawer points out in his 2010 interview with Marek Sečkař, his previous knowledge of the city was limited to two pieces of information: both Gregor Mendel and BREN light machine guns came from there. He came to find out more about Mendel and quickly realised that the material was suitable for a novel.

9.1 Benedict Lambert – the Protagonist

Although Mendel's biography alone would probably not suffice to fuel the plot of an entire novel, Mawer considers him to be the "archetype of a scientist whose ideas are ahead of his time" (Mawer 1998). His research was neglected by the academy, which, at the time was not able to embrace the visionary potential of Mendel's work. But it was not only his contemporaries' ignorance of Mendel that led to Mawer's preoccupation with the Catholic priest. Mendel's legacy is a complex and intricate one and Mawer chose to highlight this potential by employing a slightly more complex narrative trajectory along with his trademark development of parallel plots and juxtaposition of two storylines. As a result, we see Gregor Mendel's storyline interwoven with that of his great-great-great nephew, the doctor Benedict Lambert. Mendel is portrayed as the inconspicuous founder of modern genetics, relentlessly conducting experiments with garden peas, most likely unaware that his work was "one of the greatest achievements of the human intellect and imagination" (Mawer 2005, "Science in Literature"). The protagonist

60 The popularity of the Czech translation of *Mendel's Dwarf* is attributed to the success of *The Glass Room*, whose translation actually preceded that of *Mendel's Dwarf* (Mandys 2010).

of the second storyline is Dr Benedict Lambert. Benedict is a distant relative of Mendel, also a molecular biologist, and is searching for the gene at the root of achondroplasia, one of the most common types of dwarfism. Benedict happens to be the carrier of the gene that causes the aforementioned condition. His sharp, often darkly humorous quips underline the unease of those around Benedict, who are unable to disregard his condition and see him as a human being: "[p]eople seem amazed when they discover not only that I am not mentally retarded, but that I am actually more intelligent than they are" (Mawer 1997, 47). Most of the people are rather inclined to dehumanise him, perceiving him only through the prism of his condition, a victim of fate who is brave enough to name and even study it.[61] The grotesque nature of such a distorted perception of a human being is accentuated by Benedict's acerbic observations:

> The chairman rose to his feet, beaming like a circus ringmaster, and called them to silence. 'I am sure all of us appreciate Ben's coming here and sharing his insights with us.' He smiled down at me. People craned to see. 'I hope he won't mind my saying that he is not only a great Mendelian but...' Did he really look to me for agreement? I fear that he did. '... also a very brave man. Ladies and gentlemen, I give you Doctor Ben Lambert!' (Mawer 1997, 5)

Benedict's ill-fated romance with librarian Jean Piercey ("Jean. Don't laugh." (Mawer 1997, 76)) gives him the opportunity to "play God" (Mawer 1997, 250) for once and to control the tyranny of chance. In order for her to conceive a child, she needs to undergo in vitro fertilisation, with Benedict providing the genetic information and also manipulating it by selecting embryos laden with the chromosome that causes his own condition. How will he decide, and can he usurp the tyranny of chance? Can he play God? Is he entitled to do so? The novel abounds in questions, both implied and posed, often of a rhetorical nature. A number of chapters conclude with one or even more of them: "Can you possess genes for genius?" (Mawer 1997, 30); "Do appearances tell anything? Who knows, whoever knows what goes on beneath?" (Mawer 1997, 46).

61 The reviews of the novel show a curious penchant for highlighting Benedict's otherness and fail to see him as a complex human character. He is repeatedly portrayed as a freak of nature and his humanity, e.g. his sexuality, is trivialised to the point of caricature and his "brilliant" mind is repeatedly contrasted with his "misshapen form" as if the discrepancy was truly surprising. See e.g. Robin Marantz Henig's review for *The Washington Post* or Pavel Mandys's 2010 review of the Czech translation for *iLiteratura*.

As the novel switches between the storylines of the two protagonists, the reader realises that Mawer may be less interested in them than in the moral, historical, and philosophical effects of their work (Prose 1998). The novel invites the reader to ponder on the nature of scientific endeavour, opening up the ethical, moral, and metaphysical dimensions of modern genetic research, prompting some reviewers to label it a piece of "speculative fiction" (Askew 2000), or "science fiction" (Kohn 1997). Mawer himself gave some insight into the thought process behind the eventual organisation of the novel in a short piece published on his website. He claims to have deliberately juxtaposed the two parallel storylines in order to highlight the parallels and contrasts between the societies of both protagonists and the development of science, particularly genetics. According to Mawer, Benedict epitomises "the fall from grace of modern biology", which, while employing a sterile, factual, and highly intertextual academic discourse (with the novel adopting the same style of expression) has failed to prevent its own deformities, contortions, and blind branches of evolution, such as eugenics. Mawer claims that *Mendel's Dwarf* is possibly the most likely of his novels to include a moral agenda, having been written with a higher moral purpose in mind (Lauder 2015). He otherwise denies the responsibility of authors to produce literary works that inspire profound changes in society. The task of authors is to reflect society, not to instruct it (Lauder 2015).

9.2 Thematisation of Science in *Mendel's Dwarf*

Science proves to be a rich source of inspiration for Mawer's work, as well as its dominant motif and theme. Aside from historical sciences, there are two key scientific areas Mawer frequently incorporates in his writing. The first is biology, especially genetic research, which he revisits in *Mendel's Dwarf* and *The Glass Room*, but also in his latest novel, *Ancestry*. The second is nuclear physics, which is most prominently featured in *The Girl Who Fell from the Sky*, *Tightrope,* and *Prague Spring*. *Mendel's Dwarf* manages to incorporate science even into the language of the novel, parts of which are written in the form of scholarly papers, including their extensive use of footnotes and references. Although the novel addresses complex ethical and philosophical questions connected with the discussion of science, it also emphasises the disturbing clarity with which nature addresses us: "The Genetic code: It is not a code. A code is created in order to deceive. No one was trying to hide anything, no God was playing games, creating a conundrum, proposing a puzzle, writing a rebus" (Mawer 1997, 120). Mawer attempts to pair this relative simplicity of nature's communication with the "mystery of the world" (Prose 1998). As Mawer stresses in *Mendel's Dwarf*, it is precisely the inexorable logic of Mendel's contribution to science that has in fact generated a great deal of doubt and uncertainty as he "began to tease apart the very fabric of nature just as Bohr and others pulled apart the fabric of matter" (Mawer 2005). The novel thus illustrates Mawer's persuasion that uncertainty is at the heart of the modern human condition, simultaneously projected and reflected by modern science and literature alike.

9.3 The Space of Central Europe

If there is yet another typical aspect of Mawer's work to be found in *Mendel's Dwarf*, it is his ability to produce texts whose elegant finish and attention to detail evoke a self-assured grasp of the topic as well as a keen sense of space and place. Mawer's discovery of central Europe and its complex history is projected into the way *Mendel's Dwarf* approaches the nature of the place, which is done mainly by means of a number of spatial, temporal, linguistic, and historical parallels:

> I walked around the long south wall of the convent, toward the gate. Above everything – [...] stood the Spielberg Fortress, where the Austrian Emperors used to keep their political prisoners. It is interesting to reflect that while the secrets of genetics were being revealed for the first time down there in the back garden of the monastery, the secrets of democracy and subversion were being revealed for the thousandth time in the dungeons on the hill above: nature, both human and plant, under torture. Did he know about it? Of course he did. And what did he *think* about it, eh? In 1858 the Habsburgs abandoned the Spielberg as a political prison, but you can't take the stain away from a place like that. Within a century the Gestapo was putting it back to use. (Mawer 1997, 9)

A similar tendency can be observed in *Gregor Mendel: Planting the Seeds of Genetics* (2006), a non-fiction monograph which was published to accompany the two-year US tour of an exhibition created by the Field Museum in Chicago, which ended in September 2008. Approximately two thirds of the book is dedicated to a biography of Gregor Mendel and his scientific contribution, and the final part of the book connects his legacy to further developments in genetics. Mawer's gift for including didactic aspects in his texts, which is disguised by the elegance of his writing, prevents him from running the risk of being pedantic. In the following extract, he evokes the hybrid, liminal identity of a place situated in central Europe to readers who might not be familiar with it:

> The village stands at the very centre of Europe, as far from the Baltic as from the Mediterranean, as far from the Atlantic as from the Ural Mountains. In Mendel's day it was called Heinzendorf and it lay in Austrian Silesia, a province of the Austrian Empire. Nowadays the name is Hynčice and it lies in the Czech Republic. Here everything has two names. Even Mendel has two names. Known to world as Gregor Mendel, he was in fact baptized Johann. (Mawer 2006, 17)

Mawer's writing, both fiction and non-fiction, pays homage to the region's turbulent historical, linguistic, cultural, social, and political development. Its complex historical development and its positioning within the centre of competing cultural influences are projected into a unique set of qualities that feed its creative and artistic potential. The diversity of its cultural aspects indicates a tendency towards a plurality of (sometimes competing) identities and narratives. Seen from the perspective of geocriticism, a field of study focused on spatial aspects of literature, it displays an inclination towards Westphal's bifurcation and entropy (Westphal 2011, 20), which is further described and exemplified in the chapters dealing with Mawer's duo of spy novels – *The Girl Who Fell from the Sky* and *Tightrope*. The freshness and aptness of his descriptions contribute to the deepening of the reader's understanding of the sense of place and identification with the inhabitants (past and present) of the area. *Mendel's Dwarf* serves as a comprehensive introduction to a number of motifs, themes, concerns, and settings that Mawer often revisits in his works. The inspiration for the novel, namely the author's visit to the Tugendhat Villa in Brno, led Mawer to write another novel, which was a condensation of his poetics and a breakthrough in terms of his popularity, *The Glass Room* (2009).

10. *The Glass Room*: Housing Space, Architecture, and History[62]

The Glass Room (2009) marks both a turning point in Simon Mawer's writing career and to some extent also its culmination. Prior to the publication of *The Glass Room*, Mawer was little known by the general reading public. The Booker Prize shortlisting of the novel marked a watershed in Mawer's career and turned him into a critically and commercially successful novelist (Cooke 2012). *The Glass Room* revisits a number of signature aspects of Mawer's works, such as a tempestuous historical period, a culturally and geopolitically highly complex area[63], and protagonists whose identities are intertwined with radical historical, social and cultural transformation. Finally, and perhaps most importantly, the novel introduces a spectacular central conceit, which simultaneously concentrates the central dilemma of the novel and embodies the essence of its poetics. It is the eponymous Glass Room, a spacious room with walls made entirely of glass, whose stern geometrical frame braves the course of the tumultuous twentieth century in central Europe[64] and shelters the histories of individuals against the backdrop of this traumatic period.

62 Parts of this chapter were published by Tereza Topolovská in the scholarly journal *Crossroads. A Journal of English Studies* in a special volume entitled "House and Home in Literature" in 2022.

63 For more information concerning Mawer's treatment of historical details, see Topolovská, Tereza. "Through the Looking Glass: Space and Place in Simon Mawer's *The Girl Who Fell from the Sky*". In *Places and Spaces of Popular Imagination*, edited by Šárka Bubíková and Olga Roebuck. Krakow: Jagiellonian University Press, 2021.

64 At the time of its writing, it was Mawer's third venture into the area of central Europe, more specifically the realm of where the Czech Republic is to be found nowadays, with one fiction book, *Mendel's Dwarf* (1997) and one non-fiction work, *Gregor Mendel: Planting the Seeds of Genetics* (2006), situated there as well, only to be followed by his latest excursion into the tormented Czech past, *Prague Spring* (2018).

This chapter studies the ways in which *The Glass Room* develops the leitmotifs of Mawer's literary creation, i.e. his treatment of history and space and place. Mawer's approach to history, mostly recent history, inspires an enquiry into the concept of historical fiction and its contemporary understanding. The main focus of the interpretation, however, is the novel's unique spatial poetics, which echoes the topocentric qualities of Mawer's novels whilst presenting a singular portrayal of a piece of Modernist architecture. Out of a host of possible directions of research this study will take the two most prominent of these, firstly examining the relation of houses and historical narratives within the context of the spatial poetics of *The Glass Room*. Secondly, the aesthetic and ethical purism of the ideals behind Modernist architecture will be contrasted with the realities their materialisation, the fictional Landauer House was forced to endure.

10.1 The Modernist Inspiration

In spite of Mawer's thinly veiled attempts to fictionalise the setting of *The Glass Room*, the novel's depiction of the fate of the Landauer House and the family of its first owners bears a striking resemblance to the Tugendhat House and its original owners. The Tugendhat House, which was granted UNESCO World Heritage status in 2001, was designed by the German architect Mies van der Rohe between 1928 and 1930, and is considered, together with his Barcelona Pavilion, to be the peak of his European career and the embodiment of the ideals of the modernist conception of (domestic) architecture as well the articulation of the principles of the International Style (Davies 2018, 132). The disastrous impact of both WW2 and its aftermath, with its Jewish owners first being forced to flee Nazi persecution, then the house being confiscated by the Gestapo, subsequently hit by a bomb, and later seized by the Communist government and turned into a gym, was compounded by several highly unprofessional and insensitive restorations (Černá and Černoušková 2011; Davies 2018, 132; Zimmerman 2009, 45–51). Before extensive restoration, which took place between 2010 and 2012, the historical site was known as "one of the most grievous casualties suffered by the modern movement during its post-1933 extremity" (Schulze and Windhorst 2012, 135). Nowadays, the villa has become an incredibly popular historical site, with visits needing to be booked months in advance. The popularity of Mawer's novel plays an integral part in the general renown of the place.

It has inspired both a successful theatre adaptation and a less critically acclaimed film, *The Affair* (2019) (Lodge 2021), which was shot in the villa.

Mawer acknowledges the role of the Tugendhat House in the conception of the novel; upon visiting it in the early 1990s he saw the house as "emblematic of the Czechoslovakia of the interwar period – a place of progressive ideas, of culture, of light and openness – and the dreadful double disaster of Nazism followed by Soviet Communism" (Rawsthorn 2012). In the same interview, commenting on the reopening of the Tugendhat House to the public, he claimed that given its unique qualities and its narrative capacity, "the appeal for a novelist was obvious" (Rawsthorn 2012). Irrespective of the inspiration for the conception of the novel and the inclusion of a number of historical details based on extensive research, Mawer insists on the fabricated nature of the story, cemented by the employment of a generic toponym "Město", which simply means "town" in Czech (Mawer 2009, 75)[65], his use of fictional names, and some degree of deviation of the Landauers' plotline from the history of the Tugendhat family. In spite of these efforts, the choice of subject matter – the historical and spatial setting of *The Glass Room* – has been criticised by some of the members of the Tugendhat family.[66] The dispute over Mawer's treatment of history illustrates possible reservations concerning his classification amongst historical novelists, which he voices himself, and also reflects some tendencies of contemporary historical fiction.

10.2 *The Glass Room* from the Perspective of Historical Fiction

The 2009 shortlist for the Man Booker Prize for Fiction, which included *The Glass Room*, consisted entirely of works of historical fiction, testify-

65 In his 2010 interview with Marek Sečkař for *Host,* Mawer claimed that he was dissatisfied with the decision of Lukáš Novák, the author of the widely acclaimed Czech translation of the novel, to replace Mawer's neutral "Město" with Brno. For Novák, the obvious referentiality of Město to Brno outweighed Mawer's desire to "keep a formal distance".

66 Professor Daniela Hammer Tugendhat, one of descendants of Greta and Fritz Tugendhat, repeatedly expressed her dissatisfaction with the novel, accusing Mawer of robbing the family of their history. Upon the occasion of her lecture "Das Haus Tugendhat und Seine Bewohner" which took place in The Ministry of Culture on 1st October 2012, she insisted that the author should have contacted and consulted the family in the first place. In any case, he should have either avoided the history of the family altogether or abandoned his poetic licence and remained truthful to their actual history (Tugendhat 2012).

ing to the growing popularity of historical fiction. The media coverage of the shortlist opted for a critical perspective, accusing the judges of Anglocentrism and of being "reactionary" and "backward-looking" (Miller 2009). One of the judges, literary journalist and novelist Lucasta Miller explained, in her 2009 article defending the choice of the nominations, that the novels, in spite of being set in the sixteenth, nineteenth and twentieth centuries, did not linger in the past and were considered for the prize because of the "depth of sophistication and not the genre". She further declared that the quality the novelists shared was a uniquely individual voice, which contributed to the diversification of different approaches to historical fiction, and proved that although "the average historical fiction may be easier to pull off than the average novel, simply because you don't have to invent so much. [...] The best transcend genre, adding something that a nonfiction treatment could not" (Miller 2009).

Texts with similar qualities have been subjected to the scrutiny of literary scholars who focus on contemporary historical fiction, such as Elodie Rousselot or Jerome De Groot. De Groot is particularly interested in the nature of the narrativisation of the past and asserts that fiction, and novels in particular, are no longer perceived as merely fictitious and therefore dubious (De Groot 2016, 6). Quite the contrary, throughout his monographs, De Groot repeatedly demonstrates that narrativisation conditions the very understanding of the notion of pastness and thus different fictitious representations of the past act as highly useful tools for its investigation.

In accordance with this new understanding of the role of historical fiction, Mawer actively rejects the label of historical novelist (Flood 2016)[67] and stresses mainly the liberating properties of fiction that grant him poetic licence (Crown 2009). He researches the period detail meticulously whilst simultaneously adding to the dynamism of his novels' free reimagining of the past by mixing fact and fiction.[68] He thus explores "the dissonance and displacement between then and now, making the past recognisable but simultaneously authentically unfamiliar" (De Groot 2010, 3). Although his work is rarely mentioned in the recently published academic overviews of contemporary British literature, Mawer may be classified amongst authors who, like him, focus on historical

67 He paradoxically did so while receiving the 2016 Walter Scott Prize for Historical Fiction for *Tightrope* (2015), the critically well-received sequel to the spy novel *The Girl Who Fell from the Sky* (2012) (Flood, 2016).

68 Mawer frequently projects his personal experience into his writing (Pengelly 2015).

themes, narrativising the past and analysing and problematising the parallels between the past and the present, which echoes the preoccupation of the contemporary genre of neo-historical fiction. Elodie Rousselot connects the recent resurgence of historical fiction with "critical re-appraisal of specific historical periods and of their social, cultural, and political contexts" (Rousselot 2014, 1). *The Glass Room* invites its readers to relive and, more importantly, review the key moments of twentieth century Czech history – the period of the First Czechoslovak Republic, Nazi and Communist rule, the almost-liberal period of the 1960s, and the early and newly democratic 1990s. Rather than stressing the difference between the present and the past, the narrative steers towards a highlighting of the parallels between them, which Mawer considers to be one of the dominant concerns of his fiction since the similarities mediate an understanding of the present and condition our approach to the future (Flood 2016).

10.3 The Spatial Poetics of *The Glass Room*

Typically, the setting of the novel is the chief element of Mawer's poetics. His novels convincingly and self-assuredly inhabit space and time while echoing the mental processes of the protagonists and accentuating the overall thematic focus of his works. Both the temporal and spatial settings of Mawer's fiction are highly prone to profound and often rather radical transformation. Therefore, their common denominator is a profound social, historical, and cultural change, as a result of which the lives of the protagonists undergo an enormous upheaval. In the case of *The Glass Room*, the first idyllic years of the family and their new house are contrasted with the ominous atmosphere before the Munich Agreement and the German Protectorate. The following citation is taken from the chapter dedicated to the housewarming party and its atmospheric depiction of an impending storm, symbolising the looming war years: "They crowd into the space of the Glass Room like passengers on the observation deck of a luxury liner. Some of them maybe peering through the windows onto the pitching surface of the city but, in their muddle of Czech and German, almost all are ignorant of the cold outside and the gathering storm clouds, the first sign of the tempest that is coming" (Mawer 2009, 78). The Landauers are forced to flee because of their Jewish origin and their house is confiscated by the Gestapo and turned into a laboratory focusing on the study of eugenics.

Mawer comments on the striking change of circumstances by developing an equally striking contrast by juxtaposing two expressions of appreciation of the Glass Room. The first one is uttered by Liesel and Viktor upon their first visit to the almost complete room and refers to the liberating effect created by its space and light:

> Liesel and Viktor stood and marvelled at it. It had become a palace of light, light bouncing off the chrome pillars, light refulgent on the walls, light glistening on the dew in the garden, light reverberating from the glass. It was though they stood inside a crystal of salt. 'Isn't it wonderful,' she exclaimed, looking round with an expression of amazement. 'You feel so free, so unconstrained. The sensation of space, of all things being possible.' (Mawer 2009, 65)

The second time the same qualities of the Glass Room are praised, the context could not be more different from the first occasion. The room is being inspected by the Nazi scientists who want to transform it into a eugenics laboratory. The significance of the light and space suddenly acquires a shockingly dissimilar dimension: "*Gläzend!* Even more impressive than the photographs: a great open space of a place, almost the entire floor area of the whole building. Open plan. Stahl likes that. Ideal for a laboratory" (Mawer 2009, 218). Later, the house gets almost destroyed during an air raid, and the horrors of war are followed by the stifling rule of the Communist Party. The Landauer family first escapes to Switzerland and later to the United States, while the novel portrays the fate of those who stayed behind, mostly the character of Hana Hanáková, the prototypical incarnation of the femme fatale of Mawer's novels, who tries to protect the house from any further harm.

The mutual influence of the protagonists and their setting creates hybrid or liminal qualities in both, which is often also complemented by a linguistic aspect. Mawer inserts Czech and German words in the English text, illustrating the complementary nature of the characters and their setting by means of their bilingualism: "'Leave Tatínka in peace,' Liba says, ushering the children to their breakfast" (Mawer 2009, 89). Skilful employment of these aspects allows Mawer to create both convincing evocations of periods and places while inspecting their impact upon the identity formation of individual characters as well as cultures (Topolovská 2021).

Mawer's keen sense of place and space and their close connection with character development, and the tumultuous nature of his settings, all resonate with the geocritical approach and, in particular, Bertrand

Westphal's notion of nonequilibrium (Westphal 2011, 19). The choice of Mawer's settings testifies to the creative potential of heterogenising forces, which result in the creation of a rather unstable environment with a tendency towards "bifurcation and entropy" (Westphal 2011, 20). The area of central Europe, with its inherent unrest resulting from the cumulation of cultures, together with the equally unstable Mediterranean, prove to be ideal settings for him, which he further underlines by focusing on threshold historical events and periods. *The Glass Room* exemplifies these tendencies, being set in the heart of Europe in the midst of the turbulent era of the twentieth century. Mawer asserts that central Europe lacks the stability of modern English history, and that this lack has greatly enriched its arts and, most obviously, its architecture (Lauder 2015).

The Glass Room's portrayal of interwar Czechoslovakia stresses the period's focus on innovation, progress, unconstrained freedom, and cultural flowering: "They had already spoken with architects about the new house. (...) But nothing had seemed right for Victor's vision of the future, his desire not to be pinned down by race or creed, his determination to speak Czech as well as German, his insistence on reading *Lidové Noviny*, his talk of *inovace* and *pokrok*, innovation and progress" (Mawer 2009, 20). The Glass Room and the rest of the villa are perceived as a multifaceted metaphor of the era and the whole novel was even enthusiastically lauded as "a rhapsody on the Glass Room of the Landauer Villa and (...) also a rhapsody on the ideals of interwar Czechoslovakia, of the First Czechoslovak Republic" (Higgins 2009). In his 2018 article "Desire as Geopolitics: Reading *The Glass Room* as Central European Fantasy", its author, Jakub Eberle, pointed out that the desirable ideals, such as progress, modernity, and rationality, of the newly formed republic are typically associated, at least in the Central European imagination, with a Western character of society and democracy. Eberle claims that: "the narrative of the novel is grounded in a geopolitical imagination based on the familiar East/West binary, in which modernity, progress, and rationality are coded as Western, while the East is presented as backward, violent, and irrational" (Eberle 2018, 173). The novel operates on the premise of associating the concept of "Westernness" with desirable and accessible qualities and thus fuels the desire of the Czechs to be Western again (Eberle 2018, 174). "Westernness" is apparently too elusive and "this oscillation between desire and disappointment leads to the self-defeating politics of superiority/inferiority, which is so often seen in the region" (Eberle 2018, 172). Although Eberle's analysis of the novel mainly highlights the East/West binary in the light of Lacan's theory of elusive desire, he acknowledges the wider scope of *The Glass Room*'s possible interpretation: "the novel is simultaneously a story about love and loss, hope and aspiration, art and architecture, and even modernity in general" (Eberle 2018, 173). The following part of the chapter will therefore be devoted to the study of the most prominent aspects of its spatial poetics.

The spatial poetics, and in fact the whole narration of *The Glass Room,* is dominated by its double centrality. Firstly, there is the centrality of the house in relation to the narration and secondly, there is the dominant role of the Glass Room within the villa. Mawer employs the archetypal literary device of a building symbolising the history of a community, often employed by writers and even described as universal by some theoreticians (Bachelard 1994, 6). Thus, in *The Glass Room* "a real house effectively becomes the subject of a biography" (Miller 2009). Though the house may survive a precarious period, some of its inhabitants do not, and thus it serves as "a testimonial to our tragedies and our triumphs, to depravity and to all the soaring heights of which humans are capable" (Robertson 2015, 115). The home and its most canonical, archetypal representation, a house, is closely related to the study of place as a category of both scientific research and human understanding (Creswell 2015, 1). Humanistic geographers who stress the mutual conditioning of the category of place and human life, such as Yi-Fu Tuan, have been building upon the works of Martin Heidegger and Gaston Bachelard (Bachelard 1994, 8; Creswell 2015, 39). Heidegger developed the concept of dwelling as the expression of authentic human existence: "Man's relation to locations, and through locations to spaces, inheres in his dwelling. The relationship between man and space is none other than dwelling, strictly thought and spoken" (Heidegger 2011, 157), while Bachelard draws parallels between the role of the house in human life and its employment in literature, stressing the decisive, defining role the house has in the way we perceive other places in life as well as in literature. One of the most noticeable tendencies in fiction is to employ (and exploit) the integrative potential of the enormously potent archetype of the house to narrate social and individual histories. The capacity of the Landauer House from *The Glass Room* to represent the history of a family is "a literary device that has been employed to powerful effect to depict a building that has survived dramatic times, even as some of its inhabitants have not" (Robertson 2015, 94).[69] As Bill Bryson points

69 Robertson's text on the parallels between the fate of Budapest's Glass House and that of its original owners is to be found in the 2015 monograph *Global Perspectives on the Holocaust: History, Identity, Legacy*. It is no coincidence that the film adaptation of *The Glass Room* was

out in his practically oriented history of home: "houses aren't refuges from history. They are where history ends up" (Bryson 2010, 20). This statement is complemented by Francesca Saggini and Anna Enrichetta Soccio, who, in the preface of their 2012 monograph, *The House of Fiction as the House of Life: Representations of the House from Richardson to Woolf*, claim that the house has become a popular subject of scrutiny "to the point that in many ways houses seem to be situated at the very core of the creative, artistic and cultural domains of contemporaneity" (Saginni and Soccio 2012, 2). *The Glass Room* is by far not the only recent work of fiction employing the method of framing social and individual histories by means of a house. A fellow contestant for the 2009 Man Booker Prize was Sarah Waters' *The Little Stranger* (2009), a work revolving around a decaying English country house in post-WW2 England. The same year also saw the publication of a well-known biography of a house embodying the fate of Germany, Jenny Erpenbeck's *Visitation*. Inspired by a real place, the summer house of his grandmother, Thomas Harding embraced the same approach and theme in *The House by the Lake* (2015). Norman Eisen situated his account of turbulent European history in the residence of the US ambassador in Prague in his 2018 novel *The Last Palace,* Sebastian Faulks centred the plot of his two epic accounts of Austrian history, *Human Traces* (2005) and *Snow Country* (2021), in a pioneering asylum, and Yuri Slezkine's account of the tragic history of twentieth-century Russia is narrated through the story of an enormous governmental building in *The House of Government* (2017). As all these novels and earlier mentioned non-fiction works testify, the central proto-trope of the house calls for a multi-layered interpretation and surpasses the role of a setting.

The second form centrality takes in the novel is the dominance of the Glass Room, which is featured in almost every chapter of the novel. Usurping the role of centre within a centre, its prominence supports Bachelard's conception of the "house imagined as a concentrated being" (Bachelard 1994, 17). The way in which Mawer develops the central image of the Glass Room, which simultaneously acts as the leitmotif, setting, and symbol of the intellectual and aesthetic aspirations of its creator, its inhabitants[70] and their historical periods, demonstrates its versatility, corroborates its centring quality and proves that *The Glass*

screened during the London Jewish Festival in 2019 to illustrate the effect of the Holocaust on the region of Central Europe.

70 Petr Anténe attributes a similar function to universities and mainly their liberal arts departments. Not only do they provide the setting for the novels discussed in his monograph

Room surpasses purely literary qualities and aspirations to historical accuracy and ventures into the cross-disciplinary realm. The following citation illustrates the need to apply a wider scope of disciplines in the analysis of the novel because of the transgressive, genre-bending parts of the work, which mix fiction with other modes of artistic expression – poetry and architecture:

> She dreams. She dreams of cold. She dreams of glass and light, the Glass Room washed with reflection, and the cool view across the city of rooftops, the cold view through the trees, the crack of snow beneath your boots. She dreams of a place that is without form or substance, that exists only in the manner of dreams, shifting and insubstantial, diffuse, diverse:
> space
> glass, walls of glass
> a quintet of chairs, placed with geometrical precision
> a sweep of shining floor – ivory linoleum
> white and black
> the gleam of chrome
> These things move, evolve, transform in the way they do in dreams, changing shape and form and yet, to the dreamer, remaining what they always were: der Glasraum, der Glastraum, the single letter-change metamorphosing from one into the other: the Glass Room become the Glass Dream. (Mawer 2009, 304)

The excerpt relies on a prominent employment of syntactic parallelism within the repetition of the same elements of the sentence structure, beginning with: "She dreams", which secures the coherent form of an evocation of impressions. The middle part of the citation juxtaposes the individual elements of the imagery into a list, whose organisation clearly indicates a rhythm and marks both the oneiric nature of the sequence as well as its proximity to poetry. What is more, the textual and visual component of listing the individual parts of the spatial experience mediated by the text, e.g. "glass, wall of glass, a sweep of shining floor, a quintet of chairs" resembles a caption to be found in architectural plans and emphasises both the explicit and implicit architectural dimension of the text.

Campus Novel Variations: A Comparative Study of an Anglo-American Genre, but they "have often been seen as one of the pillars of this very society" (Anténe 2015, 7).

10.4 The Glass Room and the Ideals of Architectural Modernism

The highly evocative imagery of *The Glass Room* provides an apt as well as atmospheric insight into the aesthetic and ideological preoccupations of Modernist architecture. Its principles are repeatedly and aptly summarised by the character of Rainer von Abt, the fictitious architect. The qualities of Modernist architecture seep into Mawer's mode of expression and the resulting text thus acts as an intermediary between the sphere of architecture and that of language. Moreover, *The Glass Room* pertinently contrasts the utopic nature of the premises of Modernist architecture (Benton 2007, 148–223) with the realities of history and human nature. *The Glass Room* demonstrates Mawer's ability to use poetic language to effectively communicate the spatial poetics of the novel. Besides similes, the author often relies on a series of unexpected parallels (Mawer 2009, 52), such as when he underlines the organic process of designing and building a house by comparing it to the development of a baby:

> The house grew, the baby grew. The latter was a strange and rapid metamorphosis, punctuated by events of moment: the grasp of her hands, the focus of her eyes, her first smile, her recognition of Liesel and then Viktor, the first time she raised herself on her hands, the first laugh. The growth of the house was more measured: the laying of steel beams, the pouring of concrete, the encapsulating of space. (Mawer 2009, 52)

In accordance with these tendencies, Rosa Ainley described *The Glass Room* as an example of "archi-fiction" in her article for *Architecture and Culture* (2020). In her view, novels such as *The Glass Room* "look again to architecture to provide a location, to set a specific stage for the narrative, adding some notion of authenticity (this is real!) and importance (this is a highly significant building!)" (Ainley 2020, 21). In terms of fiction inspired by actual architectural works, Ainley proposes the term "artefactual" (Ainley 2020, 21) to describe works such as *The Glass Room* in which architecture surpasses the role of mere backdrop and becomes an instrument for framing complex social, cultural, political, and individual histories. This tendency is foreshadowed in the Prologue, which sees Liesel Landauer returning to the house after more than 30 years of exile and reminiscing about one peculiar quality of the Glass Room, its retractable window panes. Mawer employs this unique aspect, and mainly its effect of "temporary equilibrium", as a symbol of the former life of the Landauers in the First Czechoslovak Republic and the failed liberal ideals and aspirations of the period:

> The slow slide of the pane downwards as though to remove the barrier that exists between reality and fiction, the fabricated world of the living room and the hard fact of snow and vegetation. There is a pause during which the two airs stand fragile and separate, the warmth within shivering like a jelly against the wall of cold outside. And then this temporary equilibrium collapses so that winter with a cold sigh intrudes, and presumably, their carefully constructed, carefully warmed interior air is dispersed into the outside world. (Mawer 2009, 4–5)

The Glass Room, in addition to mediating a nuanced portrayal of Czech history by means of a house, or rather, a room, also provides an extensive commentary on Modernist architecture, its ideology, and its creators, and this acts as a second determining aspect of its spatial poetics. Although the novel covers the time span of almost the entire twentieth century, its focal point is the period of the First Czechoslovak Republic, the time when the design of the house is conceived out of the desire of a newlywed couple, Viktor and Liesel, both from upper-class, German-speaking industrialist families, to sever ties with tradition and "this clinging to the past. This is everything our new house will not be!" (Mawer 2009, 9). Driven by the desire to inhabit a domestic space that would project their beliefs in progress, the future, and the emergence of an unconstrained society governed by reason and democratic values, they let the (fictitious) architect, Rainer von Abt, build a luxurious futuristic house incarnating their beliefs: "It'll be a revolution. [...] A casting off of the past. A new way of living" (Mawer 2009, 66). The exorbitant cost of the villa was not a demonstration of wealth and privilege, but rather of the philosophical principles of both of the owners, the future inhabitants and their architect: "The whole essence of the Glass Room is reason. That is what Viktor thinks, anyway. For him, it embodies the pure rationality of a Greek classical temple, the austere beauty of a perfect composition, the grace and the balance of a painting of Mondrian. [...] There is nothing convolute, involute, awkward or complex. Here everything can be understood as a matter of proportion and dimension" (Mawer 2009, 137).

In the novel, the chief spokesperson of Modernism's desire to "reshape the world" (Vidler 2001, 52) by revolutionising the way people live is Rainer von Abt, a fictitious German architect, a "composite modernist"

(Vidler 2001, 52), acting as a synthesis of a number of pioneers of architectural Modernism, most strikingly Adolf Loos, whose disciple von Abt proclaims himself to be (Mawer 2009, 17), Le Corbusier, and Theo van Doesburg. There are both direct and indirect mentions of them in the text – either they are explicitly mentioned, or their famous quotes are cited or paraphrased by von Abt, who claims that "[s]tability is the last thing I want. This house must float in light. It must shimmer and shine. It must not be stable" (Mawer 2009, 47) or "Steel will be as translucent as water. Light will be as solid as walls and walls as transparent as air", paraphrasing Doesburg's famous statements concerning stability. Von Abt's explanation of the erotic meaning behind a cross is almost a direct quote of Adolph Loos's famous lecture turned essay "Ornament and Crime" (1913): "A horizontal dash: the prone woman. A vertical dash: the man penetrating her" (Loos 1997, 19). In *The Glass Room,* von Abt proclaims: "'This is the first work of art: the woman who lies down. [...] And this. This is the man who penetrates her. The result is the rectangular cross that underpins all my art. What could be warmer than that?'" (Mawer 2009, 24).

Von Abt is portrayed as a true trailblazer in the field of architectural concepts and the profession of architecture. Rejecting the label of architect, he considers himself to be "a poet of light space and form" (Mawer 2009, 16), who works with "nothing but ideas" (Mawer 2009, 22), "creating a work of art" (Mawer 2009, 21).[71] Echoing Loos and his abhorrence of superfluous ornamentation, von Abt can design nothing but "form without ornament" (Mawer 2009, 23), where he encloses space in "ruled lines as sharp as razor cuts, a mathematical precision that is beyond natural" (Mawer 2009, 41). Architecture, in his view, had for a long time been dominated by nothing else but "cave building", but his desire is to "take man out of the cave and float him in the air. I wish to give him a glass space to inhabit" (Mawer 2009, 18). He demonstrates his embrace of the Wagnerian concept of *Gesamtkunstwerk* by wishing not "just to design a house but to create a whole world. I want to work from the foundations to the interior, the windows, the doorways, the furnishings, the fabric of

71 Here, Mawer borrows directly from Le Corbusier and his essay "Architecture, Pure Creation of the Mind" (1927) in which he defines architecture as a material expression of thoughts. Shapes are understood as a language of architecture. And despite the employment of mostly inert materials and the embrace of a utilitarian framework, a true architect can arouse emotions (Le Corbusier 1976, 203). Both Le Corbusier and Mies van der Rohe conceived their buildings as works of art but were often considered "formalists" by their contemporaries (Davies 2018, 108).

the place as well as structure. I will design you a life. Not a mere house to live in, but a whole way of life" (Mawer 2009, 28).[72] The design of the Landauer House is conceived as a universal, international project (Mawer 2009, 64), which shall act, first and foremost, as a home: "It is not intended to be a sensation. It's intended to be a home" (Mawer 2009, 63).

The main living space of the Landauer House, the Glass Room, is repeatedly characterised as "open, infinitely extended, and thereby cleansed of all mental disturbance" (Vidler 2001, 51). Its invisible walls evoke the myth of spatial and social transparency that Modernist architecture shared with the thinkers of the late eighteenth century and creates the effect of ineffable space (Vidler 2001, 54).[73] However, in spite of the literal transparency of their main living space, which brings and merges the inside and the outside ("[t]he inside and the outside will be the same thing" (Mawer 2009, 43)), the Landauers' dreams of domestic life inside a work of art do not materialise. Although Viktor Landauer cites André Breton's *Nadja* on the occasion of the housewarming party, identifies his wife Liesel and himself with the house ("this glass house says who Liesel and I are" (Mawer 2009, 76)) and boasts that "[i]n our wonderful glass house you can see everything" (Mawer 2009, 76), these lofty ideals are not fulfilled. The house and its central living space become sites of deceit, violence, and neglect. The house is also repeatedly portrayed as a victim or as an inert witness to the dramatic events, emphasising both its no-

72 For more detailed information concerning the conception of architecture in the novel and parallels between Rainer von Abt and the masters of Modernist architecture see Topolovská, Tereza. 2013. *The Glass Room*: Architecture as a Poetic Emotion. *Prague Journal of English Studies* 2, (2013): 65–79.; Topolovská, Tereza. On the Analogy between the Language of Architecture and the Language of Literary Work: The Role of the Conception of Architecture in Generating the Poetics of *The Glass Room*. *Filologické studie*. Prague, Karolinum, 2013: 15–31.

73 In his 2001 monograph *Warped Space: Art, Architecture and Anxiety in Modern Culture*, Anthony Vidler highlights the role of Le Corbusier's fascination with the demolished Parthenon in the conception of *ineffable* space. This sublime experience of the pioneer of architectural Modernism defined his view of space. He therefore stipulated ineffability as its chief quality, dissolving walls and opening "the inside to the outside, an outside now simply framed in order to testify to its visual existence, but open more or less panoramically around the entire building. Ineffable space would then be that dreamt and idealized, worked and realized experience that matched the heights of Periclean Greece" (Vidler 2001, 55). The resulting impression of boundless, limitless, unconstrained space demonstrated its transcendent quality (Vidler 2001, 54). Le Corbusier's approach restricted the positive and purely aesthetic quality of such space and emphasised its terrifyingly sublime nature (Vidler 2001, 55). Yi-Fu Tuan stressed the ambiguous nature of open space in his *Space and Place: The Perspective of Experience*: "Space is a common symbol of freedom in the Western world. Space lies open; it suggests the future and invites action. On the negative side, space and freedom are a threat. To be open and free is to be exposed and vulnerable" (Tuan 2018, 54).

ble, classical nature as well as its factual inability to confront injustice: "the house remained indifferent, of course. Plain, balanced, perfect; and indifferent. Architecture should have no politics, Rainer von Abt said. A building just is. Below it, lapping up to the foot of the garden, were the rough tides of those political years, while the Landauer House stood beached on the shore above the tidemark like a relic of a more perfect golden age" (Mawer 2009, 100).

In spite of its purely abstract aspirations (or at least those of its designer, Rainer von Abt's), the space of the Landauer House is not portrayed as an "enclosed space, a box" (Mawer 2009, 308). Quite the contrary; it "transcends geometrical space" (Bachelard 1994, 47) as it is a lived-in space and becomes a shared experience of both the characters and the reader. Both personal and social histories intervene, and the building and the room are repeatedly depicted as silent witnesses, sometimes even victims of various kinds of atrocities. The Glass Room, in spite of its powerful sensory effect, eventually proves to be only "as rational as the people who inhabit it" (Mawer 2009, 360). By employing the complex spatial conceit of the Landauer House and, more importantly, the Glass Room, Mawer is able to provide a far-reaching commentary on the moral aspirations of architecture and art. As *The Glass Room* exemplifies, "a building just is" (Mawer 2009, 100), it cannot directly shape its inhabitants since it should not have any "politics", it may only inspire them with its perfect proportions and the impression of balance and classical beauty it radiates. The central spatial conceit of the novel, the Glass Room and its apparent indifference and neutrality, enables it to successfully frame history whilst accentuating the tragedy of "the rough tides" (Mawer 2009, 100) of those years.

The storyline of *The Glass Room* revolves around the archetypal anchoring trope of a house, in this case the fictitious Landauer House, modelled upon the famous Tugendhat House, situated in Brno in what is now the Czech Republic. Based on its integrating properties, the microcosms of the house and the eponymous room reflect the macrocosm of the world. Because of its singular, multidisciplinary character, the novel can be approached from a number of different perspectives, the major two being Mawer's vision of history and the work's topocentric qualities. As this study determines, Mawer's stance on the depiction of historical events echoes the preoccupation of neo-historical fiction, which often narrativises the past in order to be able to critically assess it and approximate it to the present. The spatial poetics of *The Glass Room* is defined by the double centrality of Mawer's narration. The Landauer House centres a narration that shelters individual and social histories. These are placed in the Glass Room, which appears in nearly every chapter of the novel.

Another vital aspect of the spatial poetics of *The Glass Room* is its presentation of the ideals of Modernist architecture. *The Glass Room* proves to be more than a skilful evocation of the artistic expression of the period. Rather, it introduces architecture as a fully-fledged element of the narration, resulting in one of the most harmonious, consistent, and evocative attempts to capture the essence of Modernist architecture, with its utopian belief in its own liberating power and its ability to promote and mediate ideas of unconstrained freedom and inevitable social and cultural progress (Benton 2007, 148–223). Moreover, *The Glass Room* contrasts the utopic premises of Modernism, especially its moral and aesthetic purism, with private and official histories. As a result, not only does the narration of *The Glass Room* exemplify a unique fusion of literature, architecture, history, and politics, but it also provides a suggestive meditation on art, its aesthetic and ethical functions, and their limits.

11. Mapping the Liminal in Simon Mawer's *Prague Spring*

Prague Spring (2018) is Mawer's third historical novel set in the region of central Europe, following *Mendel's Dwarf* and *The Glass Room*, although all three focus on different time periods and different subjects. *Prague Spring* can be seen as a continuation of *The Glass Room* and a further development of its poetic elements, including its literary references, but it cannot rival the degree of spatiality of its predecessor, manifested above all in the central conceit – the eponymous Glass Room. It provided Mawer with the opportunity to deepen his intellectual and factual connection with the region of central Europe and inform both foreign and Czech readers about a traumatic historical event with far-reaching cultural, social, and political consequences. It also allowed him to further thematise the space of central Europe and familiarise English-speaking readers with its somewhat exotic nature.

For Mawer, the region remains a source of ongoing interest, if not fascination (Vaughan 2018), as he adamantly rejects the peripheral position of its cultural space, which he rather considers to be "absolutely central" (Sečkař 2010). Thus, *Prague Spring* introduces recent historical, political, and cultural complexities of the region, namely the momentous events of August 1968. The novel's Czech translation was released only a few months after the original and, according to some of the Czech reviewers, it was an extremely substantial reflection (Konrád 2018) of the 1968 arrival of the Warsaw Pact troops, organised by the Soviet Union in order to suppress the reformist tendencies of the Czechoslovak government. Foreign reviews mainly praised Mawer's well-researched[74] atmospheric

74 In an interview with Kateřina Kadlecová for *Reflex* from 2018, Mawer cites archive materials translated into English and published by an American university, the memoirs of contemporaries in English, an American journalist's memoirs and an American diplomat's memoirs.

portrayal, enhanced by elaborate detail and his ability to evoke the haunting fragility of freedom and the horror of seeing democratic ideals crushed into dust by the wheels of history. Mawer has always excelled in the evocation of the intangible, demonstrated by how he conjures up the mounting tension in *Prague Spring* as well as the panic and general shock: "The air is stained with sound and fumes. From somewhere comes a sharp gust of gunfire. The crowd utters a collective gasp, as though there is a sudden shortage of oxygen. Some people run, others stand still" (Mawer 2018, 332).

The eventual invasion of Prague by the heavily armed troops of the Warsaw Pact and their clashes with unarmed, frustrated Czech civilians is as chilling as it is dynamic, and often the gravity of the situation is laced with absurdity, stemming from the sharp contrast between the alien, inopportune nature of the military operation and everyday life.

> Václavské náměstí, Wenceslas Square, with dawn leaching between the buildings and flooding the space. The great sloping boulevard is filling with people. Trams are stopped, while crowds gather, talking, wondering what the hell is going on when what is going on is plain for all to see as tanks gouge their way up the slope and arrange themselves as though for battle. Saint Wenceslas dominates the scene from his pedestal in front of the museum at the top end of the square, but even he, at the moment of greatest need, when he is meant to emerge from the Blaník mountain, is powerless before the armour. There is the stench of diesel, clouds of black smoke as the tanks manoeuvre, the awful clangour of their tracks. A kiosk sells bread rolls and sausages while young men and women argue with soldiers. (Mawer 2018, 331)

11.1 A Slice of History

The immediate, overall effect of *Prague Spring* on the reader is that of a slice of history written by an author who is invested in providing information and emotions that he himself experienced when witnessing the events of 1968 as an Oxford undergraduate. In his interview with Kateřina Svátková for *iRozhlas* (2018), Mawer described how the destiny of what was then Czechoslovakia affected him deeply, simultaneously arousing sympathy for the inhabitants of the country and a sense of immense tragedy. In her 2019 review, Roberta Silman praised *Prague Spring* for its ability to present the English-speaking world with intriguing and haunting aspects of Czech character and history. Mawer himself confirmed her appraisal by admitting some didactic aspects of the novel. Although Mawer typically eschews writing didactic texts that are consciously aimed at a particular group of people (Sečkař 2010), in the case of *Prague Spring*, "there are certain things that the English-speaking reader doesn't know and ought to know – the story of Milada Horáková, for example" (Vaughan 2018). In the same interview, Mawer stated that the novel's aim was not simply to describe the situation and use it as an intriguing background to the plot, but rather to inform people in the English-speaking world about the perilous situation in Czechoslovakia and, more importantly, its implications. As far as the mentor-like tone of some parts of *Prague Spring* is concerned, the reviewers were divided: while one group of mainly English-speaking reviewers praised the informative nature of the text, the other group expressed concern about its heavy-handed scholastic character, e.g. Veronika Krajíčková of *iLiteratura.cz* pointed out that the chapters dedicated to Jan Masaryk, Milada Horáková, and Czech writers, Hašek and Kafka amongst them, digress from the plot and are too obviously focused on educating the reader about Czech history. This sort of criticism is justified from the point of view of Czech readers, for whom such information may seem superfluous, but the novel had been written for a larger and more diverse audience. There are also points where it is hard to resist the urge to instruct the reader on the subject of recent Czech history, politics, and culture, especially when the author is as well versed in them as Simon Mawer. His teaching experience leads him to adopt some strategies typical of this profession, one of the most obvious of which is more or less conspicuous repetition. Thus, one is reminded of the pattern in Czechoslovak history: "1918, 1938, 1948, 1968" (Mawer 2018, 325) despite having already been informed about it in a more detailed way a hundred pages earlier: "'It seems like another betrayal, doesn't it?' Sam said. 'Munich 1938 and now Prague 1968. Do you see the pattern? Nineteen eighteen the state is created. Nineteen thirty-eight it is betrayed by the Great Powers, 1948 the communists grab power. And now here we are in 1968. It looks ominous" (Mawer 2018, 247–248). However, as noted above, Mawer's novel was regarded as one of the most distinctive pieces of fiction reflecting on the 50th anniversary of the events of 1968 (Konrád 2018).

11.2 Prototypical Protagonists

In typical Mawer fashion, *Prague Spring* weaves two storylines into a complex narrative. Thus, the story of Ellie and James, two Oxford undergraduates hitchhiking across Europe and basing their decisions on the toss of the coin, is juxtaposed with that of Sam Wareham, a sensible, grounded English diplomat posted in Prague. In his interview for Radio Prague International with David Vaughan, Mawer deliberately balanced the insight of Sam with James and Ellie's cross-class romance (she is decisively upper-class whereas his teacher parents mark him as distinctly middle-class) and their naivety, even exaggerated by the randomness of their choices. Ellie's revolutionary zeal, which she proudly flaunts as a member of ORSS, the Oxford Revolutionary Socialist Students, is contrasted with the Czech youth, whose revolutionary enthusiasm may be equally naïve but is also inevitable. There is a stark contrast between her rather capricious endeavours and the freedom of choice she and James represent and the desperate fight for freedom of the Czech youth. Sam Wareham, "a first Secretary at Her Britannic Majesty's Embassy to the Czechoslovak Socialist Republic" (Mawer 2018, 43) is a prototypical Mawerian protagonist.[75] At first, his matter-of-fact insight counterbalances the capricious antics of James and Ellie as well as the high hopes of the Czech youth. As he gets involved with Lenka Konečková, a mysterious Czech activist with a complicated past tainted by familial tragedy, he ceases to be a deliberate outsider and becomes invested in matters. As a result, he becomes involved in smuggling a group of foreigners outside the Iron Curtain and gets reprimanded by his superior for these glimmers of humanity: "Human being? But you're not a human being – you're a bloody British diplomat!" (Mawer 2018, 286). Sam's plotline, and especially his involvement with Lenka, whose dubious, inscrutable character brings hints of the femme fatale, steer the novel in the direction of genre fiction: it oscillates between historical novel, spy novel, and thriller. This quality of *Prague Spring* has been pointed out by several reviewers, including Marcel Berlins (he called it "a historical thriller with dashes of espionage" in his 2018 review for *The Times*) and Roberta Silman, who, writing for *The Arts Fuse* (2019), branded Mawer "a seasoned writer of historical spy fiction with an uncanny ability to evoke the fear and hope that existed for a short time in Czechoslovakia during the fateful year of 1968, just a little more than 50 years ago". Espionage and double identity are typical elements of Mawer's writing register, and in *Prague Spring* the urgency with which the dynamic sequences of Mawer's narration affect the reader emphasises the pervasive atmosphere of suspense, suspicion,

75 Most pronouncedly, he is reminiscent of e.g. Andrew Harding, the protagonist of Mawer's earlier novel of 1996, *A Jealous God*, set in the last, tragic days of the British Mandate in Palestine.

and fatality. Lenka, being another prototypical character of Mawer, is heavily marked with liminality, first embodying the hopes and dreams of the short-lived effort to achieve "socialism with a human face", but most noticeably so when she gets injured during the protests and eventually morphs into a symbol of the whole country[76]: "Lenka lies on the borderline between the living and the dead, neither one thing nor the other, like the country itself, neither free nor captive" (Mawer 2018, 363). In both storylines, i.e. that of James and Ellie and that of Lenka and Sam, sexuality plays an integral part of the plot. *Prague Spring* is yet another of Mawer's novels to emphasise and thematise sexuality, which he explains in terms of its elemental role in human life. Much in the vein of D. H. Lawrence, Mawer sees sexuality as instinctive and as a decisive part of human relationships. Having been interviewed by Kateřina Svátková for *iRozhlas* in 2018, Mawer argued that to deprive books of their sexual elements is tantamount to depriving them of their humanity.

The emphasis placed on the development of the romantic relationships of the two central couples is in keeping with the overall dream-like atmosphere of the novel, and also adds to the suspense as the inevitable ending encroaches on the characters' dreams and hopes. As Sam angrily quips towards the end of the novel: "What had people expected? What had Lenka and her friends, with their fifteen minutes of freedom, imagined would happen? This was reality. The last eight months had been but a dream" (Mawer 2018, 346). Some reviewers (notably Daniel Konrád, writing for *Aktuálně.cz* in 2018) interpreted the whole novel, including the eponymous historical event, as a metaphor for waking up from a callow dream, or losing one's illusions. Within the context of Mawer's works, the protagonists of the novel indeed rank amongst the youngest, and the major cultural aspects that Mawer chooses to present in the novel reflect their age. *Prague Spring* contains a great deal of musical references: there are mentions of composers of classical music, such as Dvořák or Smetana, then there is Janáček ("Who no one knows, but everyone should" (Mawer 2018, 241)), but most importantly, there is the absurd episode featuring the real-life British band The Moody Blues, who actually played a concert on Charles Bridge just hours before the tanks of The Warsaw Pact invaded the city.

---

76 The character of Lenka is reminiscent of a real-life character featured in *The Glass Room*. The character embodying the crashed ideals, hopes and dreams of young democracy of the First Czechoslovak Republic in the earlier novel is Vítězslava Kaprálová, the music prodigy who died at the age of 25.

11.3 A Roll of the Dice

Although the trajectory of *Prague Spring*'s plotline is strictly defined by its historical nature, the text repeatedly points towards chance as the main determinant of its outcome: "That's the way things work out. There's no plan, no narrative thread. They just happen. You may as well roll a die" (Mawer 2018, 300). The organising principle of the text and the events it portrays is thus concentrated in the omnipresent motif of the toss of the coin – it is how James and Ellie make their decisions while hitchhiking, it is how the chances of Lenka's survival and recovery are expressed (Mawer 2018, 386). Roberta Silman understands the emphasis on the coin that is supposed to decide the course of the journey of James and Ellie as a source of contrast between their freedom of choice and the inevitability of the historical and political events that crush the hopes of the Czechs. Mawer himself explains that he included this motif and the hitchhiking plotline because they reflect his own personal experience, replicating the journey he made fifty years earlier.[77] From the point of view of genre fiction, or rather popular fiction, *Prague Spring* bears some of the qualities of a thriller. The interweaving of the storylines, one of which highlights playfulness and freedom while the other is determined by events beyond the control of the protagonists, add to the suspense, and both storylines paradoxically illustrate a fatalistic vision. The tossing of the coin acquires a metaphorical dimension and illustrates the theme of chance in human life, which Mawer acknowledged in his 2018 interview with David Vaughan.

The role of chance in *Prague Spring*, together with its atmospheric depiction of the Warsaw Pact invasion of Prague and the way in which personal drama is interwoven with historical injustice, is reminiscent of a world-famous work by an author of Czech origin, Milan Kundera's *The Unbearable Lightness of Being* (1984).[78] In it, the author ponders on the role of chance in human life, which he illustrates through the relationship between the

77 James and Ellie's journey replicates the one Simon Mawer made with his friend in 1968. Originally, Mawer had wanted to go to Czechoslovakia, but eventually he and his friend opted for Greece, a decision he still regrets today and tried to rectify in *Prague Spring* (Vaughan 2018, Svátková 2018).

78 There are certainly more examples of intertextuality to be found in the novel. James and Ellie's plotline opens with direct references to an avantgarde play they acted in: *Fando and Lis*, a 1962 play by a Spanish playwright Fernando Arrabal, better known as its 1968 Mexican film adaptation by Alejandro Jodorowsky. The play revolves around the surreal quest of the two characters for the unreachable, mythical city of Tar. Ellie later plans their hitchhiking journey across Europe retracing the trajectory of Laurence Sterne's *A Sentimental Journey Through France and Italy* (1768) (Mawer 2018, 7-8).

protagonists of the story, Tomáš and Tereza. Their romance blossomed only after "six chance happenings" (Kundera 1999, 35) and their love and the decisions it influenced are based on "fortuitous love". Kundera's novel encompasses a number of philosophical and literary ruminations on decision making and its questionable relevance to human life. Similarly to Mawer's novel, *The Unbearable Lightness of Being* grounds its contemplation of this topic in an intimate relationship against the backdrop of the same historical event – the Prague Spring and, in the case of Kundera's novel, its aftermath. Kundera draws parallels between human life and historical events – they both occur only once, which makes it impossible to determine whether a decision made or a step taken was good or bad. He proceeds to exemplify this notion on the sequence of watersheds in Czech history – namely the years of 1618 and 1938 (Kundera 1999, 219). Should the Czechs have fought or not? Will they ever know? As Kundera concludes:

> What happens but once might as well have not happened at all. The history of the Czechs will not be repeated, nor will the history of Europe. The history of the Czechs and of Europe is a pair of sketches from the pen of mankind's fateful inexperience. History is as light as individual human life, unbearably light, light as a feather, as dust swirling into the air, as whatever will not exist tomorrow. (Kundera 1999, 220)

Instead of a poetics built upon figurative expressions of lightness and heaviness, Mawer develops a metaphorical language anchored in the tossing of a coin, which may be regarded as an apt spatial metaphor with a similar overall effect.[79]

11.4 The Intangible and the Historical Accurate

Mawer's unique ability to express the intangible is on full display in *Prague Spring* as he contrasts the role of chance with the inevitable

79 It is also not the first time that Mawer referred to Kundera's novel – he did so by means of one of the characters, Tomáš, in *The Glass Room*. Like Kundera's character of Tomáš, the Tomáš from *The Glass Room* comments on time and the rejection of its traditional division: "Tomáš does not wish to talk about the past, or the future, or anything temporal. For Tomáš there is no such thing as time. He is a doctor (a paediatrician at the children's hospital down the road) but a small, hard core of his mind is that of a philosopher rather than a physician. The philosopher has decided that past and future are both illusions, that there is only a continuous present, and the present is this view through the widnow over the city, this cigarette, this vague and milky reflection of Zdenka walking backwards [...]" (Mawer 2009, 327).

impairment of a nation's chances of establishing a democratic regime, the playful freedom of the young with the inexorable impact of historical injustice, and underlines the tension between the intimate and the public, the historical and the political. Hope, freedom, and liberty are replaced by panic and fear, culminating in the invasion of Prague: "There's a noise in the city, an undercurrent like the coming of a flood" (Mawer 2018, 329). One factor that contributes to the author's ability to capture the elusive as well as to convey a strikingly atmospheric description is the almost absolute degree of accuracy of the historical and cultural details he incorporates in his writing. He is well versed in both the factual and artistic sources of information, which he demonstrates by incorporating elements in his writing with a varying degree of implicitness. There are overtly informative chapters on Jan Masaryk, Milada Horáková, and prominent Czech literary figures, whose presence is deliberately didactic, and many inconspicuous, but highly insightful details, such as the mentions of "a cruet set of Bohemian cut glass" (Mawer 2018, 122), smoking in hospitals (Mawer 2018, 385), the phenomenon of "small wooden cabins that Czechs use as country retreats – *chaty*"[80] (Mawer 2018, 124), and witticisms based on a thorough knowledge of both Czech literature and history: "Up there, looming over everyone, was the Hrad, the Castle, where the president of the country resided and Kafka reigned supreme" (Mawer 2018, 71). Mawer also never misses an opportunity to include a linguistic playfulness, either by toying with the etymology of words or inserting a linguistic pun.[81] Although he calls himself "a linguistic outsider" in Czech (Vaughan 2018), he is able to provide a comprehensive guide to mutual German-Czech linguistic, cultural, and historical relations in the blink of an eye:

> Vltava; Moldau. As always, a German name stands like a gothic shadow behind the Czech – Praha, Prag; Malá Strana, Die Kleineseite; Vltava, Moldau – just as German history looms behind Czech history, occasionally reaching forward to tap it on the shoulder and remind the Czechs that they only occupy a narrow Slavic salient thrust into the heart of the Teutonic world. (Mawer 2018, 29–30)

80 "They were like beach huts on the English coast: the same clapboard constructions in vivid primary colours, the same defiant sense of pride. But these didn't have uniformity. They might be put together out of anything: offcuts from a timber yard, corrugated iron, tarpaper, panels from an ancient car, barrels from a brewery" (Mawer 2018, 124).

81 "One of the universals. *Prostitutka* in both Russian and Czech, and probably every other language under the sun" (Mawer 2018, 60).

All of the aforementioned aspects evoke a powerful sense of place and space, which is probably the most recognisable characteristic of Mawer's style. His description of the tanks in the streets of Prague reveals once again his densely poetic way of expression, which provides the reader with a highly atmospheric description of events.

> People gather, some just to watch in sullen silence, others to shout. The smell of diesel exhaust and despair fills the air. The figure in the turret takes no notice and after a moment drops back inside. With a roar and a cloud of black smoke the beast shifts, its tracks screeching on the tarmac and pavement. Figures emerge from a side street and run around it, like dogs at a bear-baiting. From somewhere out of sight a glass bottle arcs through the air and smashes against the flank of the beast. A blossom of flame erupts below the hull with a low wumph of exploding petrol. The machine bellows in anger, grinds kerbstones to dust and roars out of sight. (Mawer 2018, 331)

11.5 Mapping a Historical Conflict

Mawer's well-documented tendency to set the plots of his novels in geopolitically ambiguous zones is once again evident in *Prague Spring*. The area of central Europe echoes his other preferred setting, the Mediterranean, in its linguistic, cultural, and historical complexity. The historical setting of *Prague Spring* reflects this quality as it follows the brief period before the arrival of the armies of the Warsaw Pact, which was marked by a high degree of clashing attitudes and, more often than not, a high degree of tension. The imminent seizure of the country by foreign armies, the strengthening of the position of the USSR as the main political and cultural usurper, and the iron rule of communism contrast sharply with the democratic ideals that the country tentatively embraced in the 1960s. Mawer once again centres his novel in a period of transition, which he exemplifies both literally and metaphorically, since it is in the shift between states that his literary creation gains its true momentum. Sarah Crown points to similar "shuttlings" in his earlier novels in her 2009 "A Life in Books": "between faith and its absence in *The Gospel of Judas*; science and ignorance in *Mendel's Dwarf*; most explicitly of all in *The Glass Room*, where the reason and modernity of the youthful Czechoslovakia [...] are juxtaposed with the coming invasion, which plunges the country back into physical and spiritual darkness". In *Prague Spring*, Mawer develops a similar analogy to assess the political situation:

> And whatever you may see now, it's worth remembering that Dubček and his merry men all came up through the ranks during the Stalinist era, during which they accepted all kinds of horror as though it was the will of God. Now they are standing on the brink, wondering whether to jump into the unknown or turn back into the familiar arms of Mother Russia. When push comes to shove, they're likely to turn round and beg Mummy for forgiveness. (Mawer 2018, 75)

Amongst a few of the anachronist chapters that Mawer included in *Prague Spring* in order to contextualise some of the events and characters mentioned in the novel and also to enlighten the reader on certain important aspects of Czech history, there is a whole chapter dedicated to the contemporary border of the country. Fascinated by its current lack of importance, if not virtual disappearance, compared to its former role as a part of the Iron Curtain, Mawer abhors even "[t]he idea of reverting to anything resembling that state" (Vaughan 2018), hoping that the border will disappear forever. Unable to resist the temptation of a zoology-related analogy, Mawer cites the example of the red deer roaming the Bohemian Forest and Bavaria, keeping to their respective sides, presumably having been taught to do so by their parents and grandparents: "[t]hus, the last trace of the Cold War division lies only within the brains of *Cervus elaphus*, the red deer" (Mawer 2018, 199). The absurdity of the division only emphasises the precious nature and fragility of the short-lived period which preceded the tightening of the grip of the non-democratic regime.

Thus, *Prague Spring* remains a paean to the liminality of the Prague Spring as a historical period, echoing the earlier efforts that marked the First Czechoslovak Republic, famed for its liberal values, which Mawer so memorably evoked in *The Glass Room* (2009). Mawer draws on a set of staples of his literary creation – he chooses a breaking point in the historical development of a country with a multifaceted cultural, national, and political identity. He thematises liminality as a cornerstone of the poetics of the novel – it becomes the defining quality of the linguistic, historical, psychological, cultural, and spatial aspects of the novel. Many elements of *Prague Spring* echo and complete motifs and themes presented in *The Glass Room* and although *Prague Spring* cannot match its intensity, it serves as a fitting conclusion to the triptych of works that relate to the space of central Europe and its troubled history.

12. Spy Fiction as a Meditation on Identity, Space and Place in Simon Mawer's *The Girl Who Fell from the Sky* and *Tightrope*

This chapter explores the role of spatiality and the degree of reflection of the protagonist in the spatial and temporal settings of two of Mawers critically acclaimed novels, *The Girl Who Fell from the Sky* (2012) and its 2015 sequel, *Tightrope*. The aim is to study the ways in which Mawer tests the limits of the traditional genre of spy fiction by adding a number of literary elements to its pivotal aspects, achieved mainly by merging the protagonist and her endeavours with the explosive historical and geographical setting. Both novels thus accurately articulate Mawer's abilities as far as the use of spatiality is concerned, while at the same time functioning as gripping thrillers.

The Girl Who Fell from the Sky was Mawer's first novel to be published after the enormous success of *The Glass Room* and thus inevitably drew a number of comparisons. Some reviewers hinted that the new novel was a less ambitious take on history and that it lacked a "conceit" as powerful as the glass room of the eponymous novel (Miller 2012). Moreover, it apparently lacked the ambition of its predecessor and was unable to "aspire beyond itself" (Miller 2012), and its conception was most likely motivated by visions of commercial success (Miller 2012), with the author attempting to ride on the wave of attention and financial success of *The Glass Room*, hastily publishing something that would secure him "all those lovely new readers" (Cooke 2012). What the reviewers did agree on was that the form of *The Girl Who Fell from the Sky* was nothing short of brilliant (Cooke 2012, Miller 2012). One of the features that received the most critical comments was the open ending (Cooke 2012, Miller 2012), which was perceived as either unsatisfactory or simply negligent (Cooke 2012, Miller 2012).

Mawer responded to this criticism of the ending, but, more importantly, showed his devotion to the main character – Marian Sutro

(Pengelly 2015) – with a direct sequel, 2015's *Tightrope*. Much to the satisfaction of reviewers and readers, *Tightrope* tied up the loose ends of the previous novel and did so in spectacular fashion, drawing comparisons to works by universally acclaimed authors of spy novels such as John Le Carré, Sebastian Faulks, and Ian Fleming, and perhaps more importantly, winning the 2016 Walter Scott Prize for historical fiction. Mawer's inclusion in the group of famous representatives of the genre and his exceptional literary abilities should come as no surprise as both *The Girl Who Fell from the Sky* and *Tightrope* present a seasoned author of literary thrillers and cannot be said to mark a significant departure from the previous novels, such as *Chimera, Jealous God*, or *Swimming to Ithaca*. In fact, *The Girl Who Fell from the Sky* opens with a parachuting scene that echoes the one in Mawer's literary debut, *Chimera*: "The drop was like an act of birth" (Mawer 1989, 1) and "she lets go, plunging from the rough comfort of the fuselage into the raging darkness over France" (Mawer 2012, 5). As Mawer acknowledged in an interview for *the Guardian* in 2015, there is a clear parallel between the two novels, which open with a scene of an agent parachuting into foreign territory – *Chimera* has "a man who is dropped in Italy in the war and then comes back after the war to explore Etruscan archaeology. This has always been there, this idea" (Pengelly 2015).

12.1 *The Girl Who Fell from the Sky*: A Literary Spy Novel

As with *Chimera* and the majority of Mawer's works, it is rather difficult, if not impossible, to clearly demarcate the genre of both *The Girl Who Fell from the Sky* and *Tightrope*. Most reviewers acknowledged their dual identity and highlighted their considerable literary qualities. The former was labelled as "a traditional thriller, albeit an intelligent one" (Tripney 2013) whereas the latter was described as "a spy thriller – a literary one for sure" (Pengelly 2015) and "a literary novel in the armature of a thriller, and as such it follows the routes of a thriller and departs from them" (ibid). As both novels revolve around the nuclear, and later thermonuclear, race, they include science as both motif and theme. Once again, Mawer demonstrates an ability to introduce complex issues almost imperceptibly and weave them firmly into the poetics of the story: "Time passed, with that curious relativity that brought Ned's physics to mind: relative time, elastic time, the hours of discomfort stretching out like days but the whole passage of the course compressing from days into what seemed like mere hours" (Mawer 2012, 45). Even more than the science and action, the novels focus on the main character, Marian Sutro, and her identity. Both books thematise the question of identity while charting Marian Sutro's emergence from adolescence into adulthood. Ironically, it is Marian's lack of a clearly defined identity and her uprootedness that condition and secure her successful career as an agent. As Mawer organically links the individual aspects of his narratives, including the characters and their social, historical, cultural, and physical settings, he employs the character of Marian to connect the personal and the national, the intimate and the public, thus commenting on the state of wartime France and post-war England.

12.1.1 Marian Sutro – the Liminal Protagonist

The thematic focus on Marian's character and identity is confirmed by Mawer's claim that his two novels are in fact character studies. Some reviews mentioned her "genuine charisma" (Sansom 2015) and Mawer himself considers Marian to be "the most alive to him of all his characters" (Flood 2016) and one of his most cherished creations. He even thanked her in his acceptance speech for the Walter Scott Prize for Historical Fiction. There are many exceptional aspects to Marian's character but one of the most notable is the nature of her responses to exceptional situations – neither quirky, nor brilliant, as is usual for similar characters, she mostly acts upon instinct. "And yet she embodies a kind of energy, and has a steely determination and a quick-wittedness that make her remarkable" (Sansom 2015). Yet Marian is not the first authentic female character Mawer has created, she was preceded by a long line of similarly minded and complexly conceived characters, such as Hana Hanáková and Liesel Landauer from *The Glass Room*, Helen Harding from *Jealous God,* and Dee Denham from *Swimming to Ithaca*. Mawer explained his choice of female protagonists, albeit hesitantly because of possible sexist connotations, especially for suspense-laden plots, on the basis of their superior mental complexity: "Testosterone drive, the masculine thing, is actually pretty dull. It's important in a rugby match, but it's not intellectually very interesting" (Pengelly 2015). In addition, both novels highlight the high level of cultural sexism that downplayed the role of the female agents of SOE and the involvement of women in the war effort in general[82]: "Can't give women medals, I'm afraid. Because they're not recognised combatants. FANY and all of that. So we have to go for a civil list gong. OBE or something" (Mawer 2015, 46).

It was not just the convincing portrayal of a female spy that won Mawer the coveted Walter Scott Prize for Historical Fiction. The judges appraised *Tightrope* as "impeccably researched" and perfectly inhabiting "its time and place" (Walter Scott Prize 2016). What may come as a surprise, especially in this context, is that Mawer rather ironically claimed that he does not see himself as a historical novelist and "[a]ll I do is write novels about what interests me at the time [...] and the recent past is where my particular interests lie" (Flood 2016). He endeavours to narrativise the recent past so that his readers can better comprehend its influence on the present. Although he rejects the label of historical novelist, most of his works either feature narratives of the past or attempt to re-address them, processes by which Nick Bentley defines historical fiction (Bentley 2018, 95). Mawer is a vocal proponent of writing historical narratives in relation to and from the perspective of the present, and in doing so his novels can be seen as simultaneously attempting and purposefully refraining from an absolutely accurate rendering of the past (Bentley 2018, 97). One of the frequent forms this tendency takes in Mawer's works is the mixing of real-life characters with fictional ones, as in *Tightrope*, where Mawer presents the fictitious Marian Sutro as a member of the group of real-life female spies who were captured, tortured, and murdered in the Nazi concentration camps before the end of war: "Andrée Borrel, Vera Leigh, Nora Baker, Yvonne Rudellat, Cecily Lefort, Diana Rowden, Eliane Plewman, Yolande Beekman, Madeleine Damerment, Denise Bloch, Lilian Rolfe, Violette Szabo. A roll call of the disappeared" (Mawer 2015, 87). Similarly, in *The Girl Who Fell from the Sky*, the fictional scientist Clément Pelletier introduces the names of real-life nuclear physicists and their discoveries to Marian: "Hahn and Strassman started it, yes – when they did their first work on fission. At the Kaiser Wilhelm Institute in Berlin. [...] They've got the men – Hahn, Diebner, Weizsäcker, Heisenberg, above all Heisenberg. They have a group called the *Uranverein*, the Uranium Club" (Mawer 2012, 254). This skilful blending of fact and fiction, which he does not see as necessarily opposing principles, is another aspect that contributes to the perfect inhabitation of space and time in his novels.

82 The 2019 film *A Call to Spy* develops the same theme; it was written by Sarah Megan Thomas and directed by Lydia Dean Pilcher. It points out the latent sexism as well as the vital role women played in the war effort.

Apart from its flirtation with historical and biographical fiction, *The Girl Who Fell from the Sky*, inspired by the real-life story of Anne-Marie Walters and her deployment in southwest France, which she described in her 1947 account *Moondrop to Gascony*, is first and foremost a spy novel, with a wealth of well observed details, both historical and psychological. Key mental abilities described in both novels, along with states of anguish, agitation, and desperation, are subterfuge and deception. Marian realises that in order to survive, her cover story needs to be persuasive so that it "would become more real than [her] true story. The lies would become truths, and truths lies" (Mawer 2012, 81). Thus, Marian's capacity to lie becomes her most valuable asset and her life becomes "[a] pretence. Lies are the currency of what she does and is. Deceit is the capital she has stored up against discovery" (Mawer 2012, 160). Mawer considers the deception and subterfuge of the SOE and its agents as naturally "feed[ing] into interest novelists have" (Pengelly 2015). His fascination with people taking on identities and becoming "individual people" (Pengelly 2015) projects into both novels, which thus correspond to the focus of the Bildungsroman – whereas *The Girl Who Fell from the Sky* represents the coming-of-age story of a young spy, *Tightrope* functions as the story of her maturation and dubious liberation from the world of agencies, only to spend the rest of her days in exile with an assumed identity. In order to pass between any number of worlds, Marian becomes Anne-Marie, Marianne, or Alice. *The Girl Who Fell from the Sky* ends with Marian responding to her actual name, which also automatically means that she has failed as an agent (Mawer 2012, 349).

Mawer uses Marian's character to illustrate the atmosphere and the often-tragic historical circumstances, projecting suffering, unease, fear, panic, but also hope onto her. He thus manages to merge the personal and the national, the intimate and the public. One of the most efficient ways in which he achieves this effect is by blending the protagonists and their psychological states with their environment, either through their actual physical location or through the apt use of spatial metaphors, which is apparent in the titles of both novels, or the opening chapter of *The Girl Who Fell from the Sky,* entitled "Trapeze" to signify the perilous nature of her situation, but there are numerous other examples scattered throughout both novels.

12.1.2 The Spatial Poetics of *The Girl Who Fell from the Sky*

Mawer's approach to elements of his spatial poetics in both novels is evident in how fittingly he develops the dichotomy of space and place.

Both place and space tend to be perceived as generic terms that are rarely studied as self-contained categories since they are seen as either contrasting with or conditioning each other. Studied and used by a plethora of disciplines, these two phenomena became key to humanistic geography, first formalised by Yi-Fu Tuan in the 1970s. This interdisciplinary approach considers the importance of human experience and the nuances of sensory perception in defining both place and space. Although they may fuse in our experience, space is the wider, more open and sometimes more menacing of the two. Place is then its counterpart, perceived as secure, stable, and enclosed: "[f]rom the security and stability of place we are aware of the openness, freedom, and threat of space, and vice versa" (Tuan 2018, 6). Mawer illustrates this contrast when Marian flees a group of pursuers in Paris in *The Girl Who Fell from the Sky*: "She gains the sanctuary of the buildings and turns out of sight" (Mawer 2012, 208). The dichotomy of frightening space versus secure place is further developed in *Tightrope*, where it illustrates Marian's agoraphobic states resulting from her PTSD.

Besides emotional value and the natural attachment humans have to places, Tuan also connects the place-space dichotomy with movement – space allows it whereas place acts as a pause (Tuan 2018, 138). Tuan also distinguishes between place and location, since the pause in movement combined with emotional value "makes it possible for location to be transformed into place" (Tuan 2018, 6). The incentive for the pause may be found in emotional connection and thus "[t]he pause makes it possible for a locality to become a center of felt value" (Tuan 2018, 138). Tuan's understanding of these two fundamental spatial concepts can be used to elucidate Marian's motivation for joining the SOE, which remains rather obscure. She is half French and half English and although her cosmopolitan upbringing in Geneva and especially her bilingualism almost conditioned her to train as a spy, she is also portrayed as someone displaced and rather unsure of where her place is. This is reinforced by the choice of spatial metaphors – Marian is first seen dropping from an aircraft into the darkness of the occupied zone, then she is frequently compared to an acrobat: "as though it is written across her forehead that she does not belong, that she is a performer, an artiste who has swung down from the sky, the daring young girl on the flying trapeze. There is nothing to support her, no safety net beneath" (Mawer 2012, 150). To emphasise the effect of disorientation, Mawer employs another trope, that of comparing Marian to the character of Alice in Lewis Carroll's *Alice in Wonderland* (1865) and *Through the Looking Glass* (1871) (Mawer 2012; 36,

71, 75, 77, 85, 118, 140, 144). There are a number of passages that refer to the scene in which Alice fell through the rabbit hole: "That night she dreamt. It was a repeat of a childhood dream, the falling dream, now fast, now slow, like Alice down the rabbit hole. People watched her as she fell" (Mawer 2012, 69). All of these spatial tropes and images help to build the illusion of uprootedness while supporting the dynamism of both the narrative and its poetics.

Marian, always on the move or even on the run, cosmopolitan but also lacking a sense of belonging, parachutes into southwest France, and, as she spends time there, she becomes attached to the place – in terms of place and space France represents a pause in her otherwise swift movement, both through the space of the novel and through the geographical space it indicates. Marian joined the SOE and parachuted "not for Clément, not for Benoît, but for France, that strange abstraction which means so many different things to different people" (Mawer 2012, 347). Marian gradually starts to perceive France as being as close to a homeland as possible, which signals both her identification with the country and also the formation of an identity that would revolve around a more fixed, stable point. Tuan perceives the homeland as an exemplification of a place to which one ascribes feelings of familiarity and ease "with the assurance of nurture and security, with the memory of sounds and smells, of communal activities and homely pleasures accumulated over time" (Tuan, 159). This act of pausing, of inhabiting the place and the feeling of belonging: "Suddenly it's cold. She needs to move, to get things going again, to be away from here and back in Toulouse, back in Lussac, arguing with le Patron, laughing with Benoît, being where, for the first time in years, she feels like home" (Mawer 2012, 345) turns out to be rather fatal for Marian since she is captured and arrested moments later. Not only is it an illusory sense of belonging, since Marian is living in France undercover and with a false identity, but it also proves to be extremely dangerous. As a prototypical spy, Marian seems to be condemned to physical and metaphorical uprootedness, her attachment to people and place proving to have fatal consequences.

12.1.3 Liminality as a Key Feature

Seen within the context of Mawer's writings, Marian, "a hybrid. [...] An amalgam of things. [...] A bastard" (Mawer 2012, 205), embodies typical qualities of Mawer's characters – individuals and communities alike are marked by liminality, hybridity, instability, and uprootedness. As Mawer builds characters in synergy with their settings and lets them function as expressions of contemporary society, Marian's character and her coming of age are reflected through wartime Europe. Originally, liminality was concerned with anthropology. Coined by Arnold van Gennep, a Dutch-German-French anthropologist, the term was employed to describe the periods and rituals of rites of passage that represent the transition from one stage of human life to the next. Referring to the transitional space between two clear polarities, liminality has lately become separated from post-colonial discourse and it is now used mainly in connection with in-between, transcultural spaces (Ashcroft 2007, 117).

Marian's position throughout the story cannot be described as anything other than in-between. She lives somewhere between life and death, with a fifty-fifty chance of survival, and yet she is rather thrilled by the prospect: "'Fifty-fifty?' It seemed absurd. The toss of the coin. How could she not feel fear? But it was the fear that she had felt skiing, the fear of plummeting steepness, the fear she had had when her uncle had taken her climbing, the awe-inspiring fear of space beneath her feet, a fear that teetered on the very edge of joy" (Mawer 2012, 12). During her recruitment interview, Marian's desirable qualities, and in particular her "dubious, hybrid Anglo-Frenchness" (Mawer 2012, 113), are echoed even in her position on the chair: "She sat, neither forward on the edge of the chair, nor back as though she were in the sitting room at home, neither one thing nor the other but upright, relaxed and watchful [...]" (Mawer 2012, 6). The most apt spatial trope used to convey Marian's position between life and death, illusion and reality, dream and nightmare, English and French, is the metaphor of the trapeze, which is used repeatedly (Mawer 2012, 146, 150, 226). Marian is called "an artiste, a performer" (Mawer 2012, 150) swinging through the air, partly controlling the movement and partly falling. Her success, her survival, is dependent on her daring as well as her luck.

The most obvious form that Marian's hybridity takes throughout the narrative is linguistic. It is Marian's command of languages that is shown to play a crucial role in the subterfuge and spying as it plays an essential part of her cover story. While being interrogated, it is her pronunciation and slips of the tongue that could most easily give her away. Marian is shown being assessed and in turn assessing other people's command of languages. However, their efforts to categorise and classify her keep hitting the wall of her liminal nature. This mutual process can perhaps be compared to mapping. On the one hand, Marian's cosmopolitan identity earns her a job, on the other hand, it makes her perpetually suspicious – even in *Tightrope*, during a war trial, she is somewhat mockingly called "*international*" (Mawer 2015, 121), to which she replies: "There's nothing much extraordinary about living in Geneva. A whole lot of Genevois do it" (Mawer 2015, 121). Throughout *The Girl Who Fell from the Sky*, but also *Tightrope* and other novels, Mawer points out that despite "the decreasing relevance of place in a modern world marked by mobility and flow" (Cresswell 2015, 82), the world is in fact dependent on "continued variation [...] – the existence of recognizably different places inhabited by 'locals'" (Cresswell 2015, 83). Marian vocalises his belief in the existence of "only one language. I simply use the bits of it that are appropriate at the time" (Mawer 2012, 7). This statement echoes Mawer's own preoccupation with the mixing of languages and cultures and, most importantly, with deeply rooted cosmopolitan beliefs. He writes in English, but as he situates the plots of his novels in various places around Europe, he signals this by carefully mixing languages without sounding clichéd or forced: "The boy turns the valves in his hand, then glances up at her and returns her smile. '*Gut,*' he decides, then tries it in French: 'Ça va. Vous pouvez aller.' 'Pardon?' 'Allez,' he repeats, 'allez!'" (Mawer 2012, 190). The occasional fusion of English, French, and German, together with the use of specific toponyms, adds to the authenticity of the narration, which, coupled with the way in which Mawer's narratives embrace liminality, contributes to an impression of tension and urgency. This corresponds with his tendency to set his plots in regions marked by imminent historical and cultural change.

12.1.4 *The Girl Who Fell from the Sky* from a Geocritical Perspective

The process of formation of Marian's identity reflects that of the majority of Mawer's characters – just like them she is plunged into unstable, tumultuous environment. This tendency finds its theoretical formulation in geocriticism. Geocriticism develops the concepts of earlier spatially oriented disciplines, which developed since the 1970s as a result of the so-called (postmodern) spatial turn. Compared to other similarly oriented disciplines, geocriticism seems to be more flexible and inclusive as far as subject matter is concerned. Combining literary criticism with the study of geography, it explores the nature and effect of the mutual influence of physical space and its literary portrayal. It develops the idea that there is a correlation between lived and imagined spaces and that the most articulate source of the nature of their interaction is to be found in their textual renderings. The interdisciplinary nature of geocriticism and both its practical and theoretical aspects make it a suitable framework for the study of the thematic preoccupations of novelists such as Mawer.

The foundations of the discipline were laid by the French scholar Bertrand Westphal in his *Geocriticism: Real and Fictional Spaces* (2007). Westphal's approach is rather geo-centric, concerned as he is with the textual representation of existing places and spaces (Wetphal 2011, xiv) as he stresses it in his foreword to Tally-edited *Geocritical Explorations*. Mawer's novels, and both *The Girl Who Fell from the Sky* and *Tightrope* are no exception, always draw on actual places and historical events, and Westphal's approach may thus seem perfectly suited to their analysis. Mawer, however, rarely relies on the representational aspect of the spaces and places he represents in his fiction, using them to comment on and illustrate the psychological states of the characters and the atmosphere of the period. For example, in the following scene, he refers to actual sites in Paris, but rather than charting the space, they evoke Marian's naïve vision of her future self and transport the reader to the place:

> The tide was out and sea birds picked over the mud – gulls laughing and crying. She wanted to laugh and cry with them – with joy and a breathtaking kind of fear. [...] How remarkable! Marian Sutro, living under some assumed name – Colette, she fancied – might soon be standing on the bank of the Seine beside Pont Neuf and looking across the water, past l'Île de la Cité to the Louvre on the far side. All around her the people of the city would be wondering when and if the British were coming to rescue them from their misery, when in fact they would already be there, in her own small presence. (Mawer 2012, 13)

It would therefore be rather limiting to rely solely on Westphal's conception of geocriticism, and yet some of its aspects may prove productive in this study, most notably his focus on maps and their real and imaginary counterparts. Mawer thematises the process of mapping in a number of ways and highlights how vital this process is from the perspective of spy fiction. The process of mutual mapping by means of language assessment has already been mentioned. There are other examples of the process to be found in the novel. One is Marian's mapping of the terrain, which shows how her vision of reality has been distorted by her professional training. For example, instead of a bucolic description of a farm, Marian's temporary residence, the readers are presented with a plan of an escape route:

> Alice's room is upstairs under the eaves of the farmhouse. There is a low window from which she could get down onto the roof of the dairy at the back of the building. From there it would be possible to jump to the ground, go through a fence and climb the sloping meadow that lies behind the buildings. Within a few seconds she could reach the woods that cloak the hill. It seems impossible that this small world of farm and fields and forests might ever be invaded, but still she has protected the escape route just as they taught her. (Mawer 2012, 162)

Another example of a peculiar kind of mapping, which affects the reader and the characters alike, is the evocation of the effects of an atomic bomb as if it had exploded in Paris. It is the very precision of the topographic figures that adds to the power of the evocation. This scene sadly finds its real-life counterpart in *Tightrope*, where the actual effects of the atomic bomb attack on Hiroshima are indicated.

> My estimate is that the whole of the centre of a city like Paris would be totally destroyed by just one bomb; as far out as, say, Montmartre in the north and Montparnasse in the south. I mean exactly that – no building left standing. Beyond that it would be the same destruction as an ordinary bombing raid for, what? A further three or four kilometres. Within the inner area everyone would be killed. Outside that a few might survive, only to die later from the effects of radiation. (Mawer 2012, 255–6)

The specificity of the descriptions is often paired with their vividness as Mawer's tropes and images often affect multiple senses. This tendency enables and facilitates the process of internalising the literary renderings of both spaces and places, articulated by different conceptions of geocriticism, namely those of Robert T. Tally and Eric Prieto. Tally's approach is markedly less geo-centric and takes into account imaginary literary environments, which it sees as capable of reflecting social and individual psychological experiences of places and spaces. Eric Prieto, who developed the phenomenological conception of geocriticism, also focuses on the connection between the physical environment and the individual psyche and thus paves the way for a more subjectivist approach to the discipline. Even more importantly, from the perspective of Mawer's spatial poetics, he introduces the concept of "in-between places" (Prieto 2011, 13), often overlooked places, which is unexpected given their artistic potential. The spatial textures of Mawer's novels tend to be almost explosive as the focal point of his narrative is a community on the verge of historical and cultural transformation. *The Girl Who Fell from the Sky* features evocations of places that concentrate the tension and accumulation of energy associated with the imminent change. The quality of such places responds to Westphal's principles of geocriticism – namely "non-equilibrium" (Westphal 2011, 19–20), an entropic space that both allows the accumulation of energy necessary for the change and supports a multiplicity of complex narratives. Moreover, the places and spaces of *The Girl Who Fell from the Sky* and *Tightrope* correspond to another geocritical principle, that of "transgressivity" (Westphal 2011, 37) which sees places as prone to constant change, their inner dynamism contributing to their heterogeneous character, which conditions their transition back to the homogenous state. In *The Girl Who Fell from the Sky*, it is primarily the landscape of occupied France that exemplifies a heterogeneous space. Although on the surface it acts like an orderly society, the foreign occupation prevents the existence of truly homogenous qualities. While the world of the occupied territory is a "space of police and policed" (Westphal 2011, 39) in Westphals's words, it is certainly not a space of "polis and politics" (Westphal 2011, 39). Some people have lost their sense of belonging because they cannot and will not identify with the official authorities. Rules and laws are subjected to double standards and their observation is often rather inconsistent. Mawer illustrates the entropic character of the world by challenging polarities – either he discards them completely or at least switches them: "The occupation has reversed the norms – the city is reduced to penury, the countryside has become a place of riches" (Mawer 2012, 202); or "In peacetime the countryside was still and the city a hive of activity; in wartime the circumstances are reversed" (Mawer 2012, 258). Practical laws, such as the belief in the passing of time or rationality as the governing principle of the world are replaced by relativity: "The journey was one of those wartime odysseys in which time and rationality seemed suspended" (Mawer 2012, 35).

The last-mentioned example of the suspension of time, or its relative, elastic character, which allows it to move in leaps and bounds or to stand still, is reflected in the depiction of both wartime Britain and France, which seem to simultaneously observe and challenge chronological time: "Time passed, with that curious relativity that brought Ned's physics to mind: relative time, elastic time, the hours of discomfort stretching out like days but the whole passage of the course compressing from days into what seemed like mere hours" (Mawer 2012, 45). This quality corresponds to Westphal's last geocritical principle, that of "spatiotemorality" (Westphal 2011, 9). The dissonance between the chronological interpretation of place and its breach by the relativity of space-time results in a turbulent, disorganised and yet highly creatively productive space. Mawer demonstrates that the occupation distanced parts of countries, one from the other. Therefore, travelling from Paris to Toulouse is "like leaving one continent for another, crossing an ocean, making landfall in a different world" (Mawer 2012, 277). Poignantly, the narrative describes the possible end of war seeming "like a fiction, in the way that paradise is a fiction, a time and place of unlimited plenty, of peace and harmony and eternal light. An antidote to the theology of terror" (Mawer 2012, 180). In the context of Mawer's spy fiction, as well as the genre in general, the choice of spaces and places affected by the powers of relativity, the suspension of universally accepted laws, and the lack of objectivity proves to be a highly productive element, enriching the narration with evocative imagery and adding to the overall sense of urgency and threat.

Elements of both bifurcation and entropy characterise the space of the novel and, moreover, they are shown to be elements necessary for the success of the subterfuge, the cover stories, and the assumed identities that are crucial for both agents and the genre. This is apparent from the projection of this tendency into Marian's identity, which seems to be subject to fluidity and constant change. It is not only the false identities she assumes, but also the range of addresses that reflect the changing perception of Marian. In order to accommodate the full range of demands of the outside world, Marian changes identities and names in much the same way that the titular character of *Alice in Wonderland* and *Through the Looking Glass* keeps changing sizes to demonstrate the relativity of her age and standing. Marian is belittled by being called "Love" (Mawer 2012, 3), "darling" (Mawer 2012, 24), and rejects Benoît's "my little Anne-Marie" (Mawer 2012, 83). However, as Clément acknowledges, his "little Marian is not so little anymore" (Mawer 2012, 211), as Marian acts as an accomplished, cold-blooded professional, as is expected of her. Words and names are presented as essential components of these stories, allowing Marian to assume a variety of identities such as Alice, Anne-Marie Laroche (Mawer 2012, 2), Alice Thurrock (Mawer 2012, 75), or Squirrel as Ned's sister (Mawer 2012, 99). Marian also feels motherly towards a fellow spy in training, which is absurd since Yvette is "eight years older and a widow. She was a woman and Marian a mere girl, and yet the dynamic of their relationship was this, daughter and mother, protected and protector" (Mawer 2012, 42). This reversal of roles, however, is not absurd in the context of the novel's entropic space. Thus, another member of the Resistance, Benoît, is: "[a] Frenchman pretending to be an Englishman pretending to be a Frenchman" (Mawer 2012, 147). Marian and other members of the SOE and the Resistance resort to coarse language, using vulgarity as a possible outlet for stress and anxiety, but also as a code of behaviour. Saying "Good luck!" before jumping out of a plane is thus replaced by "Merde! Merde alors!" (Mawer 2012, 135). In his novel, Mawer presents espionage as a forest of symbols, stories, and codes and because of its heterogeneity and smoothness, the space of the novel proves to be a fertile soil for a multitude of stories.

The degree of entropy and bifurcation (Westphal 2011, 20) finds its natural component in the marked liminality of Marian's character. Strengthened by the frequent mentions of falling or running dreams, Mawer paves the way for the presentation of a prominent oneiric element of the story: Alice in Wonderland. The series of analogies he creates range from more to less subtle ones – Marian's field name is Alice (Mawer 2012, 140) and her family lives in Oxford, where Lewis Carroll penned his works. To illustrate the strange, convoluted reality of the war Marian has entered, Mawer repeatedly uses elements from Carroll's works – there are scenes which feature dozing and reading, with "the one state merging into other so that she was uncertain whether she had read something or merely dreamed it" (Mawer 2012, 36) and a plethora of other parallels to Alice's stories (Mawer 2012, 36, 71, 75, 77, 85, 118, 140, 144): "She stood hesitantly in the gatehouse wondering why she was here. Alice, she thought, in some eccentric wonderland. But no white rabbit scuttled across the green velvet of the lawn [...]" (Mawer 2012, 89). Theoretical works have described the key aspect of the Carrollian experience as "off-centre, diagonal, or askew" (Lerer 2009, 195), which coincides both with Marian's impression of reality, through which she walks "like a child in a nightmare" (Mawer 2012, 150), and with the liminal, entropic space of war-torn Europe.

The prevailing impression of relativity and convolution is complemented by the motif of nuclear physics, which is further thematised in *Tightrope*. Marian's brother, Ned, and her friend and love interest, Clément, are both nuclear physicists. Since they have known each other from their childhood, the first time Marian learns about the principles of the practical implications of nuclear fission is through children's games, which accentuates the ominous tone: "She did as she was told. A children's game. Crash! And there was a faint and sulphurous smell of sparks.

There! That's all there is to it. You've just blown London off the map and out of history. Vaporised" (Mawer 2012, 108). Even when Marian learns about the potential of super-high-frequency electromagnetic radiation, she is convinced of its fictitious nature. Mawer employs Marian's astonishment and disbelief in order to reflect the naivety of pre-nuclear Europe, which relegated "A super-bomb that would blow a whole city to dust. A beam of deadly rays that would kill people with light. Rockets that would hurl high explosive form one continent to another through outer space" (Mawer 2012, 27) to the realm of "science fiction [...] nonsense you read about in bad novels" (Mawer 2012, 27). The thematic and textual choices Mawer makes in *The Girl Who Fell from the Sky* in relation to the inclusion of science stress his belief in the shared core of science and fiction and highlight the sense of instability and tension, further developing the impression conditioned by the novel's spatial poetics.

The Girl Who Fell from the Sky ends with Marian waking up, only to be caught by the Gestapo. It serves as a fitting end to a narrative that balances between a dream and a nightmare, history and fiction. Marian's awakening is not only literal but also metaphorical, as for the first time in the story she makes her own decision and responds to her actual name. Ironically, it means that she gets caught. The novel itself also defies the limitations of the genre of spy fiction by adopting a more subtle, literary approach. Mawer's attention to historical accuracy and his simultaneous desire to ignore it for the sake of an engaging narrative exemplify the transgressive potential of the novel, which focuses mainly on the remarkable character of Marian Sutro. Predetermined by her multifaceted liminality, she acts as a prototypical spy, but also as a reflection of contemporary society and the period. *The Girl Who Fell from the Sky* is an expression of Marian's maturation and identity formation – she learns, loses, gains, re-gains, re-evaluates, and tests to the limit the fundamental aspects of her humanness – to belong, to trust, to be loyal, to lie, to believe, to mistrust. Mawer's ability to express these complex processes by means of spatial aspects of the narrative allows for their internalisation by the reader and exemplifies the harmonious, organic connection between the characters and their setting. From this perspective, Marian's proverbial "fall" can be seen rather as a leap of faith.

12.2 *Tightrope*

Tightrope is Simon Mawer's tenth novel (2015), published as a follow-up to *The Girl Who Fell from the Sky* (2012). Set in the aftermath of WW2 and the onset of the Cold War, *Tightrope* charts the path of Marian Sutro, a former SOE agent, who, severely traumatised, struggles to regain balance and find purpose in ordinary existence. Just as her mission and the plot of the previous novel were fuelled mainly by the nuclear race, *Tightrope* quickly reveals that its major stimulus is the thermonuclear threat. Marian is pulled back into "the game" and, given Mawer's penchant for spatial metaphors, she is no longer "the daring young girl on the flying trapeze" (Mawer 2012, 146, 150, 226) but an experienced acrobat forced to walk a dangerous tightrope balancing national, personal, and global interests, duty and obligation.

12.2.1 Place and Identity

Tightrope exemplifies Mawer's implicit and explicit reluctance to label or classify his works or himself as a novelist. Unlike the majority of reviewers, who tend to highlight the hybrid nature of the novels, which simultaneously inhabit both literary and popular categories[83], Mawer considers both *The Girl Who Fell from the Sky* and *Tightrope* as character studies. What reviewers almost always mention with regard to both novels is the amount of attention the author dedicates to period detail, texture, and his keen sense of place and time. It is place and space which once again assume the leading role in the conception of Mawer's poetics. And *Tightrope* proves that spatial aspects of the narration can contribute to the appeal of the genre of spy fiction as a whole. The spatial poetics of the novel echoes its protagonist's state of mind, just as it reflects the overall atmosphere of "suspense and disquiet" (Bubíková 2021, 8). Mawer's tendency to place his protagonists in the midst of turbulent regions and eras allows him to observe their effect on the process of the identity formation of the characters, which contributes to his works serving as rewarding sources of geocritical analysis. In order to fully comprehend his protagonists, it is necessary to interpret them within the spatio-temporal context of the story. If we are to follow Mawer's lead and read *Tightrope* as a peculiar type of character study as well as an acute observation of both wartime and post-war England and Europe, then Marian's position and approach to spaces and places within the novel must be determined.

Tightrope trades in the varied urban and rural settings of *The Girl Who Fell from the Sky* (London, Oxford, Scotland, occupied France, Paris) for

83 See Pengelly 2015, Sansom 2015, Cooke 2012.

mostly urban ones – the majority of the novel is set in London of the late forties and very early fifties. Marian returns after being tortured by the Gestapo and later escaping from a prison camp in Germany. She is supposed to be coming home, both literally and metaphorically, although this fundamental concept seems to be alien to her: "Where was she going? She had to keep reminding herself – she was going home, wherever that was" (Mawer 2015, 17). Marian's ability to perceive home and homeland as places from which she could derive feelings of stability, nurture, and security had severely atrophied. She lacks what humanistic geographers such as Yi-Fu Tuan conceived as an inherent aspect of spatial perception – she is unable to perceive England, London, or Oxford as places to which she would be emotionally or rationally attached (Low 2021, 5), or as places to which she could relate as points of stability providing an "organized world of meaning" (Tuan 2018, 179).

This disorientation and the inability to identify the centre of her existence is partly due to Marian's PTSD, which she is instructed to call "combat fatigue" rather than shell shock, although, as she insists, she has never been in combat (Mawer 2015, 41). Another reason Mawer offers as an explanation of her inability to return "home" is her hybrid identity, which both contributed to her uprootedness and secured her the position as an SOE agent in the first place. Upon her return to England, Marian views herself as having no useful skills other than languages and "an ability to kill people" (Mawer 2015, 83). Her hybridity is mostly perceived in linguistic terms (Mawer 2015, 121) and her bilingualism functions as one of her major assets in *The Girl Who Fell from the Sky* – as its narrative unfolds, it is mostly thematised through other aspects of Marian's identity and her moral authenticity. *Tightrope* focuses on the absence of a clearly defined self as Marian becomes infested with subterfuge to the extent that she loses her own self in the process. Even her name, "was hers and not hers, the name that had been covered by a whole panoply of other names – Alice, Anne-Marie Laroche, Laurence Follette, Geneviève Marchal – all hiding the one fragile fact of Marian Sutro, who sat alone at the table driven with fear" (Mawer 2015, 123). Mawer's persuasive evocation of her initial psychological state proves his ability to portray the human mind under stress and mediate the intangible. Marian suffers from flashbacks and nightmares, rendering her hard-won freedom almost unbearable: "The mere act of leaving the house was becoming ever more difficult to achieve. Sometimes it brought panic, welling inside her like a kind of vomit, an uncontrollable, visceral fear sweeping up through her heart and flooding into her head" (Mawer 2015, 92). As open spaces initially set off panic attacks, Marian seeks enclosed spaces, such as the "sanctuary" (Mawer 2015; 29, 128) of her room. Marian's perception of space faithfully mirrors her mental states as Mawer uses both spatial triggers and spatial figures in order to express her anxiety. As a result, Marian feels "like someone edging along the brink of a precipice" (Mawer 2015, 96) who finds herself "on the edge of a cliff, with nothing to stop you stepping over the edge" (Mawer 2015, 92).

> The space around her was enormous and threatening, like the Boulevard de Belleville as it had been on that day of her betrayal. Yet here there was no market, no army lorries, no soldiers lining up to sweep between the buildings in their search for her. Plane trees, yes, but the city was just Oxford on a placid midweek day in summer. Not Paris during the occupation, not the silver city tarnished to dull grey. No *barrages* and *rafles*, no grim-faced occupiers and glum Parisians, reduced to acquiescence and compliance, but a golden city of ancient stone and placid self-confidence, with birds singing and the occasional don cycling past, gown billowing. (Mawer 2015, 92)

As one of the symptoms of her PTSD, she even experiences occasional episodes of "fugue", where she forgets where she is:

> She sat on the bed for a moment and tried to gather her scattered thoughts. She knew who she was but not where she was, nor what she was doing here in this dull hotel room with the hard, narrow bed and the ghastly picture of galloping horses on the wall, and an unknown world outside.
>
> London, of course. Presumably. Presumably London. But where and why? Questions crowded in on her, threatened to overturn her, like waves overturning a fragile rowing boat. Where was she? (Mawer 2015, 191)

The use of this element of Marian's traumatism illustrates the importance Mawer ascribes to the spatial aspects of his narrative. Marian knows who she is, but it is her inability to locate herself in time and space that poignantly exemplifies the horrifying state of her tortured, traumatised mind and also implies her general disorientation. There are also the falling dreams (Mawer 2015, 133), – "the plunging, floating" (Mawer 2015, 191), "flying" (Mawer 2015, 360) dreams. Marian's psychological anguish is rendered mainly through spatial means. Mawer's approach to spatial elements in *Tightrope* echoes the potential and acuteness of those from *The Girl Who Fell from the Sky* – their multisensory character facilitates their reception, enhances the interaction between the characters and the landscape of the novel and allows them to venture beyond their referential function (Westphal 2011, 75), echoing Prieto's and Tally's conception of geocriticism.

Marian's life after her physical recovery is seemingly harmonious, but mostly it is frustratingly monotonous. Although she is advised to welcome the dreariness of everyday existence as it might help her as well as others recover from the shock of the war: "Perhaps dullness is what we need now" (Mawer 2015, 104), she sees her life as an aimless sequence of banalities, feeling that "she was drifting through a neutral space, where there was neither love nor hate, neither danger nor safety, neither peace nor war" (Mawer 2015, 104). Marian's wish for a clearer direction is quickly granted as she is contacted and recruited by a shadowy organisation which operates "in peacetime just as much as in war" (Mawer 2015, 84). The war she thought had ended rages on "except that this one doesn't yet involve killing people" (Mawer 2015, 267). With the world of safe binary oppositions overturned, London, which should have played the role of home, quickly turns into a war zone for Marian. The tube is seen as "the best way to throw off a follower, the place you could deploy the tricks of the trade with ease" (Mawer 2015, 309) and she has to remind herself constantly that it is "London in peacetime" (Mawer 2015, 353). And although the subsequent development of events places Marian into the maelstrom of the thermonuclear arms race, it also allows her to find her lost sense of self and identity. The drabness of London has been replaced by a constant observation and evaluation of its risks, and thus Marian is once again capable of approaching it as something she is able to comprehend, reading it "as a text, as an inscription of man in space" (Barthes 1971, 167). In other words, Marian once again maps the terrain as part of her professional perspective and is most likely being subjected to mapping as a spy is most likely being followed and assessed, i.e. mapped in turn. Although Westphal's conception of geocriticism mostly concerns maps and their real or imaginary counterparts, the mutual influence between maps and their users can also be seen as one of its aspects.

12.2.2 A Geopolitical Conflict from a Geocritical Perspective

The profound ambiguity of the geopolitical conflict makes it almost impossible for Marian to navigate. The inability to identify sides, evaluate their true motives, and determine the loyalties of those involved make it impossible for battle lines to be "drawn as they were during the war" (Mawer 2015, 214). This insertion of highly heterogenising forces contributes to general paranoia, but also allows for a highly unstable environment of "non-equilibrium" (Westphal 2011, 19), which, at least from the point of view of Westphal's conception of geocriticism, is rich in developmental and creative potential. It certainly rings true for Marian, who slides "as smooth as an eel, into that shadow world she had known during the war" (Mawer 2015, 218). However, just as she feels driven and her mission provides her with a long-lost structure and sense of purpose, she becomes overcome with uncertainty about the ethical and moral implications of her and the Agency's endeavours. In spite of the seemingly strict dichotomy established by the Cold War, Marian realises the moral implications of the near-entropy she faces: "She wondered what to do. In the war it had been easy. The moral boundaries were two dimensional, drawn in black and white. But now things seemed complex and diffuse, lines cross-hatched and overlapping, shapes irregular and enigmatic, drawn in shades of grey as though with a piece of charcoal. Clair-obscur" (Mawer 2015, 210). Marian's response to this ambiguity appears quite logical given the highly unstable environment – she attempts to reinstate at least some sense of equilibrium by assuming the role of double agent. In terms of character development, her ability to see the situation in its complexity points at her maturation, but also tests her sense of ethics and her loyalties to the limit. Ultimately, she needs to either betray or desert some of those closest to her and thus sacrifice the background of her family and her home country in order to protect them while securing the balance between the two sides of the global conflict.

The title of the novel cements the prominence of the spatial imagery of the novel as the "tightrope" truly acts as its central spatial metaphor. Trying to "balance out" (Mawer 2015, 240) the thermonuclear race by passing on information to the Russians, Marian "felt like walking a tightrope, feeling the balance, knowing that a slight shift either side might be fatal. She reached her foot forward and poised to transfer her weight onto it, feeling the rope wobbling. No safety net" (Mawer 2015, 269). In spite of her unenviable situation, Marian is fully capable of navigating it, no longer resembling Alice falling through a rabbit hole, which was a prominent image and another spatial figure in *The Girl Who Fell from the Sky*.

In *Tightrope*, the seemingly familiar terrain Marian traverses is paradoxically as treacherous and hostile, if not more so, than that of wartime France. With every step she takes, and every certainty taken away from her, she becomes more mature and self-reliant. Severing all familial ties, she eventually truly masters the art of espionage. As she learns along the way, the world she thought she knew may never have existed, and it grows less and less familiar every day. The black and white binaries have been replaced by the "shades of grey" (Mawer 2015, 396) of non-equilibrium, which does not bring Marian peace, but makes for a great spy novel.

The ending of *Tightrope* mirrors the conclusion of *The Girl Who Fell from the Sky*. Marian recalls the fatal mistake she made by responding to her real name when she was supposed to have been using a cover name. More than 30 years after the main events of the plot, Marian retells the story to the enchanted narrator, Sam. She used to be his childhood crush, and as the riveting climax of the novel reveals, she used him for her disappearance. At this point, Marian admits that she no longer knows "what her name is" (Mawer 2015, 399), as if to point to the hybridity seeping into the very core of her being. It is surprisingly not the first time she has wondered what her real name is (Mawer 2015, 219). During her active career as an agent back in England, she used Swallow as her code name "with its implications of flight, of speed, of swoop, but also with hints of gullibility" (Mawer 2015, 218). But even then she was beginning to see words as mere approximations of reality because, as she realised, "life has no exact meanings, only shades of meanings, hints, versions and contradictions, a confusion of love and hates, of motives and desires" (Mawer 2015, 93). Her final warning to Sam is to avoid getting involved in the dubious game of shades of grey (Mawer 2015, 396).

In the end, Marian does get a happy ending – she lives near Laq Lemans in Switzerland with a man she loved, or at least she thought she had loved. The circle closes – the Swiss region is where she came from and it shaped her decision to become a spy. Her father worked as a diplomat for the League of Nations and Marian thus acquired a fondness for democratic principles as well as her bilingualism. She lives according to a proverb she first heard years ago during her training: "*Pour vivre heureux, vivons cachés*": She becomes the embodiment of camouflage: "She was like the cricket – cryptic, camouflaged, concealed" (Mawer 2015, 154). Her extraordinary skills of mimesis contributed to her success as a spy and helped her to survive, but ultimately at the expense of her personality. As she fully embraced both espionage and later camouflage as a way of life, partly because she wanted to and partly because she was forced to, she eventually created and inhabited an illusion, both personally by assuming a false identity or even identities, and also by her choice of where to live. To close Marian's story where it started, Mawer situates her in Switzerland. This choice enhances the circular nature of the plot, but it also emphasises the illusory element of Marian's existence. Mawer describes Switzerland itself as fantastic and of a fabricated nature, bordering on Foucault's heterotopia, a counter-place which simultaneously contradicts and challenges, but also reflects, all other places (Foucault 1986, 24–27): Switzerland, "living as it does on the fantasies of all the others, has always been the least real of European countries" (Mawer 2015, 1). Marian's search for home "wherever that was" (Mawer 2015, 17), a place from which she would be able to derive meaning and a sense of belonging, fittingly ends in a country which Mawer depicts as a reflection of her uprooted, hybrid character, cementing his ability to link his protagonists almost inextricably to their environments.

Conclusion

This monograph maps the treatment of space and place in the work of Jim Crace and Simon Mawer and, by extension, it illustrates the vitality of this phenomenon in contemporary fiction. By means of comparative analysis, it seeks to examine how the individual novels of the authors relate to contemporary literary theory concerned with space and place. Addressing both noticeable similarities as well as prominent idiosyncrasies in their fiction, it demonstrates the variety of forms and approaches to the topocentric qualities of the writings of the two novelists. The central premise of this text is the fact that the crucial common denominator of Crace's and Mawer's oeuvres is their proclaimed preoccupation with spatial representations, that is, their intense concern with diverse ways of rendering imagined, real, and real-and-imagined places and landscapes in their stories. We found this thematic and narrative affinity so fundamental to their novels that we decided to make it our study's primary subject of inquiry, despite the fact that the two discussed authors are rather unlikely to know each other personally, or even to be familiar with each other's writings. Our findings and conclusions are therefore drawn predominantly from our in-depth textual analyses on the basis of the said theoretical framework.

Crace's exceptional ability to convincingly portray concocted settings as if they had real-life referents has been repeatedly noted and praised by critics and reviewers alike. Indeed, as a self-proclaimed landscape writer, he makes no secret of the fact that a meticulous construction of varied fictional environments is one of the hallmarks of his novels. Therefore, all of his novels could have been subjected to our spatial analysis, but for the sake of the study's scope, proportionality, and clarity of argument, a representative selection had to be made. In his first two novels, *Continent* and *The Gift of Stones*, Crace introduces his major thematic and narrative dyad of communities in transition in imaginary landscapes, while *Signals of Distress* and *Quarantine* most explicitly rely on the interconnectedness between the construction of their settings and characterisation. As urban novels, *Arcadia* and *The Melody* explore the mutual influence of modern, globalised city life and metamorphoses of the cityscape, and in *The Pesthouse* and *Harvest* the author makes use of the device of the mapping narrative to complement his complex rendering of fictional landscapes with yet another dimension. Consequently, four of his twelve novels have been left out of this final selection: in *Being Dead* (1999) and *All That Follows* (2010), spatial representation is rather subdued in order to give more space to their other thematic concerns, and spatial aspects of the former are examined in Stephen Palmer's article "'Dead but not departed yet': the exploration of liminal space in Jim Crace's *Being Dead* (1999)" (2012); *Six* (2003), though also an urban novel, does not treat the cityscape as thoroughly as *Arcadia* and *The Melody*, focusing instead on its protagonist's love affairs within the city, which is why it does not offer any new insights for the purposes of our study; and *eden* (2022), Crace's latest novel to date, was published when the process of our work was already in its final stages. However, with its playful yet thought-provoking dichotomy between a tranquil and everlasting paradisal garden situated on earth and the surrounding landscape inhabited by common humans, the novel offers fertile material for potential spatial analysis in the future.

There are two key points of departure for analysing the representation of space in Crace's novels: first, the environments in which their stories are set and which their protagonists occupy play a determining role in the novel's framework of meaning. In other words, they function not only as settings and backgrounds, but also as leitmotifs, subject matter, metaphors, symbols, reflections of characters' states of mind and development, constitutive elements of characters' personalities, and even self-contained characters of a kind. And second, all these environments, no matter how lifelike and authentic they may appear, are always wholly made up. Although Crace admits to some indirect sources of inspiration – existing places and areas – his fictional landscapes are never modelled on them and remain at the level of ideas that spark his imagination. As a result, these sources of inspiration and the actual landscapes of his novels are often remote, both geographically and historically. Accordingly, the literary-theoretical concepts that have proved most applicable to Crace's rendering and treatment of literary space are

Yi-Fu Tuan's humanistic geography and Robert T. Tally's and Eric Prieto's ego-centred variants of geocriticism since they provide illustrative analytical instruments to reflect the aforementioned points of departure and their further consequences for the particular narratives. However, for the sake of complexity of analysis, other relevant concepts have also been employed, particularly Zygmunt Bauman's postmodern identity patterns and retrotopia, Michel de Certeau's practices of modern urban life, Michel Foucault's heterotopia, Edward Soja's Thirdspace, and the philosophy of Transmodernism.

The selection, ordering, and approach to the literary works analysed in this monograph reflect their role within the context of Simon Mawer's oeuvre as well as the primacy of their spatial elements within their overall poetics. Accordingly, they may be grouped into three main categories. Whereas the first two categories correspond mainly with their geographical setting (the Mediterranean, central Europe), the third is based on a historical setting – WW2 and its aftermath – and also represents a genre preference – spy fiction. Other factors which contributed to the final selection of the works for analysis are their critical reception and their role within the context of the author's works, either pioneering and foreshadowing further development, or acting as a final culmination of a literary endeavour. The novels' ability to concentrate key motifs, themes, and aspects was also taken into consideration, and there was also an effort to avoid repetition as the novels tend to be built around similar principles and notions. As a result, *Chimera*, Mawer's literary debut situated in the Mediterranean, eclipsed *The Bitter Cross*, *Swimming to Ithaca,* and *A Jealous God*. Although all the novels are also situated in the Mediterranean, none of them articulates the chief elements of Mawer's poetics or thematise the spatial aspect as expressively as *Chimera*, although all of them are mentioned at some point in this monograph. A similar decision resulted in the omission of *The Fall*, because although it revolves around mountaineering and involves a prominent spatial motif that also functions as a symbol, the North Face of the Eiger, its structuring and compactness cannot rival the dynamism and sharp focus of *The Glass Room*. Neither *The Girl Who Fell from the Sky* nor *Tightrope* faced any significant competition since they function as equal components of a narrative whose uniqueness stems from its ability to merge the characters with their settings. Novels such as the most recent, *Ancestry*, or the slightly underappreciated *The Gospel of Judas*, were not considered because of their explicit lack of any prominent spatial elements. Mawer's non-fiction works, *A Place in Italy*, his autobiographical account of life in the country, and his concise biography *Gregor Mendel: Planting the Seeds of Genetics,* are mentioned only in connection with elements they complement from the author's fictional works, most notably *Chimera* and *Mendel's Dwarf.* The final selection of novels provides a representative sample of the author's poetics, employing various elements of spatiality that simultaneously echo and complement the thematic, structural, and poetic choices of Jim Crace, whose novels occupy a similar enough position within the canon of contemporary British fiction to be placed alongside Mawer's, yet are different enough to be able to provide sufficient material for critical analysis.

From the whole complex of Mawer's novels, those selected as the basis of the interpretative portion of this volume were deemed to be the most representative of the author's poetics. What *Chimera* (1989), *Mendel's Dwarf* (1997), *The Glass Room* (2009), *The Girl Who Fell from the Sky* (2012), *Tightrope* (2015), and *Prague Spring* (2018) illustrate and exemplify is the author's keen sense of place and space in his novels, and his penchant for accurate historical detail on the one hand, but also for a great deal of poetic licence on the other. The defining quality of Mawer's novels is liminality, which permeates all elements of his fiction, demonstrated most prominently through tumultuous historical periods of social, cultural, political, religious, and ideological upheaval and through his choice of characters who are geographically uprooted, linguistically hybrid, and often rather undefined in terms of identity. This tendency, together with Mawer's preference for parallel plotlines and the insertion of circular aspects into the overall arrangement of his narratives, results in the rather complex nature of his novels, which are in need of a unifying element. Mawer most often employs a powerful central conceit, which is often spatial and acts simultaneously as an anchor of the narrative while reflecting it. The frequent use of cyclical elements of the plot, emphasised by a series of analogies, highlight the circular nature of Mawer's novels, which sometimes acquire an almost mythical quality. In general, Mawer's novels present places and spaces from a number of different angles, often transcending the role of mere settings and environments for the characters to become universal expressions of spatial experience. This perspective, together with Mawer's preference for actual historical events and real places, finds its theoretical counterpart in a host of disciplines that are applicable to his novels. Their focus on human experience of time, movement, space, and place responds to the key concerns of humanistically oriented approaches, such as the humanistic geography of Yi-Fu Tuan and the phenomenology of perception, particularly in relation to the experience of intimate places as defined by Gaston Bachelard. The author's tendency to plant his fabricated stories in the soil of accurate historical details and real places and events pulls the analysis in the direction of key concepts of similarly oriented disciplines, such as geo-centred variants of geocriticism, especially that developed by Bertrand Westphal, but also deep topography and psychogeography, which are mostly concerned with the connection between the past and the present mediated by means of spaces and places, and even ecocriticism, whose inclusive and interdisciplinary variant proves productive in analysing the fusion of protagonists and their settings.

The focus of this monograph has been shaped by the importance that Crace and Mawer ascribe to spatial elements in their works. This phenomenon is characteristic of their fiction and is therefore reflected by a number of other aspects, although those may only be revealed on closer inspection. Both authors claim to eschew the constraints of traditional genres and consider their works to be novels of ideas. What they see as the central and governing element of their work is the exploration of the essence of the human condition, which assumes the form of an ethical or philosophical query. They adopt similar strategies while rendering this – they mostly set their works in the past, in times of ongoing historical, cultural, and social transformation. Their plots often revolve around protagonists who are intimately connected with their physical environments, and the character and degree of this bond permeates the poetics of these novels. Both authors cultivate a number of other analogies, not only between the characters and their surroundings, but also between the real and the imaginary, the present and the past, and the communal and the individual. The process of profound change is also mirrored in the liminal nature of the protagonists, whose in-betweenness or hybridity takes different forms and conditions their development within the novels' stories. They suffer the consequences of such a change, try to resist it, but gradually resign themselves and adapt to the newly established circumstances.

In addition to these affinities between the thematic and aesthetic properties of the novels of Crace and Mawer, there are also differences arising from the contrary points of departure of their creative processes, which are, however, motivated by similar aims. Whereas Crace transforms the past into a purely imaginary realm through which to comment on the present and its pressing issues, Mawer, in order to do the same, creates a parallel between the past and the present, or between different levels of the past, and situates his narratives in persuasive simulations of historical reality. This tendency also affects the genre of their works. Although both authors refuse to label their works, Mawer's novels can be considered genre fiction, whereas Crace's works are less clearly marked by genre-specific qualities. Unlike Crace, who projects his poetic license into all aspects of his imaginary lands, Mawer enlivens his acutely observed works by incorporating elements of popular genres, such as thrillers, spy novels, war novels, and science fiction. Thus, the two authors strive to achieve a similar result by drawing on almost opposite approaches to the past and history. Mawer manipulates some of its aspects while maintaining the semblance of authenticity, while Crace repudiates it completely for the sake of the idea he wishes to illustrate through his imaginative narrative, which is nevertheless always inspired by genuine human experience. Both approaches then raise questions not only about the degree of accuracy and veracity of their spatial representations, but also about the role of fiction in constructing an image of the past as well as its influence on the present.

The comparative analysis of the authors' narratives reveals that, despite their opposing approaches to real-life referents in terms of history and geography, i.e. the presence of actual places and historical events in the case of Mawer's works and their absence and replacement by purely fictional situations and places only vaguely reminiscent of their real-life models in Crace's, the outcomes are very comparable and their novels successfully explore fundamental questions of human existence. It can be concluded that the similarities between these authors prevail while their differing spatiotemporal conceptions invite a dialogical reading, which was one of this study's primary aspirations. Both authors clearly contribute to the ongoing discussion of identity, which is considered to be one of the key thematic aspects of contemporary fiction. Their diverse contributions provide two unique points of view, which nevertheless share a related focus on place and space. In this way, the work of Crace and Mawer contributes to the further diversification of present-day enquiry into the position of humankind in the world. This often takes the form of literary contemplation of human spatial experience, which is a testament to the complexity and dynamism of contemporary British fiction.

Bibliography

Ackroyd, Peter. "The Englishness of English Literature." *Proceedings of the XIXth International Conference of AEDEAN*. Vigo: University of Vigo, 1995: 11–19.

Ainley, Rosa. "Looking Back Again and Forward Re: Review and Reconstruction in Writing and Architecture." *Architecture and Culture,* vol.8, no. 1 (2020): 19–28.

Aliaga-Lavrijsen, Jessica, and José María Yebra-Pertusa. "Some Concluding Remarks." In *Transmodern Perspectives on Contemporary Literatures in English*, edited by Jessica Aliaga-Lavrijsen and José María Yebra-Pertusa, 237–244. New York and London: Routledge, 2019.

Allen, Nicola. "The Bald and the Beautiful: The Figure of the Shaven-Headed Female in the Fiction of Jim Crace." In *Jim Crace: Into the Wilderness*, edited by Katy Shaw and Kate Aughterson, 113–30. Basingstoke: Palgrave Macmillan, 2018.

Altman, Irwin and Setha M. Low. *Place Attachment*. New York: Springer, 1992.

Anténe, Petr. *Campus Novel Variations: A Comparative Study of an Anglo-American Genre*. Olomouc: Palacký University Olomouc, 2015.

Armbruster, Karla, and Kathleen R. Wallace, eds. *Beyond Nature Writing: Expanding the Boundaries of Ecocriticism*. Charlottesville and London: University Press of Virginia, 2001.

Ashcroft, Bill, Gareth Griffiths, and Helen Tiffin, eds. *Post-Colonial Studies: The Key Concepts*. New York: Routledge, 2007.

Ateljevic, Irena. "Visions of Transmodernity: A New Renaissance of our Human History?" *Integral Review* 9, no. 2 (June 2013): 200–219.

Atkins, Mark and Iain Sinclair. *Liquid City*. London: Reaktion Books, 1999.

Bachelard, Gaston. *The Poetics of Space*. Translated by Maria Jolas. Boston: Beacon Press, 1994.

Baldick, Chris. *The Concise Oxford Dictionary of Literary Terms*. Oxford: Oxford University Press, 2004.

Barnes, Julian. *England, England*. London: Picador, 2008.

Barthes, Roland. "Semiology and the Urban." In *Rethinking Architecture: A Reader in Cultural Theory*, edited by Neil Leach, 166-171. London and New York: Routledge, 1971.

Bauman, Zygmunt. *Life in Fragments. Essays In Postmodern Morality*. Oxford: Blackwell Publishers, 1995.

Bauman, Zygmunt. *Retrotopia*. Cambridge and Malden: Polity, 2017. E-book, pdf.

Benton, Tim. "Building Utopia." In *Modernism. Designing a New World*, edited by Christopher Wilk, 148-223. London: V&A Publishing, 2007.

Bentley, Nick. *Contemporary British Fiction*. London: Palgrave, 2018.

Bryson, Bill. *At Home. A Short History of Private Life*. London: Random House, 2010.
Bubíková, Šárka, and Olga Roebuck, eds. *Places and Spaces of Popular Imagination*. Krakow: Jagiellonian University Press, 2021.
Carroll, Lewis. *Alice's Adventures In Wonderland and Through The Looking-Glass: And What Alice Found There*. London: Everyman, 1993.
Carter, Erica, James Donald, and Judith Squires. *Space and Place: Theories of Identity and Location*. London: Lawrence and Wishart, 1993.
Caruth, Cathy. *Unclaimed Experience: Trauma, Narrative, and History*. Baltimore and London: The Johns Hopkins University Press, 1996.
Cavarero, Adriana. *Relating Narratives: Storytelling and Selfhood*. Translated by Paul A. Kottman. London and New York: Routledge, 2000.
Chalupský, Petr. "The Urban Pastoral – Hybridisations in Jim Crace's *Arcadia*." *Litteraria Pragensia* 20, no. 40 (2010): 38–53.
Chalupský, Petr. "A Parable of Humanity – Character and Landscape Construction in Jim Crace's *Signals of Distress*." *Ostrava Journal of English Philology* 4, no. 1 (2012): 33–44.
Chalupský, Petr. "The Imaginary Landscapes of Jim Crace's *Continent*." Athens Journal of Philology 5, no. 3 (2018): 201–219.
Chalupský, Petr. "The Landscape of Trauma, Pain and Hope in Jim Crace's *The Pesthouse*." *Ars Aeterna* 10, no. 1 (2018): 1–20.
Chalupský, Petr. "The Gift of Stories – Imagination and Landscape in Jim Crace's *The Gift of Stones*." *American and British Studies Annual* 12 (2019): 63–79.
Chalupský, Petr. "'Something Odd and Beautiful': Literary Cartography in Jim Crace's *Harvest*."*Brno Studies in English* 45, no. 1 (2019): 95–110.
Chalupský Petr. "'Siblings to the empty spaces in the heart': Space, Place and Landscape in Jim Crace's *Quarantine*." *Atlantis: Journal of the Spanish Association of Anglo-American Studies* 44, no. 1 (2022): 19–36.
Chalupský, Petr. "Transgressive Spatiality and Multiple Temporality in Jim Crace's *Arcadia*." *American and British Studies Annual* 15, (2022): 49–63.
Chalupský, Petr. "Spatialising the Transmodern in Jim Crace's *The Melody*." In Transmodern Literatures Of(f) the Limit, edited by Claus Peter Newman and María del Pilar Royo Grasa. London and New York: Routledge (in print).
Coverley, Merlin. *Psychogeography*. Harperden: Oldcastle Books, 2018.
Crace, Jim. *Signals of Distress*. London: Penguin Books, 1995.
Crace, Jim. *The Gift of Stones*. London: Picador, 1997.
Crace, Jim. *Arcadia*. London: Penguin Books, 1998a.
Crace, Jim. *Quarantine*. London: Penguin Books, 1998b.
Crace, Jim. *The Pesthouse*. London: Picador, 2007.
Crace, Jim. *Continent*. London: Picador, 2008.
Crace, Jim. *Harvest*. London: Picador, 2013.
Crace, Jim. *The Melody*. London: Picador, 2018.
Cresswell, Tim. *Place: An Introduction*. Somerset: Wiley, 2015.
Currie, Gregory. *Narratives & Narrators: A Philosophy of Stories*. Oxford: Oxford University Press, 2010.
Černá, Iveta, and Dagmar Černoušková. *Tugendhat – Ludwig Mies van der Rohe's Commision in Brno*. Brno: Brno City Museum, 2011.
Davies, Colin. *A New History of Modern Architecture*. London: Laurence King Publishing, 2018.
Dean Pilcher, Lydia. *A Call to Spy*. USA, 2019.
de Botton, Alain. *The Architecture of Happiness*. London: Penguin Books, 2007.

de Certeau, Michel. *The Practice of Everyday Life*. Translated by Steven Rendall. Berkeley and Los Angeles: University of California Press, 1988.

De Groot, Jerome. *The Historical Novel. The New Critical Idiom*. Abingdon: Routledge, 2010.

De Groot, Jerome. *Remaking History. The Past in Contemporary Historical Fiction*. Abingdon: Routledge, 2016.

de Lange, Attie, Fincham, Gail, Hawthorn, Jeremy and Jakob Lothe. "Introduction." In *Literary Landscapes: From Modernism to Postcolonialism*, edited by Attie de Lange et al., xi–xxv. Basingstoke: Palgrave Macmillan, 2008.

Deleuze, Gilles, and Felix Guattari. *A Thousand Plateaus: Capitalism and Schizophrenia*. Translated by Brian Massumi. Minneapolis: University of Minnesota Press, 2000.

Eberle, Jakub. "Desire as Geopolitics: Reading *The Glass Room* as Central European Fantasy." *International Political Sociology* vol.12, no. 2 (2018): 172–189.

Eisen, Norman. *The Last Palace*. New York: Crown Publishing, 2018.

Eliade, Mircea. *The Myth of the Eternal Return: Or, Cosmos and History*. Princeton: Princeton University Press, 1954.

Eliot, Thomas Stearns. *The Complete Poems and Plays*. London: Faber and Faber, 2004.

Erpenbeck, Jenny. *Visitation*. London: Portobello Books, 2011.

Fagan, Brian M., and Nadia Durrani. *Archaeology: A Brief Introduction*. 12th ed., London: Routledge, 2016.

Faulks, Sebastian. *Snow Country*. London: Hutchinson, 2021.

Fiske, John. *Reading the Popular*. London: Routledge, 1991.

Foucault, Michel. *Discipline and Punish: The Birth of the Prison*. Translated by Alan Sheridan. New York: Random House, 1979.

Finch, Jason. *Deep Locational Criticism: Imaginative Place in Literary Research and Teaching*. Åbo Akademi University: John Benjamins Publishing Company, 2016.

Foucault, Michel. "Of Other Spaces." *Diacritics* 16, no. 1 (1986): 22–27.

Frampton, Kenneth. *Modern Architecture. A Critical History*. London: Thames and Hudson, 1994.

Freeman, Mark. "Mythical Time, Historical Time, and the Narrative Fabric of the Self." *Narrative Inquiry*. Amsterdam: John Benjamins B.V. (1998): 27–50.

Freud, Sigmund. "Civilization and its Discontents." In *The Complete Psychological Works of Sigmund Freud: Sigmund Freud's Complete Works*, Vol. 21, *The Future of an Illusion, Civilization and its Discontents and Other Works*. Translated by James Strachey. London: Hogarth Press, 1978.

Gamble, Clive. *Archaeology: The Basics*. 3rd ed., London: Routledge, 2015.

Ganteau, Jean-Michel, and Susana Onega. "Introduction: Transcending the Postmodern." In *Transcending the Postmodern*, edited by Jean-Michel Ganteau and Susana Onega, 1–19. New York and London: Routledge, 2020.

Garrard, Greg. *Ecocriticism*. Oxon: Routledge, 2011.

Glotfelty, Cheryll, and Harold Fromm, eds. *The Ecocriticism Reader: Landmarks in Literary Ecology*. Athens: University of Georgia Press, 1996.

Gottschall, Jonathan. *The Storytelling Animal: How Stories Make Us Human*. New York: Houghton Mifflin Harcourt Publishing, 2012.

Greene, Kevin. *Archaeology: An Introduction*. 3rd ed., London: Routledge, 1997.

Greene, Kevin. *Archaeology: An Introduction*. 5th ed., London: Routledge, 2010.

Groes, Sebastian. 2018. "Thinking Crace: Consciousness and Cognition in Jim Crace's *Quarantine* and *Being Dead*." In *Jim Crace: Into the Wilderness*, edited by Katy Shaw and Kate Aughterson, 149–164. Basingstoke: Palgrave Macmillan, 2018.

Harding, Thomas. *The House by the Lake*. London: Penguin Random House, 2015.

Hardy, Steve. *Relations of Place: Aspects of Late 20th Century Fiction and Theory*. Brno: Masaryk University, 2008.

Harries, Karsten. *The Ethical Function of Architecture*. Cambridge: The MIT Press, 1997.

Hauptmann, Deborah. *Architecture and the Time of Space. The Double Progression of Body and Brain*. Delft: TU Delft BK, 2020.

Head, Dominic. *The Cambridge Introduction to Modern British Fiction, 1950–2000*. Cambridge: Cambridge University Press, 2002.

Heidegger, Martin. "Building, Dwelling, Thinking." In *Poetry, Language, Thought*, 141–161. Translated by Albert Hofstadter. New York: Perennial Classics, 2001.

Heidegger, Martin. *Basic Writings*. London: Routledge, 2011.

Hutcheon, Linda. *The Politics of Postmodernism*. 2nd ed. London: Routledge, 2002.

Jasper, David. *The Sacred Desert: Religion, Literature, Art, and Culture*. Oxford: Blackwell Publishing, 2004.

Jenks, Chris, ed. *Visual Culture*. London: Routledge, 1995.

Kermode, Frank. *The Sense of an Ending: Studies in the Theory of Fiction*. London: OUP, 1967.

Kundera, Milan. *The Unbearable Lightness of Being*. London: Faber and Faber, 1999.

Lane, Richard J. "The Fiction of Jim Crace: Narrative and Recovery." In *Contemporary British Fiction*, edited by Richard J. Lane et al., 27–39. Cambridge: Polity Press, 2003.

Lane, Richard J., Rod Mengham, and Philip Tew, eds. *Contemporary British Fiction*. Cambridge: Polity Press, 2007.

Lea, Daniel. *Twenty-First-Century Fiction: Contemporary British Voices*. Manchester: Manchester University Press, 2019.

Le Corbusier. *Towards a New Architecture*. Translated by Frederick Etchells. London: The Architectural Press, 1976.

Lefebvre, Henri. *The Production of Space*. Translated by Donald Nicholson-Smith. Blackwell, 1984.

Lehan, Richard. *The City in Literature: An Intellectual and Cultural History*. Berkeley: University of California Press, 1998.

Lerer, Seth. *Children's Literature. A Reader's History from Aesop to Harry Potter*. Chicago: The University of Chicago Press, 2009.

Letissier, Georges. "'The Eternal Loop of Self-torture': Ethics and Trauma in Ian McEwan's *Atonement*." In *Ethics and Trauma in Contemporary British Fiction*, edited by Susana Onega and Jean Michel Ganteau, 209–226. Amsterdam and New York: Rodopi, 2009.

Lilley, Deborah. "Pastoral Concerns in the Fictions of Jim Crace." In *Jim Crace: Into the Wilderness*, edited by Katy Shaw and Kate Aughterson, 33–48. Basingstoke: Palgrave Macmillan, 2018.

Loos, Adolph. "Ornament and Crime." In *Ornament and Crime*, 19–24. Riverside, California: Ariadne Press, 1997.

Low, Celine. "The Topos of Glass at the Intersection of Architecture and Literature" MA diss., National University of Singapore, 2021.

Lutwack, Leonard. *The Role of Place in Literature*. Syracuse: Syracuse University Press, 1984.

Mączyńska, Magdalena. *The Gospel According to the Novelist: Religious Scripture and Contemporary Fiction*. London and New York: Bloomsbury Academic, 2015.

Malmgren, Carl Darryl. *Fictional Space in the Modernist and Postmodernist American Novel*. London and Toronto: Associated University Press, 1985.

Mawer, Simon. *Chimera*. London: Hamish Hamilton, 1989.

Mawer, Simon. *The Bitter Cross*. London: Sinclair Stevenson, 1992.

Mawer, Simon. *A Place in Italy*. London: Sinclair Stevenson, 1992.

Mawer, Simon. *A Jealous God*. London: André Deutsch, 1996.

Mawer, Simon. *Mendel's Dwarf*. London: Transworld, 1997.

Mawer, Simon. *The Gospel of Judas*. London: Little, Brown, 2000.

Mawer, Simon. *The Fall*. London: Little, Brown, 2003.

Mawer, Simon. *Swimming to Ithaca*. London: Abacus, 2006.

Mawer, Simon. *Gregor Mendel. Planting the Seeds of Genetics*. New York: Abrahams in association with The Field Museum, Chicago, 2006.

Mawer, Simon. *The Glass Room*. London: Little, Brown, 2009.

Mawer, Simon. *The Girl Who Fell from the Sky*. London: Little, Brown, 2012.

Mawer, Simon. *Tightrope*. London: Little, Brown, 2015.

Mawer, Simon. *Prague Spring*. London: Little, Brown, 2018.

Mawer. Simon. *Ancestry*. London: Little, Brown, 2022.

Menigan, Tim, ed. *Frameworks, Artworks, Place: The Space of Perception in the Modern World*. New York: Rodopi, 2008.

Miller, Lucasta. "The Booker Prize's Historical Novels Aren't Living in the Past." *The Times*. October 2, 2009.

Peraldo, Emmanuelle, ed. *Literature and Geography: The Writing of Space Throughout History*. Newcastle upon Tyne: Cambridge Scholars Publishing, 2016.

Peraldo, Emmanuelle. "Introduction: The Meeting of Two Practices of Space: Literature and Geography." In *Literature and Geography: The Writing of Space Throughout History*, edited by Emmanuelle Peraldo, 1–16. Newcastle Upon Tyme: Cambridge Scholars Publishing, 2016.

Prieto, Eric. "Geocriticism, Geopoetics, Geophilosophy, and Beyond." In *Geocritical Explorations*, edited by Robert T. Tally, Jr., 13–27. New York: Palgrave Macmillan Press, 2011.

Prieto, Eric. *Literature, Geography and the Postmodern Poetics of Place*. Basingstoke: Palgrave Macmillan, 2012.

Robertson, Naomi. "The Glass House Building as an Embodiment of the Changing Fate of Jews in Budapest from 1848 to the Present." In *Global Perspectives on the Holocaust: History, Identity, Legacy*, edited by Nancy E. Rupprecht and Wendy Koenig, 93–115. Newcastle upon Tyne, England: Cambridge Scholars Publishing, 2015.

Rothberg, Michael. *Multidirectional Memory: Remembering the Holocaust in the Age of Decolonization*. Stanford University Press, 2009.

Rousselot, Elodie. *Exoticizing the Past in Contemporary Neo-Historical Fiction*. Basingstoke, Hampshire: Palgrave Macmillan, 2014.

Saggini, Francesca, and Anna Enrichetta Soccio, eds. *The House of Fiction as the House of Life: Representations of the House from Richardson to Woolf*. Newcastle upon Tyne: Cambridge Scholars Publishing, 2012.

Schulze, Franz and Edward Windhorst. *Mies van der Rohe. A Critical Biography, New and Revised Edition*. Chicago: University of Chicago Press, 2012.

Shaw, Katy, and Kate Aughterson, eds. *Jim Crace: Into the Wilderness*. Basingstoke: Palgrave Macmillan, 2018.

Silverman, Max. *Palimpsestic Memory: The Holocaust and Colonialism in French and Francophone Fiction and Film*. New York: Berghahn Books, 2016.

Sinclair, Iain. *Lights Out for the Territory*. London: Penguin Books, 2003.

Slezkine, Yuri. *The House of Government*. Princeton: Princeton University Press, 2017.

Soja, Edward W. *Thirdspace: Journeys to Los Angeles and Other Real-and-Imagined Places*. Oxford: Blackwell Publisher, 1996.

Spaulding, Amy E. *The Art of Storytelling: Telling Truths through Telling Stories*. Lanham, Toronto, Plymouth: The Scarecrow Press, 2011.

Spurr, David. *Architecture and Modern Literature*. Ann Arbor: The University of Michigan Press, 2012.

Steffens, J. (ed.). 2009. *Unpacking my Library: Architects and Their Books* New Haven: Yale University Press.

Ševčík, Julius, director. *Skleněný pokoj* [*The Affair.*] In Film production in co-production with Investito, Česká Televize, TV JOJ, 2019.
Tally, Robert T. Jr.. "On Geocriticism." In *Geocritical Explorations: Space, Place, and Mapping in Literary and Cultural Studies*, edited by Robert T. Tally, Jr., 1–9. Basingstoke: Palgrave Macmillan, 2011.
Tally, Robert T. Jr.. "Translator's Preface: The Timely Emergence of Geocriticism." In *Geocriticism: Real and Fictional Spaces*, edited by Bertrand Westphal, ix–xiii. Basingstoke: Palgrave Macmillan, 2011.
Tally, Robert T., Jr., ed. *Geocritical Explorations. Space, Place, and Mapping in Literary and Cultural Studies.* New York: Palgrave Macmillan Press, 2011.
Tally, Robert T. Jr., ed. *Literary Cartographies: Spatiality, Representation, and Narrative.* Basingstoke: Palgrave Macmillan, 2014.
Tally, Robert T. Jr.. "Adventures in Literary Cartography: Explorations, Representations, Projections." In *Literature and Geography: The Writing of Space Throughout History*, edited by Emanuelle Peraldo, 20–36. Newcastle upon Tyne: Cambridge Scholars Publishing, 2016.
Tew, Philip. *Jim Crace.* Manchester: Manchester University Press, 2006.
Topolovská, Tereza. "On the Analogy between the Language of Architecture and Language of Literary Work: The Role of Conception of Architecture in Generating the Poetics of *The Glass Room.*" *Filologické studie*, 15–31. Prague: Charles University in Prague, Karolinum, 2013.
Topolovská, Tereza. "*The Glass Room*: Architecture as a Poetic Emotion." In *Prague Journal of English Studies* 2, no. 1 (2013): 65–79.
Topolovská, Tereza. *The Country House Revisited: Variations on a Theme from Forster to Hollinghurst.* Prague: Karolinum Press, 2017.
Topolovská, Tereza. "Through the Looking Glass: Space and Place in Simon Mawer's *The Girl Who Fell from the Sky.*" In *Places and Spaces of Popular Imagination*, edited by Šárka Bubíková and Olga Roebuck, 47–63. Krakow: Jagiellonian University Press, 2021.
Topolovská, Tereza. "The Glass Room: Housing Space, Time and History." *Crossroads. A Journal of English Studies*, no. 36 (2022): 22–36.
Topolovská, Tereza. "Reading Buildings: The Textual Turn of Architecture as a Parallel to the Spatial Turn in Literary Studies." *Ars Aeterna*, vol. 14, no.1 (2022): 58–70.
Tuan, Yi-Fu. *Space and Place: The Perspective of Experience.* Minneapolis: University of Minnesota Press, 2018.
Turner, Victor. *The Forest of Symbols.* New York: Cornell University Press, 1970.
Vickroy, Laurie. *Trauma and Survival in Contemporary Fiction.* Charlottesville and London: University of Virginia Press, 2002.
Vidler, Anthony. *Warped Space. Art, Architecture, and Anxiety in Modern Culture.* Cambridge, MA – London: The MIT Press, 2001.
Walters, Anne-Marie. *Moondrop to Gascony.* Wiltshire: Moho Books, 2009.
Waters, Sarah. *The Little Stranger.* London: Virago Press, 2010.
Westphal, Bertrand. *Geocriticism: Real and Fictional Places.* Translated by Robert T. Tally, Jr.. New York: Palgrave MacMillan, 2011.
Westphal, Bertrand. "Foreword." In *Geocritical Explorations. Space, Place and Mapping in Cultural Studies*, edited by Robert T. Tally Jr., ix–xv. Basingstoke: Palgrave Macmillan, 2011.
White, Jonathan. "Introduction." In *Landscape, Seascape, and the Eco-Spatial Imagination*, edited by Simon C. Estok et al., 1–21. New York and London: Routledge, 2019.
White, Kenneth. "Elements of Geopoetics." *Edinburgh Review* 88, (1992): 163–178.
Williams, Raymond. *The Country and the City.* London: The Hogarth Press, 1985.
Wilk, Christopher, ed. *Modernism. Designing a New World.* London: V&A Publishing, 2007.
Zimmerman, Claire. *Mies van der Rohe. The Structure of Space.* Cologne: Taschen, 2009.

Internet Sources

antae Editorial Board. "'You Want to Mess with People's Heads': An Interview with Jim Crace." *antae* 2, no. 1 (2015): 5–14. https://www.um.edu.mt/library/oar/bitstream/handle/123456789/12872/2-1-2015-1.pdf?sequence=1&isAllowed=y. Accessed 8 November 2018.

Askew, Simon. "*Mendel's Dwarf*: Review." *Spike Magazine*, September 1, 2000. https://spikemagazine.com/0900mendelsdwarf/. Accessed 5 January 2021.

"Autor Skleněného pokoje se vrátil do Československa, prožívá pražské jaro." ["The Author of Glass Room comes back to Czechoslovakia, he experiences Prague Spring."] *ČT24*, August 21, 2018. https://ct24.ceskatelevize.cz/kultura/2572468-autor-skleneneho-pokoje-se-vratil-do-ceskoslovenska-proziva-prazske-jaro. Accessed 21 November 2021.

Barnacle, Hugo. "The Glass Room by Simon Mawer." *The Sunday Times*, February 8, 2009. https://www.thetimes.co.uk/article/the-glass-room-by-simon-mawer-gg9r2xqvttl. Accessed 30 December 2021.

Barry, Aoife. "Jim Crace Interview: 'I'm an un-tortured writer and that isn't very sexy.'" *The Journal*, June 21, 2015. https://www.thejournal.ie/jim-crace-interview-2166986-Jun2015. Accessed 10 December 2021.

Battersby, Doug. "The Melody by Jim Crace – Alarm Bells." *The Financial Times*, February 16, 2018. https://www.ft.com/content/e4793488-0ccb-11e8-bacb-2958fde95e5e. Accessed 10 December 2021.

Begley, Adam. "A Pilgrim in Craceland." *Southwest Review* 87, no. 2 & 3 (2002). http://www.jim-crace.com/Adam%20Begley%20article.htm. Accessed 29 June 2018.

Begley, Adam. 2003. "Jim Crace: The Art of Fiction no. 179." *The Paris Review* no. 167 (2003). https://www.theparisreview.org/interviews/122/jim-crace-the-art-of-fiction-no-179-jim-crace. Accessed 29 June 2018.

Berlins, Marcel. "Review: Crime Fiction Round-Up." *The Times*, August 11, 2018. https://www.thetimes.co.uk/article/review-crime-fiction-round-up-claire-accessory-to-murder-pddkbs0qh. Accessed 21 November 2021.

Biblio Blog. "An Interview with Jim Crace." October 22, 2007. https://www.biblio.com/blog/2007/10/interview-jim-crace. Accessed 29 November 2018.

Bookgroup.info. "Jim Crace: interview." 2007. http://www.bookgroup.info/041205/interview.php?id=38. Accessed 29 November 2017.

"Book Review: *Prague Spring*, by Simon Mawer." *The Scotsman*, July 31, 2018. https://www.scotsman.com/whats-on/arts-and-entertainment/book-review-prague-spring-simon-mawer-1427419. Accessed 21 November 2021.

The Booker Prizes. "Simon Mawer and Rewriting History." *The Booker Prizes*, June 24, 2016. http://themanbookerprize.com/news/simon-mawer-and-rewriting-history. Accessed 21 November 2022.

Brookner, Anita. "Pure, but Never Simple." *Spectator*, February 28, 2009. https://www.spectator.co.uk/article/pure-but-never-simple. Accessed 15 January 2021.

Cooke, Rachel. "*The Girl Who Fell from the Sky* by Simon Mawer – Review." *The Guardian*, May 4, 2012. https://www.theguardian.com/books/2012/may/04/simon-mawer-girl-fell-sky-review. Accessed 6 March 2020.

Cross, Stephanie. "Jim Crace, author of Booker-shortlisted *Quarantine*: 'I'm leaving Craceland'." *The Independent*, February 10, 2013. https://www.independent.co.uk/arts-entertainment/books/features/jim-crace-author-of-booker-shortlisted-quarantine-im-leaving-craceland-8488415.html. Accessed 10 July 2018.

Crown, Sarah. "A Life in Books – Simon Mawer." *The Guardian*, October 3, 2009. www.theguardian.com/culture/2009/oct/03/simon-mawer-life-in-books. Accessed 1 November 2021.

ČTK. "Nový román o pražském jaru od autora Skleněného pokoje si britský tisk chválí." ["British Press Applauds the new novel by the author of The Glass Room."] *Lidovky.cz*, August 21, 2018. https://www.lidovky.cz/orientace/kultura/novy-roman-o-prazskem-jaru-od-autora-skleneneho-pokoje-si-britsky-tisk-chvali.A180820_223959_ln_kultura_Ceh. Accessed 21 November 2021.

Dowling, Tim. "A House Through Time Review – a Compelling Way to Trace Social History." *The Guardian*, January 5, 2018. https://www.theguardian.com/tv-and-radio/2018/jan/05/a-house-through-time-review-a-compelling-way-to-trace-social-history. Accessed 23 February 2018.

"Drama ve vile Tugendhat. Do Skleněného pokoje se první odvážilo Brno." ["Drama in the Tugendhat Villa."] *ČT24*, February 7, 2015. https://ct24.ceskatelevize.cz/kultura/1500106-drama-ve-vile-tugendhat-do-skleneneho-pokoje-se-prvni-odvazilo-brno. Accessed 30 December 2021.

Ehrenreich, Ben. "An Interview with Jim Crace." *The Believer*. January 1, 2004. https://www.thebeliever.net/an-interview-with-jim-crace. Accessed 10 July 2018.

Flood, Alison. "Simon Mawer's *Tightrope* Wins Walter Scott Prize for Historical Fiction." *The Guardian*, June 20, 2016. https://www.theguardian.com/books/2016/jun/20/simon-mawers-tightrope-wins-walter-scott-prize-for-historical-fiction. Accessed 6 March 2020.

Grimble, Ed. "An Interview with Jim Crace." *Epigram*, March 2, 2016. https://issuu.com/epigrampaper/docs/epigram_297. Accessed 12 May 2021.

Guidarini, Lisa. "An Interview with Jim Crace." *BookBrowse*. March 2013. https://www.bookbrowse.com/author_interviews/full/index.cfm/author_number/1836/jim-crace. Accessed 12 July 2018.

Hewitt, Emma. "Interview: Jim Crace." *Cherwell*. November 15, 2013. https://cherwell.org/2013/11/15/interview-jim-crace. Accessed 12 July 2018.

Higgins, Bernadette. "Czech History Through a Glass Darkly." *Radio Prague*, November 22, 2009. www.radio.cz/en/section/books/czech-history-through-a-glass-darkly. Accessed 14 March 2021.

Holderness, Graham. "Jim Crace, *Quarantine*, and the Dawkins Delusion." *Critical Survey* 22, no. 3 (2010): 69–91. https://www.jstor.org/stable/41556386. Accessed 12 May 2021.

"An Interview with Jim Crace." *The Free Library*, 2012. https://www.thefreelibrary.com/An+Interview+with+Jim+Crace.-a0326854557. Accessed 10 December 2021.

"ISLE." *Interdisciplinary Studies in Literature and Environment*. https://academic.oup.com/isle. Accessed 26 May 2020.

Jim Crace Website. "Penguin Books interview with Jim Crace." 2002. http://www.jim-crace.com/Interview.htm. Accessed 29 November 2017.

Kadlecová, Kateřina. "Simon Mawer: Nereformovatelný komunismus? Havlův pohled ignoroval důležité věci." ["Simon Mawer: Unreformable Communism? Havel's Point of View Ignored Important Things."] *Reflex*, December 17, 2018. https://www.reflex.cz/clanek/rozhovory/91876/simon-mawer-nereformovatelny-komunismus-havluv-pohled-ignoroval-dulezite-veci.html. Accessed 14 November 2021.

Kelly, Richard T. "*The Glass Room*: Review." *The Financial Times*, January 5, 2009. https://www.ft.com/content/8e6d0130-d6c7-11dd-9bf7-000077b07658. Accessed 30 December 2021.

Kemp, Douglas. "Historical Novel Society: Review: *Prague Spring*." *Historical Novel Society*, November 2018, Issue 86. https://historicalnovelsociety.org/reviews/prague-spring/. Accessed 21 November 2021.

Kermode, Frank. "Into the Wilderness: Review of *Quarantine*." *The New York Times*. April 12, 1998. http://www.nytimes.com/1998/04/12/books/into-the-wilderness.html. Accessed 29 June 2018.

Kohda Hazelton, Claire. "*Tightrope* Review – Simon Mawer's Skilful Evocation of a Mind under Stress." *The Guardian*, August 9, 2015. https://www.theguardian.com/books/2015/aug/09/tightrope-review-simon-mawer-skilful-evocation-mind-under-stress. Accessed 6 March 2020.

Kohn, Marek. "Tough on the Causes of Crime. Book Review." *The Independent*, July 18, 1997. https://www.independent.co.uk/arts-entertainment/books/book-review-tough-on-the-causes-of-crime-1251369.html. Accessed 30 December 2021.

Konrád, Daniel. "Mawerův roman o roce 1968: Pražské jaro jako ztráta iluzí, mladí přejeté tanky." ["Mawer's Novel About 1968: Prague Spring as Disillusionment, Youth Run Over by Tanks."] *Aktuálně.cz*, December 4, 2018. https://magazin.aktualne.cz/kultura/literatura/simon-mawer-prazske-jaro-1968-kniha-zlin-recenze/r~8ba4db7af7dd11e884f6ac1f6b220ee8/. Accessed 20 December 2021.

Krajíčková, Veronika. "Mawer, Simon: Pražské jaro." ["Mawer, Simon: Prague Spring."] *iLiteratura.cz*, March 18, 2019. http://www.iliteratura.cz/Clanek/41293/mawer-simon-prazske-jaro. Accessed 20 November 2021.

Langerová, Jana. "Události roku 1968 jiným pohledem." ["Events of 1968 from a Different Point of View."] *Kultura21.cz*, January 8, 2020. https://www.kultura21.cz/mluvene-slovo/20132-prazske-jaro-recenze. Accessed 15 January 2022.

Lauder, Silvie. "Autor Skleněného pokoje: moje srdce je v Česku." ["The Author of The Glass Room: My Heart is in the Czech Republic."] *Respekt*, April 5, 2015. https://www.respekt.cz/tydenik/2015/15/romany-nas-trenuji-v-empatii. Accessed 30 December 2021.

Lawless, Andrew. "The Poet of Prose – Jim Crace in Interview." *Three Monkeys Online*. http://www.threemonkeysonline.com/the-poet-of-prose-jim-crace-in-interview/4/. Accessed 29 June 2018.

Lodge, Guy. "The Affair Review: Architecture is the Star of a Muddled Europudding Melodrama." *The Variety*, March 5, 2021. https://variety.com/2021/film/reviews/the-affair-review-1234922610/. Accessed 30 November 2021.

Mączyńska, Magdalena. "Toward a Postsecular Literary Criticism: Examining Ritual Gestures in Zadie Smith's 'Autograph Man.'" *Religion and Literature* 41, no. 3 (2009): 73–82. https://www.jstor.org/stable/i25746538. Accessed 14 May 2021.

Mahmood, Sameerah. "Interview with Jim Crace." *Writers in Conversation* 2, no. 1 (2015). https://dspace.flinders.edu.au/xmlui/bitstream/handle/2328/35172/Crace_Mahmood.pdf?sequence=1&isAllowed=y. Accessed 5 July 2018.

Mandys, Pavel. "Simon Mawer: Mendelův trpaslík." ["Simon Mawer: *Mendel's Dwarf*."] *iLiteratura.cz*, October 3, 2010. http://www.iliteratura.cz/Clanek/27131/mawer-simon-mendeluv-trpaslik. Accessed 20 November 2021.

Marantz Henig, Robin. "A Book that Will Make You Terrified of Your Own House." *The New York Times*, December 31, 2018. https://www.nytimes.com/2018/12/31/books/review/rob-dunn-never-home-alone.html. Accessed 1 January 2019.

Mawer, Simon. "Science in Literature." *Simonmawer.com*, 2005. www.simonmawer.com/ScienceandLiterature.htm. Accessed 6 November 2021.

Mawer, Simon. "Theo van Doesburg: Forgotten artist of the Avant Garde." *The Guardian*, January 23, 2010. www.theguardian.com/artanddesign/2010/jan/23/theo-van-doesburg-avant-garde-tate. Accessed 1 December 2022.

Mawer, Simon. "Once Upon a Life: Simon Mawer." *The Guardian*, November 28, 2010. https://www.theguardian.com/lifeandstyle/2010/nov/28/simon-mawer-once-upon-a-life-climbing. Accessed 1 December 2022.

Mawer, Simon. "The Aesthetic Brain." *Nature*, vol. 484 (26 April 2012): 444–445.
Mawer, Simon. "Simon Mawer – Biography." *Simonmawer.com*. http://www.simonmawer.com/biographical.htm. Accessed 21 June 2023.
Miller, Lucasta. "*The Girl Who Fell from the Sky* by Simon Mawer – Review." *The Guardian*, May 11, 2012. https://www.theguardian.com/books/2012/may/11/girl-fell-sky-simon-mawer-review. Accessed 6 March 2020.
Myerson, Jonathan. "*Ancestry*: A Novel by Simon Mawer review – one for all the family." *The Guardian*, August 1, 2022. https://www.theguardian.com/books/2022/aug/01/ancestry-a-novel-by-simon-mawer-review-one-for-all-the-family. Accessed 6 December 2022.
Naidu, Vayu. "Words are My Picture and My Music." *The Hindu*, 2014. https://www.thehindu.com/todays-paper/tp-features/tp-literaryreview/words-are-my-picture-and-my-music/article5539575.ece#.UuBKyI8vm3k.gmail. Accessed 20 June 2018.
Palmer, Stephen. "'Dead but not Departed Yet': the Exploration of Liminal Space in Jim Crace's *Being Dead* (1999)." *Mortality* 17, no. 1 (2012): 51–63. https://www.tandfonline.com/doi/full/10.1080/13576275.2012.651833. Accessed 15 May 2021.
Pengelly, Martin. "'Women are more interesting than men': Simon Mawer on *Tightrope*." *The Guardian,* November 1, 2015. https://www.theguardian.com/books/2015/nov/01/simon-mawer-tightrope-trapeze-marian-sutro. Accessed 6 March 2020.
"*Prague Spring* Review." *Publishers Weekly*, 2018. https://www.publishersweekly.com/978-1-59051-966-0. Accessed 21 November 2021.
"*Prague Spring* Review." *Nine Voices*, December 10, 2018. https://ninevoices.wordpress.com/2018/12/10/prague-spring/. Accessed 21 November 2021.
Proctor, Minna. "Jim Crace." *BOMB Magazine*, 2000. https://bombmagazine.org/articles/jim-crace. Accessed 8 June 2018.
Prose, Francine. "Get Out the Chromosomal Map." *The New York Times*, March 22, 1998. https://archive.nytimes.com/www.nytimes.com/books/98/03/22/reviews/980322.22proset.html. Accessed 30 December 2021.
Purdon, James. "The Glass Room by Simon Mawer." *The Observer*, April 25, 2010. www.theguardian.com/books/2010/apr/25/the-glass-room-simon-mawer. Accessed 4 October 2021.
Rawsthorn, Alice. "Reopening a Mies Modernist Landmark." *The New York Times*, February 24, 2012. https://www.nytimes.com/2012/02/27/arts/27iht-design27.html. Accessed 4 July 2023.
"Román Skleněný pokoj ožije ve filmu z vily Tugendhat. Rodině se fiktivní příběh nelíbí." ["The Glass Room comes to live in film adaptation from the Tugendhat Villa. The family does not appreciate the fictitious story."] *ČT24*, February 6, 2018. https://ct24.ceskatelevize.cz/kultura/2382961-roman-skleneny-pokoj-ozije-ve-filmu-z-vily-tugendhat-rodine-se-fiktivni-pribeh. Accessed 30 December 2021.
Sansom, Ian. "Smorgasbits." *London Review of Books* 23, no. 22 (November 15, 2001): 13–14. https://www.lrb.co.uk/v23/n22/ian-sansom/smorgasbits. Accessed 15 June 2018.
Sansom, Ian. "Design for Living." *The Guardian*, January 24, 2009. www.theguardian.com/books/2009/jan/24/simon-mawer-the-glass-room. Accessed 1 November 2021.
Sansom, Ian. "*Tightrope* by Simon Mawer Review – Meet the Female James Bond." *The Guardian*, September 24, 2015. https://www.theguardian.com/books/2015/sep/24/tightrope-simon-mawer-review-novel-female-james-bond. Accessed 6 March 2020.
Scottish Centre for Geopoetics. http://www.geopoetics.org.uk. Accessed 15 December 2017.
Sečkař, Marek. "Letting in the Light." An interview with Simon Mawer. *Eurozine*, November 2, 2010. https://www.eurozine.com/letting-in-the-light/. Accessed 21 November 2021.

Self, Will. "The Deep Topography of Nick Papadimitriou." *Will Self*, February 18, 2011. https://will-self.com/2011/02/18/the-deep-topography-of-nick-papadimitriou/. Accessed 10 September 2021.

Shore, Marci. "The Russian Revolution Recast as an Epic Family Tragedy." *The New York Times*. August 18, 2017. https://www.nytimes.com/2017/08/18/books/review/yuri-slezkine-the-house-of-government.html. Accessed 23 February 2018.

Silman, Roberta. "Book Review: "Prague Spring" – The Fragility of Freedom." *The Arts Fuse*, April 2, 2019. https://artsfuse.org/182855/book-review-prague-spring-the-fragility-of-freedom/. Accessed 1 January 2022.

Slezáková, Alena. "Hodiny, kdy dopadla sekera na naděje pražského jara." ["The Hours, when an axe crushed the hopes of Prague Spring."] *iDnes.cz*, November 24, 2018. https://www.idnes.cz/kultura/literatura/simon-mawer-prazske-jaro-kniha-zlin.A181123_151151_literatura_kiz. Accessed 21 November 2021.

Stemporowski, Jakub. "The City and the Country, the Myth and the Reality in Jim Crace's Novel *Arcadia*." Unpublished master's thesis. Toruń: Nicolas Copemicus University, 2002. http://www.jim-crace.com/stemporowski%20thesis.htm. Accessed 8 January, 2010.

Svátková, Kateřina. "Milostný příběh na pozadí pražského jara. Simon Mawer představil nový román zasazený do srpna 1968." ["Love Story on the Background of Prague Spring. Simon Mawer introduced a New Novel situated in August 1968."] *iRozhlas*, 25 November 2018. https://www.irozhlas.cz/kultura/literatura/simon-mawer-prazske-jaro-srpen-1968-skleneny-pokoj-spisovatel-kniha-roman_1811251011_gak. Accessed 21 November 2021.

Tayade, Vishal. "An Interview with British Writer Jim Crace." *Indian Rumunantions*, 2011. http://www.indianruminations.com/contents/interviews/an-interview-with-british-writer-jim-crace-by-vishal-tayade. Accessed 7 November, 2018.

Teske, Doris. "Jim Crace's *Arcadia*: Public Culture in the Postmodern City." In *London in Literature: Visionary Mappings of the Metropolis*, edited by Susana Onega and J.A. Stotesbury, 165–82. Heidelberg: Universitätsverlag C. Winter, 2002. http://www.jim-crace.com/ Arcadia.htm. Accessed 21 December, 2009.

The International Institute of Geopoetics. http://institut-geopoetique.org/en. Accessed 15 December, 2017.

"Things I Heard Simon Mawer Say." *Nine Voices*, June 22, 2019. https://ninevoices.wordpress.com/tag/simon-mawer/. Accessed 21 December 2021.

Tripney, Natasha. "*The Girl Who Fell from the Sky* by Simon Mawer – Review." *The Observer*, June 16, 2013. https://www.theguardian.com/books/2013/jun/16/girl-fell-sky-mawer-review. Accessed 6 March 2020.

Vaughan, David. "Simon Mawer's *Prague Spring*: A Complex Love Story amid the Drama of 1968." *Radio Prague International*, August 12, 2018. https://english.radio.cz/simon-mawers-prague-spring-a-complex-love-story-amid-drama-1968-8144155. Accessed 21 November 2021.

"The New York Public Library's 43rd Annual Books to Remember List." "25 Books to Remember from 1998." https://www.nypl.org/collections/nypl-recommendations/lists/btr1998. Accessed 20 December 2022.

The Walter Scott Prize for Historical Fiction. "The Winner of the 2016 Walter Scott Prize is Announced!" June 18, 2016. https://www.walterscottprize.co.uk/simon-mawer-wins-2016-walter-scott-prize/. Accessed 21 November 2021.

Wilkinson, Tom. "The Writing on the Wall: the Language of Buildings." *The Architectural Review*, January 23, 2019. https://www.architectural-review.com/essays/the-writing-on-the-wall-the-language-of-buildings. Accessed 23 January 2020.

Williams, John. “This is the Sorcery of the City: Review of *Arcadia*.” *Birmingham* 13 (July 1992). http://www.jim-crace.com/birmingham.htm. Accessed 21 December, 2009.
Wroe, Nicholas. “At the Watford Gap it hit me that the English landscape was absolutely drenched in narrative.” *The Guardian*, August 16, 2013. https://www.theguardian.com/culture/2013/aug/16/jim-crace-interview. Accessed 21 November 2021.

Lectures and Conference Papers

Hammer-Tugendhat, Daniela. “Das Haus Tugendhat und Seine Bewohner.” Guest lecture. Prager Gäsprache organized by Das Österreichische Kulturforum Prag, 1 October 2012, Veranstaltungssaal des Tschechischen Kulturministeriums, Prague, Czech Republic.
Mawer, Simon. Book Signing. May 17, 2010, The Luxor Book Palace, Prague, Czech Republic.
Rodríguez Magda, Rosa María. “The Crossroads of Transmodernity.” International Conference *Transmodern Perspectives on Contemporary Literatures in English*, University of Zaragoza, April 26–28, 2017.

Index